ENGLISH RECUSANT LITERATURE
1558–1640

Selected and Edited by
D. M. ROGERS

Volume 338

ST. PETER OF ALCANTARA
A Golden Treatise
1632

Ordo Baptizandi
1636

ST. PETER OF ALCANTARA

A Golden Treatise of Mentall Praier

1632

The Scolar Press

1977

ISBN 0 85967 374 x

Published and printed in Great Britain by
The Scolar Press Limited, 59-61 East Parade,
Ilkley, Yorkshire and
39 Great Russell Street,
London WC1

NOTE

The following works are reproduced (original size) with permission:

1) St. Peter of Alcantara, *A golden treatise*, 1632, from a copy in the library of St. Edmund's College, Ware, by permission of the President.
References : Allison and Rogers 644; STC 19794.

2) *Ordo baptizandi*, 1636, from a copy in the library of St. Edmund's College, Ware, by permission of the President.
References : Allison and Rogers 722; STC 16162.

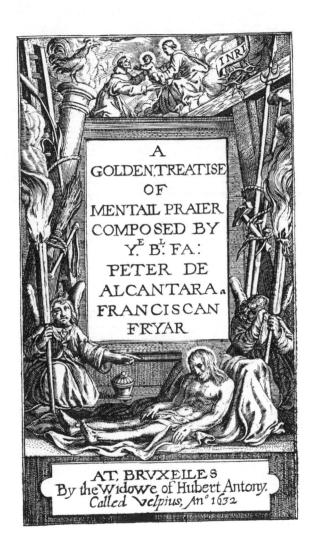

A

GOLDEN TREATISE

OF

MENTAIL PRAIER

COMPOSED BY

Y.ᵉ B.ˡ FA:

PETER DE

ALCANTARA a

FRANCISCAN

FRYAR

AT. BRVXEILES
By the Widowe of Hubert Antony.
Called Velpius, Anᵒ 1632

A
GOLDEN TREATISE
OF
MENTALL PRAIER,

With diuerse spirituall rules and directions, no lesse profitable then necessarie for all sortes of people.

First composed by the venerable and blessed Father, FR. PETER DE ALCANTARA, of the Seraphicall Order of *S. Francis*. Beatified the 18. of Aprill. 1622.

Translated into English by G. VV.

To which is prefixed a breife relation of the life , and death of the same Father written by G. VV. of the same Order and observance.

AT BRVXELLES,

By the Widowe of HVBERT ANTONE, called *Velpius*, sworne Printer of the Court, at the signe of the golden Eagle by the Palace. 1632.

Permissu Superiorum.

TO THE RIGHT
HONOVRABLE
AND TRVELY
VERTVOVS LADY,
THE LADY
ELIANOR
POWES, &c.

All prosperitie in this vvorld,
and euerlastinge glorie in
the vvorld to come.

MADAM,

Although the greatnes of your blood doth chalenge much

res-

THE EPISTLE

respect, yet I knovve by experience, that your LADI-SHIP thinketh vertue to be only and true nobilitie; and that to be Gods seruāt, you esteeme it your greatest glorie. This therfore vertuous and religious dispositiō of yours, beinge the only loadstone that dravveth my affection to loue, and honour you, hath emboldened me to present vnto your LADISHIPS veivve, this little treatise of mentall prayer, vvith the life of the Authour, vvhich longe since, and alvvayes from

the

the firſt time I tooke it in hand, I intēded to shrovvde vnder the vvinges of your protećtion, but beinge hin-dred by ſome occaſions, vvherin holy obedience hath emploied me , I could neuer compas my deſires till novve. I novve ther-fore ſend it to your LADI-SHIP deſiringe you to ac-cept of it , not for my de-ſertes, vvhich indeede haue bene none to claime ſuch a fauour, but for the digni-tie of the matter of vvhich it treateth (though I am afraied made much vvorſe

a 4   by

by my vnskilfull pen) as alfofor the fanctitie of the Authour vvho made it, and your LADISHIP vvill increafe my many obligations tovvardes you, and alvvayes oblige me to reft and remaine.

MADAM,

Your honors poore beadfman,

GILES VVILLOVGHBY.

A

BREIFE RELATION

OF

THE LIFE AND DEATH

OF

THE BLESSED FATHER

Fr. PETER DE ALCANTARA, a

FRANCISCAN FRYAR.

VVritten by G. VV. of the same Order &
observance.

THE PROLOGVE.

Ifericordias Do-
mini in æternum
cantabo. (a) *I will* (a) *Psalm.* 88.
singe the mercies of
our Lord for euer, *saith that*
Kingly Prophet DAVID:
And

THE PROLOGVE.

And not without cause: for so great and vnspeakable, are the mercie-workes of the almightie, which out of the bowells of his infinite goodnes, he hath shewed to man-kinde from the first instant of his creation, that the toungues of men and Angells are neuer able to ex-presse them.

How wonderfull was this be-nefit; that creatinge man after his owne (b) image and likenes, (c) he would haue made him partaker of eternall felicitie, and vested with his originall iustice, vvithout (d) death or any passage by misery would haue associated him with the com-panie of Angells, if he had not, by his ovvne default, violated the lawes of his creatour ? notwith-standinge this act of malice, the diuine

(b) Gen. 1. 26.
(c) Magister sent. lib. 2. dist. 20.
(d) Gabriel. lib. 2. dist. 19. quæst. vnica, art. 2.

diuine clemencie would not suffer
the worke of his powerfull handes,
so to perish : but he accordinge to
the diuersitie of times , (e) alwaies
ordeined opportune remedies, to reduce wanderinge man to the right
way of his owne saluation. Nowe
manifestinge his diuine pleasure by
the meanes of Angels : nowe sendinge the Patriarchs replenished
with his heauenly grace , who by
their good example , might stirr
them vp to pietie : then sendinge the
Prophets illuminated with his holy
spirit, not only to preach the present
benefits exhibited to mankinde, but
also to foretell the future incarna-
tion of the Sonne of God , with the
mysterie of his death and passion,
by meanes of which man should
be loosed from the power of Sathan,
                                    and

(e) Scotus lib.
4. dist. 1. qu.
7. n 2.

and eased of the heauy loade of his tranſgreſsions.

Thus farr hath that impenetrable abyſſe of the diuine clemencie, ſweetly diſpoſed all thinges, requiſite for the ſauinge of the ſoule of man. But if we will extend our thoughtes a little further, and call to mind the great benefits, ſtill heaped vpon man, after the aſcenſion of our bleſſed Sauiour, we ſhall finde them innumerable. VVho is not aſtoniſhed at the vocation of mankinde, that the Apoſtolicall trumpet of a fewe men, ſoundinge to humane eares, the Euangelicall truth, through the wholl world, ſhould rouze vp (f) ſoules makinge thē* happy & thrice happy to forſake all worldly vanities? to betake themſelues to a ſtate of perfection;

(f) (Religoſi) Ecclesiæ pars ſelectior, & ſapientior; ſiquidem ij ſalꝑ liſunt, quā reliquū mortalium vulgus, qui ſeipſos à mundi cōſortio ſegregarunt, vt tꝯ tā ſuam Deo conſecrārunt. Nazianz ora in laudē Baſilij *Beati illi certè, ac ter beati, vt qui Dei amore flagrārunt, at ḡ ob eius amorē omnia pro nihilo duxerūt, ſiquidē lacrymas profudērunt dieḡ; ac noſte in luctu verſati ſunt, vt æternam conſolationem adipiſcerētur:

fection; to *sell all they haue and* carnes *suas fame & sitt, & vigilijs*
giue to the poore : *to liue in perpe-* *confecerūt, vt*
tuall chastitie, and simple obedience: *illic paradisi dilicie, &*
to spend their dayes in rigorous pe- *gaudia illos*
nance, watchinge, fastinge and *ex iperent.*
prayer, and finally to renounce all *Damascen. in b st B. Iosa-*
the seeminge pleasures (for (g) *true* *phit.*
there are none) which the flatte- (g) *Consolatio mūdi vilis, &*
ringe world could afford vnto thē. *ad nihilū vti-*

These thinges are dayly putt *lis, & quod magis metuē-*
in practice by many, who professe *dum est, vere*
the gospell of Christ. *For where* *& salubris consolationis*
Catholique Religion *flourisheth,* *impedimentū.*
we see diuerse Monasteries of *D Ber. in ser.*
men and women, filled with reli- *vir. Natiu sic se habēt vni-*
gious soules, who consecrate them- *uersa sub so-*
selues a perpetuall sacrifice to the *le, vt nihil sit in eis vere*
almightie. *iucundū, om-*
nis siquidem
How many religious doe vve *laboris reme-*
see honoured vvith Preistly *fun-* *dium, alterius laboris initiū*
Ction, *(an office requiringe more* *est. Idem in*
se m de pri-
mordijs &
medijs nouiss.
Vide plura
apud Hieron.

then

Platū de bono stat. relig. l. 3. cap. 1.
(h) *Quo non oportet esse puriorem tali fuentē sacrificio? quo solari radio non splendidiorem manū carnem hanc diuiden-tem? os quod igni spiritali repletur, lin-guā quæ tre-mendo nimis sanguine ru-bescit. Sic D. Chrys. hom.* 83. *in Mat.*

then humane (h) *puritie and a burthen scarcely to be supported by Angels shoulders) executing their charge vvith great integretie of minde, carefull of their ovvne, and zealous of the sauinge of their neighbours soules, vvho by their holy doctrine and exemplare liues, preach to the Christian vvorld a reformation: vvho spare noe paines or tedious trauells, to propagate the*
faith

And Pope Gelasius vvritinge to Elpidius Bishop, doth excellently set dovvne the great purity required to Preistly function sayinge: *Sacrosancta Religio quæ Catholi-cam continet disciplinam, tantam sibi reuerentiam vendicat, vt ad eam quilibet nisi pura conscientia, non audeat peruenire: nam quomodo ad diuini mysterij consecrationem cælestis spiritus inuo-catus adueniat, si sacerdos & qui eam adesse deprecetur crimi-nosis plenus actionibus reprobetur?* 1. q. 1. c. *SACROSANCTA.* Although a vvicked Preist doth consecrate and administ-ter the Sacramentes truely, yet he sinneth greiuiously in cōsecratinge, & administratinge vnvvorthily. *Sacrificia im-piorum eis ipsis oberunt qui offerunt impiè.* 1. q. 1. c. *PERISAIAM. necesse est, vt esse munda studeat manus, quæ diluere sordes cu-rat: ne sacta quæque deterius inquinet, si sordida ipsa stercoris lu-tum tenet. Greg. in negesto.* l. 2. *Epist.* 24. *& ponitur* 1. q. 1 cap. *NECESSE EST.*

THE PROLOGVE.

faith of IESVS CHRIST, *to* heathens and infidells; vvho couragiously labour in God almighties vineyard, expofinge their liues for the name of IESVS. Indies both eaft and vveft are vvitneffes of their zealous and heroick fpirits, there they fealed the truth of the gofpell vvith the effufion of their facred blood. Yea vvhat aftes memorable in the church of God are there, vvherin (i) thefe men haue not had a very greate ftroke. And finally they fo well employ, and multiply thofe talentes, vvhich the great commaunder of heauen and earth, hath beftovved vpon them here, that affuredly they may expeft an eternall revvard in the Kingedome of heauen hereafter.

(i) *Hieron. Platus de bono ftatus relig. l. 2. c. 3* &c.

But

But that which is more admirable, to see a multitude of the weaker sexe, to abandon all worldly pleasures: they who in the world might haue swoome in brauery, and haue had all thinges at their owne command; to inclose themselues in a retired Cloister, there to spend their dayes in penance, and to consecrate the very flower of their springinge youth, a sweet smellinge sacrifice to their celestiall spouse CHRIST IESVS. *These truly are those that* (k) *fill and beautifie the garden of paradise with lillies of puritie: these are the* (l) *flowers of our holy mother the Catholique Church, which make her glorious and fruitfull. These are they, that make that happie chaunge, a moments fadinge pleasure, for an im-*

mor-

(k) Nuptiæ replēt terram virginitas paradisum. D. Hieron.

(l) Flos est ille Ecclesiastici germinis, decus atque ornamentū gratiæ spiritualis, læta, indolis, laudis & honoris, opus integrum atq; incorruptum; Dei imago respondens, ad sanctimoniam Dñi, illustrior portio gregis Christi, gaudet per ipsas, atque in illis largiter floret S. Matris Ecclesiæ gloriosa fœcunditas, quantoq; plus gloriosa Virginitas numero suo addit, tanto plus gaudium matris augescit. Cypr. de habit. virg. l. 4 c. 24

mortall crowne of glorie.

Thus we see perpetuall riuers
streaminge from the fountaine of
God almighties mercie. But let vs
descend a little further into his
aboundant charitie, and take notice
of his fatherly prouidence, that in
proces of declininge times, when
the blood of our redeemer, hath oftentimes begun to wax cold in the
hearts of men, he would not suffer
it altogether to be extinguished, but
accordinge to varietie of times, neuer ceased to repaire his church by
the ministery of some elected seruāts,
whom he sent into this world as second Apostles, who by their example, and doctrine might drawe men
out of the mire of their sinnes, re-
newe the feruour of our blessed Sauiours passion, and reduce collapsed

b   disci-

THE PROLOGVE.

discipline to her former rigour. Many hath he sent for this end, and amongst many this blessed Saint, S. PETER DE ALCANTARA, a man from his very cradle consecrated to Euangelicall perfection; he was a faithfull labourer in our Lords vineyard, with great fidelitie performinge his commanded taske, as it will plainly appeare by that which followeth in his life.

CHAP.

Chap. I.

OF THE BIRTH
AND
EDVCATION,
OF BLESSED
ALCANTARA,

And of his enteringe into Religion.

(a) *Ciuitas Hispaniæ militiæ ordinis Alcantarensis clara. Iste ordo prout constat expriuil. illi concesso an. Dñi 1174. fuit institutus à Dño Gomesio Hernandes tempore Ferdinãdi 2. Regis, & approbatus ub Alex. 3. Lucio 3. & Innoc. 4. Rod. qq.Reg. to 1. qu. 4. art. 4.*

T HIS blessed Saint was borne at (a) *Norba Cæsarea*, vulgarly called A L-CANTARA, in the yeare of our Lord 1499. in the reigne of Pope ALEXANDER the sixth, and FERDINANDO Catholique Kinge of *Spaine*. His Father was called BACHILIER GARAVITO, and his Mother MARIA VILLELA DE SENABRIA , both of good qualitie , but especially honoured for their vertues.

b 2　　　　They

They brought vp their younge Sonne in the feare of God, and sowed in him the seedes of vertue ; they put him to schoole where, as he profited in learninge, so his obedience towards his parentes did likwise increase. Although he was a child, yet he withdrewe himselfe from the common sportes of children, and sorted himselfe amongst men, whome he sawe inclined to deuotion. In these his tender yeares he addicted himselfe, to the workes of mercie : he applied himselfe seriously to learne the Christian doctrine : he often visited churches, and holy places, he frequented the Sacramētes, and continually emploied himselfe in good workes : all which did aboundantly presage his future sanctitie, but more confirmed it, by that which followed immediately, for he was skarce sixtene yeares of age, when, before he knewe, he began to loath the world, and when the younge sparkes of his vertues began to breake into a flame of deuotion. He opened the dores of his soule to the inspirations of the holy Ghost : and as he excelled his fellowe studentes in science, so he knewe that all (*b*) science, was ignorance without the right knowledge of God.

(b) *Quid profuerit ea quæ egenda sunt scire ei, qui ea ad opus non perducit.* D. *Chrys.ho.* 13. *ad Rom.*

God.Therfore from that time forward
he applied his minde to heauenly wiſedome , and buſied himſelfe cheiſly to
knowe what ſhould be moſt acceptable
to his ſacred Maieſtie.

About that time , there was a famous
and reformed monaſtery of FRANCIS-
CANS in the prouince of S. GABRIEL,
three miles from VALENTIA, whether he addreſſed himſelfe , there to
bringe his good deſires to a ioyfull pe-
riode. But as he went alonge towards
this place, he came to a great riuer , called *Tiartar* , which without boate, was
impoſſible to be paſſed ouer. He ſeeinge
this vnexpected barr, to ſtop his happy
iournie, looked about,hopinge to eſpye
ſome waterman , who might carry him
ouer , but when he could ſee none , to
giue him any aſſiſtance : he caſt his eies
to heauen , and with great anxietie lamented this vnhappie hindrance. Behold! vpon the ſuddaine (as he himſelfe
related)(c)he was miraculouſly trãſpor- (c) *Marianus*
ted on the other ſide of the riuer, with- *in eius vita*
out any notable motion, that he could *cap. 1.*
perceiue.

This miracle was not vnlike to that,
when the riuer of Iordane ſtood ſtill
for the Children of ISRAEL to paſs;

or when S. PETER walked vpon the
waues of the sea: and indeed, it was no
small beginninge of God almighties
many fauours, exhibited to this blessed
Saint.

This obstacle beinge remoued, he
passed the other part of his way, (the
holy Ghost beinge his guide) without
any difficultie, and at length ariued to
his desired harbour, this solitarie monasterie, situated amongst great rocks,
which they comonly call *Los Manxere-
des*, where he came to the Fathers, and
asked the habit of S. FRANCIS of
them, who did graunt it to him with as
much charitie, as he begged it with humilitie.

But when this blessed Saint considered his poore habitation, sequestred
from the companie of men, and abstracted from all worldly tumoultes.
And when he sawe himselfe vested in
his penitentiall weede, we may well immagine with what meditatiõs he spur-
red himselfe forward in God almighties seruice. He spake to his owne soule
these or the like wordes, behold,,
thou hast nowe accõplished thy de-,,
sire,thou art nowe arriued to the land ,,
of promise, and climed vp to the ,,
(d)hi- ,,

(d) highest mountaine of God almighties fauour to mortall mā in this vale of misery (that is) the sacred state of a religious life, where, by howe much more thou art sequestred from the pleasures of the flatteringe world, the more thou enioyest the fredome of thy spirit. Thou art nowe come to the house of God, in which it is better for the to be an abiect then to dwell in the courtes of Princes; all occasiõs of offendinge thy creatour are nowe taken a way, thy soule is nowe sure not to be defiled with the pitch of euill conuersation. Thy companie nowe are (e) terrestriall Angels, who, though they liue on earth, yet they haue their conuersation in heauen, all whose actions incite thee to nothinge else but to aspire vnto perfection. Thou findest here no snares to entangle thee in worldly vanities, no flatterers to applaud thee when thou doest offend, or any thinge else to withdrawe thy affection from the Cross of CHRIST. Thy beloued spouse hath brought thee nowe into this holy desert, to recreat thy soule with his heauenly consolatiõs (f) here abstracted from all wordly tumoults,

(d) Hæc terra montuosa, & in sublimi sita quantum à delicijs seculi vacat tantò maiores habet delicias spiritus. D Hier. l. 2. Epistolarum. Epist. 8. ad Eustochiã.

(e) Quo nomine appellem nescio, homines cælestes an Angelos terrestres degentes in terris, sed conuersationem habentes in cælis. D. Bernard. serm. ad fratres de monte Dei.

(f) Anima à corporeis cu-

b 4   it may

piditatibus li-
bera in aula
mentis poßit
diuinæ vacare
sapientiæ, vbi
omnī strepitu
terrenarum
silente cura-
rum, in medi-
tationibus
sanctis, & in
delicijs læte-
tur æternis.
S. Leo in ser.
8. de ieiunio
10. mensis, &
eleem.

(g) In Reli-
gione homo
viuit purius,
cadit rarius,
surgit velo-
cius, incedit
cautius, quie-
scit securius,
irroratur cre-
brius, purga-
tur citius, mo-
ritur confidē-
tius, munera-
tur copiosius.
Idem. Hom.
simile est re-
gnū ælorum,
homini nego-
tiatori
(h) S. Fr. Ver-
ba exhort. ad
fratres.

it may attēd only to diuine wisedome „
& the noise of all temporall cares, be- „
inge hist & silent , it may be wholly „
emploied in sacred contemplation, & „
rauished with eternall pleasures. God „
almightie hath nowe wafted thee „
ouer this troublesome sea, and placed „
thee heere, in the quiete harbour of „
thy saluation, in which state in respect „
of thy former , thou art farr more „
sure to (g) fall seldomer, rise sooner, „
stand more securely , liue more „
sweetly, and dye more confidently. „
Goe too , I say, why standest thou „
still ? why camest thou hether ? Con- „
sider thy course habit, and see what „
penance it exacteth ? Looke vpon „
the place, and reflect what spirit it „
teacheth thee ? be couragious and „
make no delay, thy death is certaine, „
and thy hower vncertaine, the iudge is „
at hand, (h) Alas! the pleasure of this „
world is short, but the punishment for „
it perpetuall. A little sufferinge here „
and infinite glorie hereafter. Thus, „
this newe soldiar of C H R I S T spent
his tine, in holy discourses, sometimes
of God almighties maiestie, sometimes
of his owne miserie: although his precedent conuersation to Religion was a

mir-

mirrour of perfection, yet he stoode not still in that grace, he had already gotten, but continually aspired to higher, in which he farr excelled his fellowe nouices. Two vertues were cheifly eminent in him: simplicitie and puritie. He likwise had a perfect obliuion of all wordly thinges. He greedily desired, and willingly accepted of the inferiour, and basest employmentes of the monasterie. Neither did he esteeme it a dishonour to him to cast himselfe at the feete of the Friers, but was most willinge to serue euery one at their beck. In this his first yeare he laied such groundes of humilitie, that in his wholl life after he was a rare example, and patterne of this vertue. Neither when he was promoted to superioritie, did he leaue of his humble exercises. Thus goinge from grace to grace, from vertue to vertue, his good example was a burninge lampe to giue others light, to immitate his vertues, that the wholl monasterie began euerie day more and more to flourish in regulare obseruance, and in the opinion of the world, to get a great name of sanctitie.

CHAP.

CHAP. II.

Of his naturall gifts , and of his prudence, and mortification of his eies.

HE was an elected veſſell, beautified with all the iewells of vertues , and as his minde was replenished with ſupernaturall gifts, ſo his bodie wanted not its naturall graces. He was of a ſpare bodie , but comely, he had a graue and modeſt looke , his eies were ſparklinge , tokens of the fire of diuine loue, which was in hiſſoule inuiſible to the eie. There was not one member in that man , which was not ſubordinate to the rule of reaſon. His ſpeech was meeke and humble, his conuerſation Angelicall. He had an excellent naturall witt, ioyned with a happie memorie : he had likwiſe a ſingular good iudgement (as appeared in his gouernment:) he was couragious in goinge through with buſines which did tend to God Almighties honour and the good of religion : he was gratefull to all, giuinge

uinge to euerie one their due respect: he was dexterous in his actions, modest in correctinge: and a peace maker, reconcilinge those who vpon any occasion, had bene at iarrs. In his sermons he was hott but mouinge: in hearinge of confessions he was a helper , a counsailer, and a comforter: in his ordinary speech he was not fawninge, nor bitinge, and his conuersation without any pertinacie: and to côclude all in a fewe wordes: he was a man of an other world , of whome we may iustly say as (*a*) A L E- XANDER HALENSIS saied of S. BONAVENTVRE. That he was a man, in whome *Adam seemed not to haue sinned.* He was a reformer, Prelate, Master, and patterne of perfection , of the Seraphicall Order of our holy Father S. FRANCIS, who through so many Prouinces, and remote Kingedomes, illustrated this sacred institution ; as an other Apostle preordained by God Almightie for this happie end.

(*a*) *Antonius Possenimus in Sacro apparatu de scriptoribus Ecclef. tom. 1. de Bonauent.*

CHAP.

CHAP. III.

Of his religious simplicitie, and mortification of his eies.

BVt to defcend to particulars, wherin his religious fimplicitie was manifefted. He was fo abforped in God almightie, that he minded nothinge of exteriour thinges. When he was a younge brother keepinge the keyes of the pauntrie, for the fpace of fix months, there was in the pauntrie grapes and pomgranades, which lay fo palpably, that none could choofe but fee the, but he for that fpace neither fawe, nor fmelt, much leffe touched them: beinge asked why he did not giue them vnto the brothers, he humbly anfwered, that he knewe of none that were there. An other time, liuinge fower yeares in an other cloifter, he neuer tooke notice of a great tree which ftood in the middeft of the court, which was obuious to euery ones eie. Being a yeare in an other place, and asked what his cell was made of, he anfwered,

ſwered, he knew not whether it was of
ſtone, or brick, or vvood. And a chap-
pell vvhich he frequented aboue others,
yet he knevve neither ſituation, forme,
or any ornament vvhich did belonge
thervnto. He vvas vvont to ſay to bleſſed THERESIA his ghoſtly child,
that he knevve neuer a brother in his
monaſterie, but only by his ſpeech. Moreouer he vvas ſo mortified in his eies,
that vvhere ſoeuer he vvas, he knevve
no difference in places, no diſtance of
cells, and finally he vvas a dead man to
all exteriour thinges. Neither vvas this
mortification any ſtupiditie of nature,
or vvant of ſenſes, but his continuall bu-
ſyinge his thoughts vpō God almighty,
a more noble, and higher obiect. Who
could but thinke this chaſt child of
S. FRANCIS to haue made a coue-
nant vvith his eies, not to behold a virgine? and vvell he might be ſtiled that
ſonne of a doue, vvhoſe eies vvere vvaſ-
hed vvith the milke of innocency. He
kept ſuch a continuall guard ouer his
eies, that he neuer knevve any vvoman
by her face. There vvas a certaine noble
matron famous for her vertue , vvho
vvas vvont at PLACENTIA, ſome
times to viſite the holy Father , for his
ſpi-

Spirituall counsell she meetinge him at ABVLA, saluted him, and expressed to him the difficulties of her state , he modestly denied, that he euer sawe the vvoman. If euer he opened his eies, it vvas in the quire , though he had so good a memory, that he knevve most part of the office vvithout booke. Beinge Superiour he did particularly correct this imperfection vvith seueritie. Knovvinge, nothinge to be more preiudiciall to the soule , then to set open those vvindovves, at vvhich, doth enter the greater part of sinne , that doth defile the heart of man.

CHAP.

CHAP. IV.

VVith vvhat austeritie and mortification the holy Father liued.

BECAVSE for the most part this holy Father liued in solitarie conuentes, most remote from vvorldly tumoults, or rather heremitages, all his rigourous penance, could not be taken notice of by any. Neuertheless vve vvill sett dovvne some, vvhich he could not hide from those, vvith vvhome he conuersed.

He did vvare for seauen yeares together a haire shirt full of hard knotts, S. THERESIA affirmeth that he vvore it tvventie yeares.

Besides plates of Iron, and other things vvhervvith he tyranized euer his tender flesh. His disciplines vvere so frequent and bloodie, that he seemed rather the trunke of a tree then a humaine bodie. He vvould neuer couer his head although it rayned neuer so fast, or the

sun

fun shined neuer fo hott. His diet was fo flender, and meane, that in his youth, and old age he did eate nothinge but browne bread, and the moft muftie crufts that he could finde. If fometimes he recreated himfelfe with a fewe boyled hearbes, he would not be fo delicious as to eate them with oyle. Beinge fuperiour he caufed as many beanes and peafe to be boyled at once, as should ferue the conuent for feauen dayes together, which aufteritie his fubiects moft willingly embraced, beinge glad in fome meafure to immitate their cheife. But he feafoned his owne portion with ashes, or fome vngratefull liquour, leaft his pallate should take pleafure in his meate.

Mother THERESIA hath heard his companions fay, that fome times he liued eight dayes together without any meate or drinke, efpecially when with more violence, he addicted himfelfe to deuotion. For he fuffered in his prayers frequent raptes and extafies, of which (faith she) I am wittneffe. He neuer dráke wine|but water, though for the infirmitie of his ftomach it was prefcribed to him by the Phifitian: but he conftantly refufed it fayinge that nothinge was fo

repu-

repugnant to holy pouertie , and abstinence, as flesh and wine, the one beinge an enemy to chastitie , the other to contemplation, both which , as longe as he liued , by Gods grace he would enioy. I will sett downe for the satisfaction of the deuout reader the wordes of euer blessed THERESIA, the glorie and foundresse of the discalsed Carmelites, to whome he was some times ghostly Father , of whome she confesseth to haue receiued much spirituall comfort; whose authoritie , by reason of her renouned sanctitie , and liuinge at the same time with him, is without controull. Her wordes be these. *(a) God almightie bereaued vs of a man of admirable example, vvhen he tooke out of this life, Father* PETER OF ALCANTARA, *the vvorld it seemeth could endure no longer so great perfection , they say that our health is not so good, that novve those times be past , this holy man vvas of this time , he vvas fatt in spirit , as those of other ages , he had also the vvorld vnder his feete , for though vve doe not goe barefoote , nor doe such austere penance as he did, there are many thinges (as I haue saied else vvere) to treade dovvne the vvorld vvith all . And our Lord teacheth them , vvhen he seeth such a minde , as he*

(a) **Ex vita B. Theresia** *cap. 27.*

gaue

gaue in great meaſure to this holy man,
vvhich I ſpeake of , to continue 47. yeares
together in ſuch auſtere penance , as all
knovve. I vvill declare ſome part of it , for
I knovve that it is all true. He told it to me
and to an other , from vvhome he concealed
little , and the cauſe vvhy he told it me , vvas
the great loue vvhich he bare me, and vvhich
our Lord gaue him to defende me , and en-
courage me, in the time of ſo great neceſſitie,
as that vvas, vvhich I haue ſpoken of , and
vvill declare further ; it ſeemeth to me, that
he told me , that he had ſlept no more but
an hovver and halfe betvvixt day and night
for the ſpace of 40. yeares, and that this vvas
the greateſt difficultie he fovvnd in his penance at the beginninge , to overcome his
ſleepe , and for this cauſe he did alvvayes.
Either kneele or ſtand , and vvhen he ſlept it
vvas ſitttinge leaninge his head againſt a little
peece of vvood , vvhich he had driuen into the
vvall , he could not lye dovvne though he
vvould, for his cell as is knovvne,vvas no longer
then fovver foot and an halfe , in all theſe
yeares he neuer did put on his capuce , hovv
great ſun-ſhine or raine ſoeuer it vvas, neither
had he any thinge on his feet , nor other garment, but his habit of courſe cloth , vvithout
any other thinge next his skin , and this as
ſtreight as could be endured, and a ſhort cloke
                                        of the

of the ſame vpon it , he told me that vvhen it vvas very cold he did putt it of , and opened the dore and little vvindovve of his cell , that aftervvard vvhen he did putt his cloke on againe , and shutt his dore , he might giue ſome contentment and recreat his bodie, vvhich before vvas frozen vvith cold. He did very ordinarily eate but once in three dayes ; and he asked me at vvhat I maruailed , for it vvas verie poſſible , for one that accuſtomed himſelfe to it. His pouerty vvas extreame, and likevviſe his mortification in his youth , &c. VVith all his ſanctitie he vvas verie affable, though he vſed not many vvordes, if he vvere not ſpoken too , for then he vvas verie pleaſinge, hauinge a good vnderſtandinge. And a little after. His end vvas like his life preachinge and admonishinge his Fryars. VVhen he ſavve death dravve nighe, he ſaid the Pſalme: Lætatus ſum in his quæ dicta ſunt mihi; and kneelinge dovvne departed. Since our Lord hath let me enioy him more then in his life, giuinge me aduiſe and counſell in many thinges I haue ſeene him many times in exceedinge great glorie ; the firſt time he appeared vnto me, he ſaied: O happie penáce which did merit ſuch a reward ! and many other thinges. A yeare before he died, he appeared to me beinge abſent , and I knevve that he should dye, and I ſent him vvord beinge ſome leagues

from

from hence. VVhen he gaue vp the ghost, he appeared to me and sayed, that he vvent to rest, I beleeued it not , I told some of it , and eight dayes after the nevves came that he vvas dead, or rather began to liue for euer. Behold here his austeritie endeth vvith so great glorie, he seemed to comfort me more novve , then vvhen he vvas in this vvorld. Our Lord told me once, that nothinge should be asked in his name, vvhich he vvould not heare. I haue seene many thinges fulfilled vvhich I haue desired him to aske of our Lord; he be blessed for euer. Amen. And in the 30. Chapter of her life she sayeth as flolloweth : *Our Lord vouch-safed to remedy a great part of my trouble, and for that time the vvholl , by bringinge to this place the blessed Father* PETER OF ALCANTARA, *of vvhome I haue alreadie made mention, and spoken somethinge of his penance , for amongst other thinges, I vvas certified, that for* 20. *yeares he had vvorne a cilice of plate continually. He is the authour of certaine little bookes of prayer, vvhich are novv much vsed in the spanish tongue, for as one, that hath exercised it vvell he vvrote very profitably, giuinge most excellent rules to those, vvho addict themselues to prayer. He obserued the first rule of* S. FRANCIS *vvith all rigour, and other thinges vvhich I haue related before.* Thus she. And so much

much shall ſuffice to ſpeake of, but part
of his rigourous penance, it was his feruent zeale, and loue of God, not ſtrēgth
of bodie, which made this crabbed way
of penance eaſy. to his Heroick ſpirit:
whoſe example may (though not in ſo
great a meaſure as he did) iuſtly moue
vs, to shake of that old and ſelfe-loue
excuſe of ours, in ſayinge, our bodies are
weake , when alas ! our willes are frozen , and ſo nice , that we are afraied to
expoſe our carcaſſe but to a poore triall,
the heathen S E N E C A will check our
indeuotion, who ſayeth : (b) *Not becauſe*
certaine thinges are hard, therfore vve dare
not doe them , but becauſe vve dare not doe
them, therfore they are hard.

(b) *Non quia*
diffiilia quæ-
dam ſunt, ideo
non audemus,
ſed quia non
audemus, ideo
difficilia.

CHAP.

CHAP. V.

Of his great puritie, and humilitie.

THE man of God increasinge in his rigorous penance, did not only mortifie in part, but wholly subdued his passions, and made his senses subordinate to the rule of reason, he suffered nothinge to enter into his soule, which might separate, or in the least kinde withdrawe his affectiō from his beloued spouse, for (as much as was possible for pilgrime man) he enioyed the spirit of God; golden peace and diuine consolation satt vpon his winges of contemplation, and where others make their bodies masters, he made his a slaue vnto his spirit. Hence it came to pass, that many of both sexe, drawne with the fragrāt odour of his vertues, flocked to him, as to an other Apostle, to whose counsells and admonitions they obeyed, as to a diuine oracle.

Vpō a time the count ORAPSANE a deuout nobleman, came to visit him.
And

And fallinge into discourse, how much God almightie was moued with the sins of the world, out of his zeale breaketh into these speeches. O Father! what doe you thinke ? what will be come of this wicked world ? doe you thinke the diuine iustice, can conteine it selfe any longer from reuenge ? behold howe vertue is oppressed, and sin triumpheth? how wilfully doe we hoarde vp anger against the day of anger ? to which the man of God modestly answered and sayed , noble Sir, doe not afflict your selfe, a remedy will easily be found to cure this disease , the point of the difficultie consisteth only in you and me, for the generall perdition of mankinde, floweth from this fountaine , that all and euery one dissemblinge or cloakinge their owne sins, accuse the wholl, when the wholl can not be said to sin at all, but particular persons in the wholl. Wherfore men crye out against the wickednesse of the world , that all are naught, and none that doe good, when if they would but looke into their owne particular , they should finde matter enough of sorrowe , and to moue them selues to doe penance for their owne faults : but nowe because they blame the

c 4   wholl,

wholl, they neglect their owne particu-
lares, and iustifie themselues with a fot-
tish presumption. Therfore, noble Sir,
let your Lordship , and I mend one a
peece , and then a great part of the
world wilbe amended, we shall appease
the angery iudge , and repaire a great
part of the ruine of mankinde by our
good example.

When CHARLES the fifth recol-
lected himselfe in a certaine monasterie
of the HIERONYMITES, vnderstandinge of the sanctitie and integrety
of this holy Father , he sent for him,
with an intent to make him his ghostly
Father. But he hūbly refusinge so great
an honour, alleaged some reasons, why
he thought this employment not to be
fittinge for him. At which deniall the
Emperour beinge a little moued , with
anger, saied, we charge you, Father, that
you would take care of our soule. He
seeinge this suddaine alteration of CE-
SAR, fell downe at the feete of his maiestie, and earnestly desired him, to differre
the busines to what day or houre he
would please to appoint , that in the
meane time he might cōmend it to God
almighty; which the Emperour graun-
ted, then he tooke his leaue of the Emperour,

perour, and saied, this renouned C E-
S A R, shalbe a signe vnto you, that it is
not accordinge to God almighties will,
which you haue desired, if I doe not retourne at the appointed time. Then pas-
singe to his former solitude, as he went,
he complained with many sighes and
groanes, to God almightie, fearinge by
the diuises of Sattan, to be drawne from
the embrasinges of his beloued spouse
C H R I S T I E S V S. He sent vp his fer-
uāt prayers to the almightie throne, and
saied these like wordes: Lord, I haue „
not therfore left the world, and beta- „
ken my selfe to this holy desert, that „
now at length my name should be re- „
nowned in a Princes court, and liue „
in honour, that am a poore F R A N- „
C I S C A N F R Y A R. Why should „
my eares be troubled with the flatte- „
ringes of courtiers, who came to spea- „
ke my fault in religion? I confess that „
this office may be exercised without „
sinne, but whether it be expedient „
for my soule, sweet I E S V S, tell me? „
and when he entred into his cell. „
Lord, I beseech thee pull me not from „
hence, whether thy omnipotent hand „
hath brought me. Here I am safe, here „
I am rich ; because I enioy thee who „
　　　　　　　　　　　　　　　　alone „

alone canſt ſatiate my ſoule. Alas! with- ,,
out thee what is the wholl empire? ,,
and with thee this poore cell , is a ,,
Kingdome of contēt. Here let me liue: ,,
Here let me die. Lord let it pleaſe thee ,,
what I wish for, becauſe all is thine, ,,
what ſoeuer I deſire. If thou granteſt ,,
me my petition, let this be a ſigne vnto ,,
me, that C e s a r moleſteth me no ,,
more. So riſinge, as beinge heard, did
appeare no more before him. Neither
did the Emperour euer ſolicite him after.

The ſame requeſt did the illuſtrious
Princeſſe I o h a n n a, ſiſter to P h i l-
l i p the ſecond, Catholique Kinge of
Spaine , make vnto this holy Father,
whome he likewiſe denied after the
ſame manner. Thus whileſt he fled honours, he was moſt honoured of all, and
reuerenced of euery one.

And what candide ſynceritie he vſed,
in contemninge proferred honours ,
men of no ſmall qualitie obſerued, that
thoſe who honoured him, he would no
more regard their ſpeech then a ſimple
ideot, and would labour to diuert them
from that, to ſome other diſcourſe. He
had rather be called a ſinner then a holy
man, and he himſelfe would (but without ſcandall) lay open to the world his
im-

imperfections, vnder vvhich, his vertues and graces vvere cloaked. But God the searcher of secrets, by hovve much he did striue to hide them, the more he made his fame to shine in the vvorld, to the astonishment of all. For he vvas a man vvhome God had chosen accor-dinge to his ovvne heart, by vvhose in-dustrie, and from vvhose spirituall loines did springe, many great seruantes of IESVS CHRIST, and many re-novvned martyrs of our holy Order.

CHAP.

CHAP. VI.

Of his feruant prayers and raptures, & of his spirit of prophesie.

GOD almightie was alwayes present with him, and he with God. His soule was like a fyerie fornace , made hott with the fuell of the crosse of CHRIST. It was not in his owne power, to conteine himselfe , but what thinge soeuer he either sawe , or heard, which might delight his beloued IESVS, though it were but a farr of, his heart-stringes would beginne to treble, and his vitall spirits leaue him , and frequently fall into extasie. He was accoustomed for a wholl houre together , to say his prayers with his armes stretched out in manner of a crosse, sighinge and weepinge, till at last he would be besides himselfe, eleuated from the ground, and vnited only to his God. He was oftentimes in this manner rapt, when he was in the quire at mattins. But his deuotion was much more augmēted at the aulter, when he celebrated the dreadfull sacrifice,

fice, then would riuers of teares gush in aboundance from his venerable eies, that would moue the moſt ſtonie and obdurate heart of any of the ſtanders by, vnto compunction. After maſſe he would withdrawe himſelfe into his cell, where he hath beene often heard to haue had greuious conflicts with deuils: who oftentimes appearinge in a viſible shape, would followe him vp and downe with a terrible furie.

In talkinge of God almightie, his ſoule would be preſently inebriated with diuine ſweetnes, and aſcendinge by degrees from one word to an other, as, what was God incarnated for me? was God made man for me? was God veſted with humane flesh for me? and the like. He would forthwith breake into exclamations, and hurryinge himſelfe into his cell, would for the ſpace of aboue three howers together, looſe the vſe of his ſenſes. (a) One day, a brother, that was newely made Preiſt, practiſinge in the garden to ſinge maſſe, when he heard him ſinge theſe wordes of S. IOHNS goſpell. (*Et Verbum caro factum eſt.*) He was eleuated into the aire two cubits high, and flewe through fower dores with the violence of this motion, at length

(a) *Marianus in vita B. Alcant. cap. 10.*

length settinge himselfe vpon his knees, before the blessed Sacrament for a longe space together remained in extasie.

This therfore vvas ordinarie to the freind of God, that vvhen he heard any thinge of the humanitie of our blessed Sauiour, or any deuout vvord of the holy Scripture, it vvould cause him raptures. Neither could he help them, though he did striue much against them, especially in the presence of others, but his heart vvould become like meltinge vvax in the middest of his bovvells. He vvas often in seinge the Crucifix, moued vvith such compassion that his armes a cross vvould be rapt, vvith little cloudes glitteringe about his heade.

He would some times prophesie, to some the loss of honours, to others sudden death, to other purgatorie. Which would fall out the verie day and hower he told them.

The first time he sawe S. THERESIA he told her what contradictions and afflictions she suffered from her ghostly Fathers, and other spirituall persons, who would needs perswade her, that she was seduced. And moreouer, that she was to suffer much more, in the same kinde. He likewise

for-

of blessed Alcantara.
forteold what should be successe in the
Indies.

CHAP. VII.

Of his patience.

HE traced the steeps of our blessed Sauiour , and all his glorious Saints, (*a*) all vvhich did neuer merit their crovvnes vvithout carryinge of the cross of CHRIST.

He vvas an other patient IOB, in sufferinge the temptatiōs and afflictiōs, the infirmitie of man is subiect vnto, he vvas in a particulare manner loadē vvith the heauie burthen of them , notvvithstandinge his feruant spirit , patiently supported, and victoriously triumphed ouer all his difficulties mauger all the force of Sathan. His frequent combates, his persecutions, his sicknes, his longe and tedious trauells , the difficulties he did vndergoe in erectinge his prouince, vvould take vp too much time to relate. He vvas so greedie of sufferinge, that he esteemed himselfe happie , to

bare

(a) Quis Sanctorum sine patientia coronatus? solus in deliciis Salomon fuit, & ideo fortasse corruit. Diu. Hieron.

bare afflictiōs for the name of IESVS,
sayinge, that there vvas no vvay so sure
and easie to attaine vnto perfection, as
the carryinge of the cross of CHRIST.
He vvould therfore begge of God almightie that he might neuer be vvithout some affliction. Thus did our couragious champion trample vpon all his
(b) Psal. 90. enemies. (b) He kicked the *Aspe* and
Basiliske, he vvalked vpon the *Lion* and
the *Draggon*, vvhilest he vanguished all
his foes, not so much by resistinge, as by
sufferinge.

CHAP.

CHAP. VIII.

Of his charitie towardes his neighbour.

HIs charitie towardes his nei-
bour vvas vnspeakable, for this
cause he ofte visited hospitalls
to serue the sick, assistinge them both
spiritually and corporally , and oftentimes miraculously restoringe them to
their former health. After he had made
an end of his deuotions, the residue of
his time he spent , in comfortinge the
afflicted, in cherishing the feable, and finally in any thinge he could immagine,
might cōfort his neighbours, either corporally or spiritually, so that innumerable people of all conditions, and sexes
continually flocked vnto him for his
charitable assistance.

CHAP. IX.

Of his pouertie.

(a) *S. Franciscus non solùm paupertatis commodis libentissimè fruebatur, sed etiam ita honorabat & colebat, quasi rem eximiam & cui nulla humana dignitas posset cōparari. Itaq; vt D. Bonau. scribit, eam in omni sermone modò Matrē, modò Sponsā, modò Dominam appellabat, sæpe et:ā Reginam, propterea quod in rege regum eiusque genitrice, adeo insigniter effulsisset. Hieron: Platus de bono stat. relig. lib. 2. cap. 3.*

HE vvas a rigid obseruer of holy pouertie, vvhich in immitation of his patron (a) S. Francis, he not only loued, but honoured so farr that he vvas vvont to call it the Euangelicall pearle, vvhervvith he enriched his nevve erected prouince, in that lustre as the obseruance vvas in the infancie of our Seraphicall Order, from vvhich time, and by vvhose example, most prouinces through the Christian vvorld haue excelled in this particulare point, as much as in their former splendour. He permitted his bretheren to haue nothinge in their cells but of mere necessitie, and to the preachers he permitted them no more but tvvo or three bookes, vvith the Bible and a crucifix.

He vvas vpon a time asked by S. Theresia vvhither or no she should found her Monasteries vvith rentes and yearely reuenues, to vvhich
diuerse

diuerse persons of qualitie had aduised her. He answered, that it vvas an iniurie to God the authour of Euangelicall counsells, to aske the aduise of men touchinge the obseruance of them, or to doubt vvhither or no they vvere obseruable. And vvith all encouraged her to be constant in that feruant desire, she had begun in embracinge holy pouertie. To vvhose counsell she vvillingly obeyed. And after our Lord appeared to her in prayer, and declared, that it vvas his vvill that her Monasteries should be founded in holy pouerty. His letter to her I thinke it not amisse to set dovvne at large, vvhich follovveth.

A letter

A letter of the blessed Father FR. PETER DE AL- CANTARA , *to the holy Mother* THERESA OF IESVS, *who demanded his counsell, whither she should founde her Monasteries with rents or no.*

THE holy Ghoſt giue you his grace and loue, &c. I receiued yours, deliuered me by DON GONZALES D'ARANDA. And am amazed, conſideringe your zeale , and pietie: in committinge to the direction of learned lavvyers , that vvhich is no vvayes their profeſſion , or belonginge vnto them : you should doe vvell to take their aduice concerninge the deci- dinge of a proceſs or of ſutes in lavv, and tēporall affaires, but in that vvhich concerns perfection of life , vve ought to treate only vvith thoſe vvho practiſe the ſame. For ſuch as the conſcience of euerie one is , ſuch are his exerciſes and

vvor-

vvorkes. Concerninge the Euangelicall counsells, may I demand vvhither they be obseruable or noe? For that the coūsells of God cannot be but good , neither can the obseruance therof seeme difficult, vnlesse to those, vvho gouerne themselues accordinge to humane prudence , hauinge lesse confidence in God then they ought. For he , vvho hath giuen the counsell, vvill consequently giue force and meanes to accomplish the same. And if your zeale and feruour dravve you to embrace the counsells of CHRIST IESVS , obserue them vvith the greatest integritie, and perfection that possible you can: seeinge they were equally giuen to both sexes. It can not be, but the same meritt and reward will be rendered vnto you, as to others that haue truly obserued them. And if there be seene any want or necessitie in the Monasteries of poore Religious Women , it is becauschy they are poore against their wills , and not through faulte of their vowe of pouertie, or followinge of the Euangelicall counsells. For I accoumpt not much of their simple pouertie, but of their patient sufferance of the same for the loue of God. But I more esteeme of that pouertie

d 3   which

which is defired, procured, and embraced for the fame loue. And if I should
thinke or otherwife determinatly beleeue , I should not hould my felfe a
good Catholique. I beleeue in this, and
in all other thinges taught by our bleffed Sauiour , and that his counfells are
good and profitable, as proceedinge frō
God , and though they oblige not to
finne, they binde neuerthelefs that man
to be more perfect that followeth thē,
then if he had not yndertaken them at
all. I hold them poore in fpirit , which
are poore in will , as our Sauiour hath
faied, and my felfe proued ; how be it
I beleeue more from God thē of myne
owne experience , that those, who by
the grace of God , are with all their
hearts poore, leade a life most happie as
confidinge and hoping in him alone.
His diuine Maieftie giue you light to
vnderftand this truth , and to practife
the fame. Beleeue not thofe that shall
tell you the contrarie, for want of light
and vnderftandinge, or for not hauinge
tafted, how fweet our Lord is to thofe,
that feare and loue him , renouncinge
for his sake all vnneceffarie thinges of
this world , for they are enemies of the
Croffe of C H R I S T, not beleeuinge
the

the glorie which accōpanieth the same.
I also pray our Lord to giue you this
light , that you be not wantinge in the
beleife of this truth , so much manifested. And that you take not counsell,
but of the followers of CHRIST
IESVS. Although others thinke it
sufficient if they obserue the thinges
they are bound vnto, yet they haue not
alwayes greater vertue and perfection
by their worke. And though the counsell bee good , yet that of our blessed
Sauiour is much better. Who knowes
what he counselleth and giueth grace
to accomplish the same: and in the end
reward to those who hope in him and
not in rents and goods of the earth.

From Auila this 14. *of April* 1562.

d 4   CHAP.

Chap. X.

Of his confidence in God almighties prouidence.

HIs admirable confidence in God almighties prouidēce, did accompanie his rigid and Euāgelicall pouertie, and it oftentimes miraculously appeared, both at home and abrode.

(a) *Marianus in eius vita. cap. 6.*

(a) He liued some times in the conuent of *Sancta Maria de Rosario*, which is situated in a woody place, by the riuer *Tentairis*, six Italian miles remote from any companie, at all times it was hard to come vnto by reason (b) the way is very steepe and crooked, neuerthelesse it was a place of great deuotiō, whether the inhabitāts of the country did much resort; but now by reason of a great snowe, the like was not seene in the memorie of man; the Monasterie was so inuironed on euery side, that the Fryars could not goe out to get their victualls, neither could any come to them to bringe prouision. They cried to heauen

(b) *Ea est itineris ad eum ob loci solitudinem, atque viarū anfractus difficultas, vt vix accolis atque assuetis pateat. Gonsaga 3. parte Chrō. ord. S. Franc. in prou. sancti Iosephi.*

heauen to the Father of the poore, that beinge destitute of all humane aide, he only out of his infinite mercie would be pleased not to forsake them. The holy Father desired them to goe into the church, and settinge themselues vpon their knees, before the blessed Sacrament, to pray to God that he would put a remedy to their hard affliction. He with great confidéce animated his Bretheren, sayinge: Be couragious, Bretheren, God almightie will not be longe, he will come without delay. He had no sooner vttered these wordes, but an other most violent storme of snowe fell so fast, that frustrated their hopes of all humane assistance. But he that conteineth not his anger longe, did not delay to comfort his afflicted childeren. Behold! a little space after the storme was ouer, the porter heard the bell of the gate of the conuent to ringe, he went to open the dore, but espied no bodie, he retourned back againe, thinking it to be the winde, that had stirred the bell, or that his fancie seemed to heare the noise when he heard it not; checkinge himselfe with foolishnes, that he could immagine, that it was possible for any to come to the conuét in so deepe a snowe.

W hi-

Whileſt he was thus diſcourſinge with himſelfe, it range againe ſo hard that all heard it, notwithſtandinge it was a great winde. Then retourninge againe to the gate, and openinge it, he found a basket filled full of newe white bread, he looked about to ſee if he could eſpy any body, but no creature appeared, for it was a deepe ſnowe, where the footinge of any perſon could not but appeare. He left the basket, and with ioy ran backe into the conuent, to carry the good newes vnto the Fryars; who would not beleeue, vntill the holy Father, commaunded all the Brothers, to goe in manner of proceſſiõ, to ſee what God almightie had done for his ſeruantes: When they came, they found all true, as the porter had related to thẽ. But their benefactour did no where viſibly appeare. They carried the baſked in, and after thankeſgiuinge refreshed themſelues, with the bread which the Father of heauen had miraculouſly beſtowed vpon them. Vpon which they liued many dayes, vntill the extremity of the ſeaſon, was paſt and that they could goe out to begg almes accordinge to their cuſtome.

(c) An other time trauailinge in the (c) *Marianus* extremitie of the heate of summer, vpon *ibidem cap.7.* the mountaine vulgarly called *Siera Morena*, he, with his companion grewe so faint, for wāt of some thinge, to quench their thirst, that they were ready to sinke vnder the burthē of their tedious iourny. He said vnto his companion: Brother, let vs betake our selues to prayer the only remedie, to incline the God of mercie to take compassion vpon our miserie. Whilst they were vpon their knees at their prayers, from a thicket came runninge out a mad bull, who made towards them amaine, they seeing themselues in this great danger of their liues, betooke themselues to flight, but the bull persued them ouer hedge and ditch, hard at their heeles, till at last he forced them to a place, where was a fountaine of water, when they came in sight of that, the bull forgettinge his former fury, stoode still like an innocent lambe, he breathed himselfe a while, and went an other way. But they admiringe this great miracle of the omnipotent, that sendeth his willd beasts to teach the poore, refreshed themselues and went on their iourny with alacrity, their soules more com-

comforted with this vnexpected benefit of God almighties prouidence, then
their bodies ftrengthned with the water which they drunk for their fufte-
nance.

(d) *Marianus*
ibidem.

(d) Hauinge occafion to goe from
De las Lucuas to *Del Pico* : as he was in his
iournie it began to fnowe, which fell fo
faft that it was not poffible for him to
goe forward or backward , fo that he
was enforced to remaine the wholl
night in that extremitie of cold and
fnowe. But the feruour of his deuotion,
wherwith he implored the diuine affiftance, caufed him to pafs ouer the night
without tedioufnes. But that which
was more admirable. Behold ! in the
morninge when it was day, one might
fee, that the fnowe did not fo much as
touch or wett him, but it congeled ouer
his heade in a miraculoufe maner like a
canopie, and of each fide too wales of
fnowe frozen in a curiousmanner, defended him from the iniurie of the
weather, as though he had bene fhutt
in a beautifull chamber.

These fewe miracles I haue fet
downe collect out of many, which God
almightie hath bene pleafed to worke
by the meanes of his glorious feruaunt.

(e) As

(e) As teftimonies, not only of many fingular prerogatiues of graces exhibited to this holy Father in his owne particular. But alſo that we admiringe theſe ftraunge and vnaccuftomed manner of God almighties proceedinges with this bleſſed man, the truth wherof beinge cõfirmed by many approued authours. May be incited to immitate his vertues whome God hath honowred with the grace of workinge miracles.

(e) Miracula voco quicquid arduũ aut inſolitum ſupra ſpẽ vel facultatẽ mirantis apparet, quædam admiratiõe faciunt, quædam gratiam magnam beneuolentiãque conciliãt Aug. de vtil. cred. prope finem.

CHAP.

If thou shouldeſt obiect vvith Caluin *in præfat. inſtit.* that the miracles of our Sainctes in the Catholique Church, are partly fained, partly diabolicall. I anſvver, that the ſame thinge the Phariſies obiected to our bleſſed Sauiour, that he caſt out deuils in Beelzebub the prince of the deuils. More ouer it is moſt deuiliſh to blemiſh the integritie of the ancient Fathers and Sainctes, vvith ſuch an impudent and foule aſperſion , as thoſe vvho vvrote the liues of other Saints, as Nycenus of Taumaturgus, S. Athenaſius and S. Hierom, of S. Anthonie, Seuerus of S. Martine, S. Gregorie of S. Benet, S. Bernard of S. Malachias, S. Bonauenture of S. Francis. VVhoſe authoritie if vve ſhould deny no faith or credit is to be giuen to any hiſtorie in the vvorld. VVhich abſurditie none, but men out of their vvitts, or blinded vvith malice, vvill admitt S. Auguſtine confirmeth vvhat I ſay. His vvordes be theſe: *Au dicet aliquis iſta falſa eſſe miracula , nec fuiſſe facta ſed mendaciter ſcripta; quiſquis hoc dicit, ſi de his rebus negat, omnino vllis literis eſſe credendũ, poteſt etiã dicere nec Deos vllos curare mort alia. De ciuit. Dei l. 10. c. 18. Quædã facta non niſi à proteruientibus negari poſſunt, vt ſunt miracula facta à Sylueſtro corã Conſtantino tam in curatione lepræ eius, quã in diſputatione eius contra Iudæos: quæ facta tanquã celeberima mundũ non latuerant. Scot. in prol. q. 2 n. 11.*

CHAP. XI.

Of his knowledg in holy Scripture, and of his preachinge.

HE was so well versed in the holy Scripture , that for the most part , he could repeate it without booke, and in explicatinge it, he was so cleare, and with all so mouinge that one might iudge his learninge , to be rather supernaturally infused in prayer, then naturally gotten , by the ordinarie meanes of studie (*a*) for he quickly learned what he was taught seeinge he had the holy Ghost for his master. He wrote some spirituall workes , wherin he had a speciall gift of God almightie, both to direct those who tend vnto perfection , in their iourny towardes heauen, as also to inflame their wills to aspire to that eternall good. In this particulare science, he was cheifly eminent and wrote profitable and learned tracts of this matter.

(*a*) *O quam velox est sermo sapientiæ, & vbi Deus magister est, quam citò discitur quod docetur. B. Leo ser 1. de Pentecoste.*

He

He had such a rare gift in preaching : so inuectiue against sinne, and withall so comfortable, to those who were pullinge their feete out of the snare of vices, that God almighty was pleased to worke by his meanes, many wonderfull effects in the soules of his auditory.

In the citty of *Abula* there was a young gentleman, that was giuen vnto, and as it were buried in all the sportes and vanities of this wicked world. But especially in the vild and pernicious loue of wanton womē. Cominge in his pompe vpō a festiuall day of that place, by chaunce mett the holy Father, who when he vnderstood of his corriualls the qualitie and sanctity of him, went towardes him with others to salute him with great respect, and withall begged his prayers, but God knoweth, with what intention, for he still obstinately remained in his filthy desires. But the holy Father in his sermon touched the soare of his soule vnto the quick (yet not reuealinge any person) in so much, that the holy Ghost did so worke with him, that this prodigall child vnderstandinge the Father was to goe away from that place, the next day, made

made hast, to gett pen and inke to write his sins, the next day cometh to the Father, and saluteth him, giuinge him a longe (*b*) scroule of his sinfull life, and desireth him for the loue of God, that he would vouchsafe to pray for him, that God would haue mercie vpon his soule, and that he would not punish him for euer accordinge vnto his deseruertes. The holy Father receiued his paper, and promised that he would pray for him. So each departed their way. But he had scarce turned his backe, but the Father earnestly begged of God almightie his conuersion, of which he was presently sensible : for before he came home, the spirit of God did so inflame him, that he abiured his former conuersation, and loathed the pleasures, that before he loued so much, and beinge retourned to his house, flunge off his braue cloathes, toare his chaine from his neck, and vested himselfe in meane and country cloathes, without any shame appearinge so to all the world, all admiringe the suddaine chaunge of the right hand of the highest; and as afterward he liued well, perseueringe to the end, so he dyed happily; he dispersed his patrimonie,

(*b*) The younge mā out of humility manifested his sins to the holy Father out of the Sacrament of confession.

monie amongst the poore , and built many monasteries and hospitalls, as testimonies of his conuersion.

He had such efficacy in his preachinge, that many common Women, drawne with the sweetnes of his spirit, chaunged their sordid and base manner of liuinge into holy and pious conuersation. Others as well of the nobility, as amongst the meaner sort of people, renouncing all pleasures for the loue of I E S V S, shrowded themselues in cloisters, where they might be secure from the contagion of worldly vanities. And many consecratinge their virginitie to their celestiall spouse, like lillies amögst thornes, perseuered in the open world amidst the dangers therof, with immoueable constancie.

c   CHAP.

CHAP. XII.

Of his religious zeale and of his death.

THE Reuerend esteeme of his vertues encreased so much, euen in his owne Cloister, that there many times (enioyned by obedience) performing the office of Guardian with great integrety , was at length by the suffrages of all the Fathers , elected twice Prouinciall of the prouince of S. GABRIEL, where he mad a happie and notable reformation. But after his three yeares expired , he betooke himselfe againe to his poore heremitage, where he fatted his soule with sacred contemplation , perseueringe in readinge the ancient Fathers , watchinges, fastinges, and regulare discipline. But the more he hid himselfe in these obscure places, the more the fame of his learninge and sainctitie did shine abroade. And in testimonie that God almightie would not haue this resplendāt light, to be put vnder a bushell , but to
be

be ſet vpon a candleſtick, to giue light
to others, to followe his glorious foot-
ſteppes, and to the end, that he might
not only enrich his owne ſoule with
the treaſures of vertue, but alſo inſtruct
others, both by his doctrine and exam-
ble, to aſpire to heauen, the ſea Apo-
ſtolique did vouchſafe to honoure him
with a commiſſion, by vertue of which,
he ſhould erect, and foūde a newe prouince vnder the title of S. IOSEPH.
Which before his death, he was ſo happie to ſee, not only multiplied in number of conuentes, and religious men (by
his great labour and trauaile)but alſo to
be perfectly eſtabliſhed in regulare ob-
ſeruance, and true monaſticall diſci-
pline.

At laſt, the number of his meritts beinge compleat, his iuſt maſter, whom
he had ſerued ſo longe with great fidelitie, was pleaſed to call him, to reward
his labours with an eternall crowñe of
glorie, and to reape in ioy what he had
ſowed in teares. He fell ſick in the Conuent of S. ANDREVVE DE MON-
TE ARENO, where God almightie
vouchſafed to let him knowe the
hower of his death. And before his departure he called his bretheren, exhor-

tinge them to perseuerance in that happie course, which they had vndertaken for the loue of God, and the sauinge of their owne soules. He the receiued vpon his knees with aboundance of teares the sacred *Viaticum* with singulare deuotion, and a little after, his infirmitie increasinge, he receiued also the Sacrament of extreame Vnction. The blessed Virgin and S. I o h n (to whome all his life time he was verie much deuout) appeared to him, and gaue him assurance of his saluation. Which euer-comfortable newes, he no sooner vnderstood, but his heart was rauished with ioy, and his mouth filled with gladnes; and out of that aboundance of content breaketh out into these wordes of the Prophet

(a) *Psal.* 112. D a v i d : (a) *Lætatus sum in his quæ dicta sunt mihi: in domum Domini ibimus:* I haue reioyced in those thinges that are saied vnto me : we will goe into the house of our Lord. In fine the happie hower beinge come, he yealded his blessed soule into the handes of his maker, and by the passage of a temporall death, trauailed to an eternall life the 18. of October, vpon the feast of S. L v k e 1562. the 63. yeare of his age, and the 47. of his entrance into holy Religion.

His

His body after his death became more beutifull, shininge with great claritie, and sendinge fourth sweete odours. The people from all partes flocked to behold this sacred spectacle, and greedie after so rich a prey, clipped peeces of his habite, which they conserued as holy reliques. His bodie was no sooner in the graue, but his sepulchre began to be renouned with many (b) miracles which for breuity sake I omitt to speake of because I would not be too tedious to the deuout reader.

(b) *Cum puerulus Æthiops inutilis penitùs atque contractus ad illius sepulcrū ab eius hera vxore quondam Martini de Friars ac præfati oppidi Arrenarum accola, adductus esset eius meritis Deo opt. max. id operante integræ sospitati restituitur. Et Ieonora Gonsalua eiusdem oppidi inquilina à paralisi qua grauißimè laborabat ad eius quoque sepulcrum liberatur. Franc. Gonzaga 3. parte Chron. ordinis Seraphici. Vide plura apud Ioannem de sancta Maria in vita B. Alcant. c.30.*

(c) His soule was no sooner out of his body, but presently he appeared to S. Teresia, to bringe vnto her the ioyfull tidinges of his receiuinge into heauen. Many times after he appeared to her, and once amongst the rest he saied vnto her: O HAPPY PENANCE THAT (d) DESERVED SVCH A GLORIOVS RECOMPENCE!

(c) *In eius vita cap. 27.* (d) *Opera nostra nō habent bonitatē meritoriā gloriæ ex sua natura, nec à nobis sed à Deo.* For our vvorkes are to be taken, a toofeld respect.

e 3 (e) Hap-

1. As they are in ther proper nature & dignity. 2. As they haue Gods promise & acceptance. If vve consider them in the first sence, so they doe not merite, saluation: if in the secōd, they doe. This I say, to ansvvere the obiection

of ignorant protestantes, vvho might take occasion to carpe at this vvord *(deserued)* and vvho likvvise thinke that vve so dignifie our vvorkes that therby vve thinke to merite heauen, abstractinge from the merites of our blessed Sauiours passion vvhen it is certaine, our doctrine is, that the

(e) Happie indeede was his penance, that chaūged sorrowes into pleasures: mourninge into mirth : teares into ioyes, and a momentarie crosse into an eternall crowne. The same blessed T H E R E-S I A (as we haue said before) affirmed, that she receiued more comfort , and consolation from him after his death, then in time of his life. And that his soule flewe immediately to heauen, without any passage by purgatorie. All these thinges beinge well examined, and verified, by persons , without all exceptiō, worthy of creddit, his holines, for the glorie of God , honour of the Saint , and benefit of the faithfull, vouchsafed to pronoūce him beatified: to the end , that as he had a perfect fruition of glorie, in the Church triumphant , so he should want no praise or reuerence, in the Church militant. He was

cheifest reason of merite is founded in Gods promise, not mans vvorke, and our vvorkes, so to merite, and to be ennobled, cheifly by vertue of ther principall agent our blessed Sauiours passion. *Conradus Klingius de locis com l.1. c.35. Stapelton. controuers. l.10.c.12. Bellarm.l.1. de iustificat. c.21. & l.5.c.11 cum comuni Doctorum.* (e) If the conuersion of sinners, and of greuious sinners, be so pleasinge to almighty God, that the Angels of heauen doe reioyce at it accordinge to S. Bernard *Supernas beatorum mansiones attingit pænitentiæ odor (ita vt teste ipsa veritate) magnum gaudium sit inter Angelos Dei super vno peccatore pænitentiam agente:*

was beatified the 18. of April 1622. and his office is celebrated in the Conuentes of his order the 19. of October.

gaudete pœnitentes, pusillanimes confortamini: vobis dico quos nuper onuersos de sæculo, & à vijs vestris prauis recedentes, ex-

F I N I S.

cepit mox amaritudo animi pœnitentis. Ac velut recentium adhuc vulnerum dolor nimius excruciat ac perturbat. Securæ manus vestræ distillant myrrhæ amaritudinem in salubrem hanc vnctionem, quia cor contritum, & humiliatum Deus non despiciet. D. Bernard. super Cantica serm. 10. I say if such à conuersion be so pleasinge to God, hovve glorious may vve iudge this holy Fathers penance to be, vvho from his cradle to his graue, liued innocently and austerly? So that vve may iustly say of him as the Church of *S. Iohn, Antra deserti teneris sub annis, ciuium turmas fugiens petisti, ne leui saltem maculare vitam, famine posses.*

BENEDICTVS DEVS.

BEA-

BEATIFICATIO

B. P.
DE ALCANTARA.

Gregorius Papa XV. ad perpetuam rei
memoriam.

IN Sede Principis Apostolorum nullis licèt nostris suf-
fragantibus meritis à Domino constituti, pijs fidelium
votis, quibus virtutum Dominus in seruis suis hono-
rificatur, libenter annuimus, eaque fauoribus prose-
quimur opportunis. Cum itaque instantibus non solum claræ me-
moriæ Philippo III. & charißimo in Christo filio nostro Philippo
IV. Hispaniarum Regibus Catholicis, sed etiam ferè omnibus
Hispaniæ regnis, venerabiles fratres nostri S.R.E. Cardinales sa-
cris ritibus præpositi, de mandato nostro causam serui Dei Petri
de Alcantara, Ordinis Min. strictioris obseruantiæ Discalceato-
rum nuncupatorum, ac Prouinciæ S.Iosephi eiusdem Ordinis Fun-
datorü, iuxta seriem trium causarum Palatij Apostolici Audito-
rum ad effectum canonizationis examinauerint, ac multis desuper
habitis seßionibus, referente dilecto filio nostro Marco Antonio,
tituli S. Eusebij Presbytero Cardinale Gozzadino nuncupato, ple-
nißimè constare de validitate processuum, fama sanctitatis, fide,
puritate, cæterisque virtutibus non in genere solùm, sed etiam in
specie, reliquiarum ac sepulchri veneratione, plurimisque tan-
dem miraculis pronunciauerint, censuerintque posse nos quando-
tunque voluerimus, eundem Dei seruum, iuxta Catholicæ Ec-
clesiæ ritum, Sanctum, atque in cælis regnantem declarare, om-
nibusque fidelibus solemni canonizatione proponere venerandü.
Prædictus vero Philippus IV. Rex, & dilecti filij Minister Ge-
neralis, & Fratres Ordinis prædicti nobis humiliter supplicari
fecerint,

fecerint, vt donec ad canonizationem dicti Petri deueniatur, idem Petrus Beatus nuncupari ac de eo tanquam de Confessore non Pontifice Missam ac officium vt infra celebrari & recitari respectiue possint, indulgere de benignitate Apostolica dignaremur. Nos supplicationibus huiusmodi inclinati de eorundem Cardinalium consilio, vt idem Dei seruus Petrus de Alcantara in posterum Beatus nuncupari atque de eo tanquam de Confessore non Pontifice die 19. Octob. qua ipsius obitus memoria celebrabitur vbique terrarum ab vniuersa religione Minorum obseruantium vtriusque sexus respectiue Missam celebrari atque officium recitari possint. In oppido verò de Alcantara illius diœcesis vbi natus atque in altero de Arenas Abulensis diœcesis vbi corpus eiusdem requiescere accepimus, omnibus tam regularibus quam secularibus Clericis sub ritu tamen semiduplici idem omnino liceat. Ac demum in Prouincia prædicta S. Iosephi, cuius autor extitit, ab ipsis dicti Ordinis Discalceatorum fratribus, etiam cum octaua veluti de Patrono, officium pariter ac Missa iuxta Breuiarij ac Missalis Romani Rubricas celebrari possint, Apostolica auctoritate tenore præsentiam perpetuo concedimus & indulgemus. Non obstantibus constitutionibus & ordinationibus Apostolicis, cæterisque contrarijs quibuscunque. Volumus autem vt præsentium transumptis etiam impressis manu alicuius Notarij Publici subscriptus, & sigillo personæ indignitate Ecclesiastica constitutæ munitis eadem prorsus fides adhibeatur quæ præsentibus adhiberetur si forent exhibiti vel ostensæ. Datum Romæ apud S. Petrum sub annulo Piscatoris die 18. Aprilis 1622. Pontificatus nostri anno secundo.

Copia vera desumpta ex tomo 4. Bullarij
Laertij Cherubini impresso Romæ
an. 1631.

FA-

FACVLTAS
SVPERIORIS.

Librum verè pium Meditationum B. PETRI DE ALCANTARA, Ordinis Fratr. Min. in linguam Anglicanam à religioso Patre Fr. *Ægidio Villoughby*, eiusdem Ordinis Prouinciæ nostræ Angl. filio, fideliter translatum, per omnia concordantem exemplari Latino inuenèrunt RR. PP. Theologi, quibus à nobis commissa fuit eiusdem examinatio, ideoque prælo dignum censui, ad instructionem populi Christiani, qui in tot controuersijs fidei, his pijs maiorum nostrorum exercitijs penè destituitur. Habet insuper adiunctam vitam ipsius B. PETRI è varijs authoribus à prædicto Patre *Ægidio* collectam, de qua idem sit iudicium. Dat. in nostra residentia Londini 1. Aprilis 1632.

Fr. IOANNES GENINGES,
Minister Prouincialis.

APPROBATIO.

MEditationes hæ B. PE-
TRI DE ALCAN-
TARA, in linguam Anglica-
nā à Religioſo Patre Fr. Ægidio VVilloughby, Ordinis Mi-
norū S. FRANCISCI tran-
ſlatæ, vti & vita dicti B. Patris
ab eodem auctore ex proba-
tis auctoribus collecta, lucem
videre merentur. Actum hac
10. Aprilis 1632.

HENRICVS CALENVS,
S. Theol. Licent. Archipr.
Brux. Librorum Cenſor.

ERRATA.

Pag.	Line.	Faults.	Corrected.
5	3	teaceth	teacheth.
11	2	iuspirations	inspirations.
15	17	hart	art.
30	7	tumpett	trumpett.
30	24	at housand	a thousand.
32	6	theatninges	threatninges
32	30	*incuruimine*	*incuruemini.*
43	17	vvortly	vvorthy.
49	11	*cribaret*	*cribraret.*
80	20	meditatig	meditatinge.
81	9	ony	my.
81	11	crucifieth	crucifie.
85	10	transgression	transgressions.
131	21	the	then.
134	20	medition	meditation.
135	15	discouse	discourse.
137	19	tutret	turret.
141	6	often felt	often is felt.
150	25	ractes	actes.

A
GOLDEN TREATISE,
OF
MENTAL PRAIER.

Compofed by the Reuerend & holy Father
Fr. Peter de Alcantara,
of the Seraphicall Order of
S. Francis.

Chap. I.

IN this Chapter wee will briefly fett downe the fruite of prayer and meditation, that men confidering the benefit of them, may be incited with a prompte and more willing mind to frequent thefe holy exercifes.

It is moft certaine, that the malice of our owne heartes, is the principall caufe that hindreth vs from attaining to our beatitude

A   *and*

and euerlasting happines, because it maketh vs slovve to godly actions, dull to vertuous exercises, and suggesteth a greater difficultie in them then there is, which if it vvere not, a man might vvalke vvithout any molestation in the way of vertue, and at length without labour attaine to his desired end.

Rom. 7. Hence it is, that the Apostle sayth : *I delight in the lavve of God acording to the invvard man: but I see another lavve in my members repugnant to the lavve of my mind , and captiuateinge mee in the lavve of sinne.*

The efficacie of deuotion. This therfore is the prime roote and cause of all our miseries, against which there is no remedie more conuenient , and efficacious, then deuocion, which acording to S. Thomas, is nothing else, but a certaine promptitude and facilitye of the minde to doe well. It doth exclude from our minde this tedious difficultie , and maketh vs with alacritye applie our selfes to vertuous actes. Therfore not without cause wee may tearme it spiritual food , recreatiue and heauenly deawe , a pleasant instinct and supernatural affection of the holy Ghost , which doth so roborate and transforme the hartes of men , that it doth begett in them a new gust and fealing of spiritual thinges , and on the contrary a tedious loathing of worldly vanities.

Day.

Daylye experience manifesteth this particular vnto vs. For wee see the soules of those who arise from profound and deuout prayer, to bee Strengthened with admirable resolutions, adorned with newe graces, and replenished with firme purposes of amendment of life, and frequenting pious exercises, they burne with an ardent desire of seruing and louing him with their wholl heart, whom in their prayer they found the God of all goodnes and benignitye, desiring to suffer any grieuious and burdensome crosse whatsoeuer it bee, yea to sheadd their bloud for his sake. To conclude, prayer is a bath, an open place, a bedde of pleasure, wherein the soule recreateth and refresheth her selfe.

If you aske mee, what bee the chiefest meanes to attaine vnto this heroicall vertue of deuotion. I answere with the same Doctour, that it is gotten by serious meditation and contemplation of heauenlye thinges. For the ruminating of these in the soule, with a more attentiue and profound consideration, doth begett in the will that disposition which wee call deuotiõ, which effectually rouzeth and pricketh a man forward to euery good worke. For this cause the exercise of prayer and meditation was frequent and familiar to men of

By vvhat meanes deuotion is gotten.

A 2   san-

ſanctity, as iudging it the eaſieſt meanes to cōpaſſe deuotiō, which although it be but one only ſimple vertue , yet it diſpoſeth and maketh vs fitt for all others , and as it were with ſpurres pricketh vs forward to the performance of euery good worke.

Bonau. in the Med. of the life of Chriſt cap.73.

I call S. BONAVENTVRE to witneſſe what I ſay : his wordes are theſe. The ineſtimable vertue of prayer is able to obtaine all good, and remoue all hurtfull things. If thou will patiently endure aduerſity; bee a man of prayer: If thou wilt ouercome tribulatiō and temptatiōs, bee a mā of prayer: If thou wilt trāple vpō thy peruerſe inclinatiōs; bee a mā of prayer: If thou wilt knowe the deceiptes of Sathan, and auoid thē; bee a mā of prayer. If thou wilt liue ioyfully in the worke of God , and trace the way of labour and afflictiō; bee a mā of prayer. If thou wilt exerciſe thy ſelfe in a ſpiritual courſe, and not walke acording to the deſires of the fleſh ; bee a man of prayer. If thou wilt put to flight thy vaine and trifling fancies ; bee a man of prayer. If thou wilt fatt thy ſoule with holy thoughtes, good deſires, feruour, and deuotion; bee a man of prayer. If thou wilt eſtablish thy heart with a manly Spirit, and conſtāt purpoſe in the ſeruice of God ; bee a man of prayer. To conclude , if thou wilt roote

out

out vice, and bee indued with vertues; bee
a man of prayer. In it is receaued the Vnction of the holy Ghoſt, which teaceth all
thinges. Alſo if thou wilt clime vp to the
toppe of contemplation , and enioye the
ſweet embracinges of thy beloued ſpouſe;
be a man of prayer. For by the exerciſe
of prayer, wee come to that contemplation
and taſte of heauenly thinges. Thou ſeeſt,
of what great power and vertue, prayer is.
For the Confirmation of all which , omit-
ting the Teſtimonie of holy Scriptures, let
this bee an euident proofe vnto the , that
by dayly experience, wee heare and ſee il-
literate and ſimple perſons, to haue attained
the foreſayd and greater thinges by the
vertue of prayer. Thus S. BONAVENTVRE.

I beſeech you , can there bee found a
richer treaſure or a more fertile fielde deſired? Heare an other Doctour no leſſe
for Religion and ſanctitye, who vpon the
ſame matter ſayth : By prayer the ſoule is
cleanſed from ſinne, replenished with charity , confirmed in fayth , roborated in,
and refreshed in Spirit. Prayer eſtabliſ-
heth the inward man , pacifieth the heart,
knoweth the trueth , conquereth temptations, expelleth ſorrowe , reneweth the
ſences, ſtirreth vp languishing vertue, put-
teth to flight tepidity , and ſkoureth the

ruft of vices. In prayer the quicke fparkles of celeftial defires are inceffantly fent forth from the burning coales of diuine loue. The priuiledges of prayer are rare, the prerogatiues admirable. Prayer vnlocketh the gates of Heauen, manifefteth diuine fecrets and alwaies findeth free acceffe to the eares of God. I will adde no more for thofe thinges which haue alreadie bene fayd, aboundantly expreffe the fruites of this holy exercife.

Chap. II.

Of the matter of prayer.

HAVINGE take notice of the vtility of prayer and meditation, wee will nowe declare the matter about which meditation is to bee converfant : for feeing it is ordained to this end, that the foule of him that meditateth, may bee excited to the feare and loue of God, and the keeping of his commaundementes : the matter of meditation ought to bee fuch , as doth next difpofe to this end and fcope. And although euery creature, and the whole Scripture it felfe bee able to minifter

nifter this matter vnto vs, yet speaking generally , the misteries of our holy fayth,
contained in the *Creed*, are most efficacious
and profitable to attaine vnto this end. For
these on the one side, cōtaine God Almighties benefittes, the later iudgement, the paines of hell, and the glorie of Paradise; all
which , like sharpe prickes doe spurre vs
on to the loue and feare of God : On the
other side; they comprehende the life and
Passion of our Lord and Sauiour, which is
the springe and fountaine of all our good.
These two thinges contained in the Apo-
stolicall *Creed* , for the most part yeilde
matter of meditatiō, and therfore I thinke
prayer and meditation ought chiefly to be
conuersant about thē, although euery one
in particular may haue certaine pointes,
which may more specially inflame and excite the soule to the loue and feare of God.

Beeing therfore perswaded with this
reason , that I might the better conduct
younge beginners, and vntrained soldiars
into this way of mentall prayer , and that I
might giue vnto them altogether prepared, and (as it were to litle children) fore-
chowed matter of meditation, I haue selected two kindes of meditatiōs, almost takē
out of the misteries of our faith , the one
seruing for the morning, the other for the

euening : that as the body is comonly fedd
with two meales ; soe the soule may be
strenthened and nourished with two spiritual refections, by the meditation and
consideration of heauenly things. Some
of these are of the Passion and Resurrection of our Lord IESVS CHRIST, others
of the misteries of our fayth, as I sayd before; But those who can not haue the opportunity, to meditate twice a day , after this
manner, they may vse them, to wit; they
may take to their consideration the 7. former Meditations in the one weeke , and
the latter in an other weeke ; or they may
chiefly insist vpon those of the life and
Passion of our Sauiour: although the other
be not to be neglected, especially in the be-
gining of a soules conuersion , to whom
they are proper, when the feare of God,
contrition and horrour of sinne , is chiefly
to be regarded and sought after.

Here

Here follovve the 7. former Meditations.

A Meditation for Munday.

THis day thou shalt call to memory thy sinnes, and shalt exercise thy selfe in the knowledge of thy selfe, that on the one side , thou maiest truly ponder the greatnesse of thy offences, and on the other side, thou maiest looke into thy basenes, and thy owne nothing, and acknowledge that all the good which thou hast, is from God. This consideration will gett thee submission of mind, and true humility the mother of all vertues.

First therfore waigh with thy selfe, the multitude of the sinnes of thy former life, and namely those sinnes which thou hast cōmitted whē as yet thou wert not illuminated with the diuine splendour to know God Almightie rightly. These if thou dost examine with exquisite diligence , thou wilt finde to bee so many in number, that they will exceede the haires of thy head: for in this time thou leadest the life of a heathen, ignorant of the diuine powre, and as it were without any knowledge of his sacred Deity.

Then

Then confider how thou haft behaued
thy felfe about the tenne commaundeméts
and the 7. deadly finnes, and thou wilt finde, that there is no precept of Almightie
God, which thou haft not violated, nor any
mortal finne, into which thou haft not fal-
len, eyther in thought, word, or deed. After that, call to minde God Almighties benefittes, which he hath beftowed vpon
thee in the whole courfe of thy former
life, and fee whether thou canft giue a
good accompte of them or no.

Tell mee I pray the, how thou haft confumed the dayes of thy infancy, thy youth
and the flower of thy manly age? how haft
thou employed thy 5. exteriour fenfes, and
inward faculties of thy foule, giuen vnto
thee by God, only to bee bufied about his
holy feruice, and the contemplation of
heauenly thinges, what haft thou turned
thine eyes vnto, but to beholde vanityes?
what haue thine eares liftned after but lies
and tales? what hath thy tongue vttered
but mnrmuringes, and blafphemous fpea-
ches? what hath thy taft and feeling bene
delighted in, but wanton pleafures? how
haft thou vfed the remedy of the holy Sacramentes, giuen vnto thee, as a fingular gif-
te? what thankfgiuing haft thou reftored
for foe many benefittes which he hath
                                    hea-

heaped vpon thee? what alacrity haſt thou
vſed to ſatisfie his holy iuſpirations ? how.
haſt thou ſpent thy health of body and naturall forces? how haſt thou diſpenſed thy
goodes of fortune ? what good vſe haſt
thou made of the commodity, and proferred occaſions to liue well ? what care haſt
thou had of thy neighbours welfare ?
what workes of mercye , or of bountye,
haſt thou done vnto them ? what wilt
thou anſwere in that terrible daye of iudgement , when thou muſt render a ſeuere
accompte of all theſe thinges ! o withered
tree deſtinated to eternal flames , except
thou doeſt penance! what excuſe wilt thou
then frame , when thou muſt giue an accompte of euery yeare , of euerye month,
of euery weeke , of euerye daye, of euery
moment ?

Thirdly conſider, thoſe ſinnes , which
thou haſt euery day committed, after God
Almighty hath illuminated and opened
the eyes of thy ſoule to meditate vpon
heauenly thinges : and thou shalt finde
that the old *Adam* hath yet borne a great
ſway in thy actions, and that ſinfull roote
to haue procreated in the, many and peruerſe habits.

Diligently ponder , how vngratefull
thou haſt bene to God Almighty, how vn-
mind-

mindfull of his benefites , how contrary
thou haſt behaued thy ſelfe againſt his holy inſpirations, how ſlouthfull and remiſſe
in his diuine ſeruice : in which thou ſcarce
haſt euer vſed due alacrity and diligence,or
ſuch purity of intention as it is requiſite,
nay haſt thou not ſerued God for worldly
reſpectes and commodity ?

Enter into conſideration how rigid
thou art to thy neighbour,and how indul-
gent to thy ſelfe ? how thou loueſt thy
owne will,how thou adheareſt to thy ſen-
ſuality,how chary of thy honour , and of
euery thing that belongeth vnto thee.
Waigh well with thy ſelfe, how euery day
thou groweſt more arrogant , more ambi-
tious , more vaine, more prone to anger,
more deſperatly bent to malice, more prone to delightes and pleaſures, more muta-
ble , more vnconſtant, more propenſe to
carnal ſinnes,and a greater louer of earthly
vanities. Conſider thy inconſtacy in good,
thy indiſcretion in wordes, imprudence in
deedes , in heigh and difficult matters pu-
ſillanimity ſometimes, and often audacious
temerity.

In the fourth place, after thou haſt take
notice of the number and order of thy ſinnes, pauſe vpon them a while in thy minde, and waigh euery one in the ballance of
                                        due

due confideration, that thou maieft perceaue with what mifery thou art on euery fide enuironed. Which that thou maieft the
better doe ; confider thefe three circum-
ftances in the finnes of thy former life. Firft
a gainft whom thou haft finned. 2. Why
thou haft finned. 3. How thou haft finned. Which if thou doeft diligently penetrate, thou wilt finde that thou haft offended God, whofe maieftie and goodnes is
immenfe, who hath obliged man vnto him
with fo many benefites, as there are fandes
in the fea, or drops of water in the Ocean.

Why haft thou finned, or what violent
occafiō hath enforced thee to any cryme ?
a litle momentary pride : a foule reprefen-
tation of pleafure; fome fmale commoditye
placed in thy fight, and oftentimes, no oc-
cation at all , but euil cuftome , and mere
contempt of God.

But alas how haft thou finned ? with
fuch facility , with fuch notable audacity,
with fo litle feare and confcience, yea with
fuch fecurity and pleafure, as though thou
hadeft to doe with no other then a woo-
den God , who regardeth not thefe fublu-
nary thinges , neyther vnderftandeth or
feeth any thing, what is done vpon the face of the earth. Is this the honour due vnto his fupreme maiefty? is this a remunera-
tion

tion of his benefittes ? doest thou with
such seruices requite his whippinges , his
buffettinges , and pretious bloud sheadd
vpon the Crosse for thy sake ? o wicked
wretch that hast offended so great a maiesty , more miserable , that for so sleight a
cause, and most deplorable , that thou art
not sensible of thy vtter Ruine ; that after
sinne thou fearest not damnation , and so
neglectest to doe penance.

Moreouer it is very profitable,to insist a
while vpon this consideration , and that
thou esteeme thy selfe nothing , and cer-
tenly perswade thy selfe that thou hast nothing of thy selfe but sinne; all other thinges to be the giftes of God Almighties
bountie. For it is most euident,that all our
good,both of grace and nature doth flowe
from him: for he is the Author of the grace of predestination (ewhich is the fountaine and originall of all others) of the grace
of our vocation,of concomitant and perse-
uering grace , and of the grace of euerlasting life. What hast thou then, that thou
canst boast of,but sinne? only this nothing
thou canst attribute to thy selfe , all other
things belong to God : Whence thou maiest clearly and manifestly perceaue what
he is, and what thou art, and hence coniecture , what diffidence thou oughtest to
haue

haue in thy selfe , and what confidence in God; to loue him, and to glorifie thy selfe in him, and not in thy selfe , but so farr as his grace doth freely operate in thee.

These thinges being digested with attē-tiue meditation, as much as thou canst, vrge thy selfe, to a contempt of thy selfe : imagine that thou art like an emptie reede shaken with euery blast of wind , without grauity, without vertue, without constancy, without stabilytie, and finally without any thing. Thinke thy selfe to bee a *Lazarus* foure dayes dead, a stincking and abhominable carcasse, swarming with vermin, so filthy that passers by are forced to stoppe their nostrels, least they smel such a nastye sauour. Beleeue me, thou hart more abhominable , before God and his holy Sain-ctes. Thinke thy selfe vnworthy to lifte vp thine eyes to Heauen; to tread vpon the earth , or that the creatures should serue thee; yea not worthy to eat bread or breath in the aire. Cast thy selfe with the sinfull woman in the Ghospel, at our Blessed Sauiours feete : presenting thy selfe vnto him with a cōfused and blushing countenāce, no otherwise thē the womā takē in adultery before her husband, and with inward sorrowe, and true compunction, begg pardon of thy sinnes : that for his infinite

mer-

mercy and goodnes, he would vouchſafe to receiue thee againe into his fauour, and that thou maieſt dwell in his howſe for euer.

A Meditation for Tvveſdaye:

THis day thou shalt meditate vpon the miſeries of the life of man , out of which conſideration, thou wilt take notice of worldly vanities, and learne how much the glorie of them ought to be deſpiſed, ſeeing they are built vpõ ſo weake a foun-dation, as our fading life, whoſe miſeries, becauſe they be innumerable , ,thou shalt take but ſeauen of the principall for thy Meditation.

First therfore conſider the shortnes of the life of man, being reſtrained within the limittes of threeſcore and ten or fourſcore yeares, whatſoeuer the ouerplus be, it is but labour and ſorrow , as the Prophet ſpea-keth : Out of this time, if thou doeſt ſub-tract thy infancy, which time thou liuedſt rather the life of a beaſt, then a man ; the time that thou ſpendeſt in ſleepe, for then thou árt depriued of the vſe of reaſon, which only diſtinguisheth man from other creatures , and thou wilt finde thy life to bee farr shorter then euer thou didſt ima-gine.

gine. This time if thou doeſt compare with
the eternity of the world to come , thou
wilt find it to be leſſe , then a moment.
Coniecture then the foolish madnes of the
louers of this worlde, who that they might
enioye one only momentary pleaſure of
this tranſitory life, doe not feare to expoſe
them ſelfes to the loſſe of eternitye.

Then take to thy conſideration the vncertainty of this life (which is a ſecond mi-
ſerie) for not only it is moſt short, but the
breuitie it ſelfe is moſt vncertaine and
doubtful. For who is there, that attaineth
to the age of three or foure ſcore? how ma
ny are extinguished at their very entrance
into the worlde ? how many periſh in the
flowere of their youth ? You knowe not
ſayth CHRIST, whē your Lord is to come:
whether in the firſt watch or 2. or 3. or in
the cocke crowing. Which that thou maieſt the better vnderſtand , call to minde
eſpecially thy domeſticke friends, and
other mē placed in dignity and authority,
whom inexorable death hath at diuerſe
ages (ſome yonger, ſome older) ſuddenly
taken out of this worlde , irritating their
vaine and longe-life-promiſeing hopes.

Ponder 4. the inconſtancy and mutabi-
lity of this preſent life, neuer continuing in
one ſtate. The diſpoſitiō of the body often

changeth , not alwaies enioying health,
but subiect to frequent diseases: but if thou
reflect vpon the minde, thou shalt see that
like the troubled Ocean it is tossed vp and
downe with the boisterous windes of her
vntamed passions , inordinate appetites,
fluctuatinge cogitations, which vpō euery
occasion doe disturbe her quiet. Consider
lastly, the instability of the goods of fortune (as they tearme them) to how many
chaunces they are obnoxious, neuer suffe-
ring the temporall substance to stand still
in one stay , therby to make men happy
and prosperous; but like a wheele is turned
vp side-downe, without any intermission.
Consider also the continuall motiō of our
life, neuer restinge night nor day, but goeth
forward without ceasinge , and euery day
more and more wasteth it selfe , so that it
may not vnfitly be compared to a candle;
which by little and little consumeth it selfe,
and when it giueth the clearest light, the
sooner it approcheth vnto its end , also to
a flower , which springeth vp in the morninge, at noone fadeth, and at night wholly withereth away. Which God Almightie
speakinge by the Prophet ISAIE , of this
mutation, excellently shaddoweth in these wordes : *Omnis caro fænum, & omnis gloria
eius quasi flos agri.* All flesh is hay , and all
the

the glorie of it is like a flower of the feild.

Which words S. HIEROME expoundinge saith , if one doth rightly consider the fraylty of the flesh, and that we growe and decrease accordinge to the moments of howres, neuer remaininge in one state, and that the very thinge we now speake , doe, or write , passeth away as part of our life, he will not doubt to confesse that all flesh is hay, and the glorie therof as a flower, or the greene medowes. He that is now an infant will by and by be a little childe, then presently a younge man, growinge towardes his decreped age, through vncertaine seasons, and before he hath contented him selfe in youth , stealeth old age to come vpon him. The beutifull woman which did drawe after her wholl troops of gallāts in her youth , her face is now fourrowed with deformed wrincles , and she that before was a pleasure , is now vgly to behold.

Consider 5. how deceiptfull this life is, (which is the worst condition of all deludinge the louers of the world with a miserable blindnes) for we thinke it amiable, when in it selfe it is vgly : we thinke it sweet, when it is full of gall and bitternes: when it is circumscribed with in the shor-

Hieron. l. 11 Com. in Isa. cap. 40.

test

teſt limits, we thinke it longe. When it is full of miſery, we thinke it ſo happie, that there is no danger, no hazard that mē will not expoſe themſelues vnto, for the con-ſeruation of it, yea with the loſſe of eter-nall glorie, when they doe not feare to co-mitt thoſe ſinnes which make them vn-worthie of ſo great felicitie.

Conſider ſixthly, that beſides the bre-uitie, and other fore-mentioned conditiōs, that ſmall time wherin we liue, is ſubiect to innumerable miſeries both ſpirituall and corporall. That it may well be called a tor-rent of teares, and oceane of infinite mo-leſtations. S. HIEROME reporteth how XERXES that potent kinge, who ouer tur-ned mountaines, and made bridges ouer the ſeas, when from a high place, he be-heald that infinite multitude of men, and his innumerable army, he wept, to thinke that not one of thoſe men there preſent, should be aliue after a hūdred yeares. And preſently addinge, ô that we could but aſcend vnto ſuch a turret, to behold the wholl earth vnder our feete, then would I manifeſt vnto thee, the ruins of the world, nation riſinge againſt nation, and kingedo-me againſt kingdome, ſome tormented, others ſlaine, ſome drowned, others led into captiuitie. Here marryinge, heer

mour-

mourninge, some borne, others dyinge, some aboundinge in wealth, others begginge. And not only the mighty army of XERXES but all the men of the world, in a short space to be turned to dust and ashes.

Take notice a little , of the labours and infirmities of the body, the cogitations and passions of the minde: the diuerse dangers in euery state, and all seasons threatninge the ruine of man: and thou wilt euery day, more clearly vnderstand the miseries of this life, that when thou seest, what is to be hoped for in this world , thou maiest with a noble courrage contemne it.

The last of all these miseries , is death, both in respect of soule or bodie, a thinge most terrible: for in this moment the body is disrobed of all the thinges, in this world. And the soule in this point receiueth the ioyfull or fearefull sentence of eternity.

These thinges well considered , thou wilt be instructed how short and miserable the glorie of this world is , and how it ought to be hated and despised of thee.

A Me-

A Meditation for VVeddensday.

THis day thou shalt meditate on death: the confideration of vvhich is very profitable to attaine vnto true vvifedome, to beate dovvne finne ; and to excite men timely to caft vp their accompts vvhich they are to make in the latter day.

Confider firft the vncertainty of that hovver vvherin death is to feaze vpon thee, thou knovveft not the day , nor the place , nor the ftate vvher in it shall finde thee : only thou beleeueft that thou muft die , for other thinges thou art vvholly ignorant of; except that it oftentimes fetteth vpon a man vvhen he little dreameth of it, and thinketh it to be furtheft of.

Confider fecondly, that greiuious feparatiõ,vvhich shall be at the point of death, not only from euery thinge of this prefent life,vvherin thou tookeft content, but alfo betvvixt the foule and body,vvhofe fociety vvas moft anciẽt , moft louinge and deare. If a man taketh it greiuioufly to be banished , to be thruft out of his natiue Soile,and to be depriued of that aire vvherin he firft breathed , although he should carry all others, his deareft thinges vvith him,hovv farr more bitterly vvould he take that ge-

r   !!

nerall exile , vvherin he muſt be vveaned
from all vvorldly thinges, his hovvſe, his
meanes, his father, his mother, his childrē,
his freinds, vncertaine vvhether he him
ſelfe muſt goe. Then shall he be depriued
of the light and the commerce of all humane creatures ?

If the oxe vvhen he is diſioyned from
his fellovve vvith vvhome he vvas vvont
in the ſame yoake to be coupled , vvith
bellovvinge doth expreſs his ſorrovve,
vvhat ſobbs, vvhat ſights vvilt thou fetch,
vvhen thou shalt perceiue thy ſelfe to be
violently pulled from theſe thy confede-
rats.

Conſider alſo that anxiety vvhervvith
the minde of the dyinge is tormented,
vvhen abſtracted from al corporall buſines, he only thinketh vvhat shall become
of his body, and vvhat shall betyde his ſoule, hovv his body muſt be caſt ſeauen foot
into the earth, to be eaten of vvormes; and
vvhat vvill become of his ſoule, vvhere it is
to remaine ; he is altogether vncertaine:
vvhich cogitation doth ſurely much trouble the minde of him that dieth , vvhen he
certainly knovveth there is heauen or hell
to be expected , and he at equall diſtance
frō them both, neither can he tell vvhich of
theſe tvvo contraties vvill fall to his share.

B 4 An

An other no leſſe affliction followeth, that preſently he muſt giue a ſtrict accōpt of all his forpaſſed life , to the eternal iudge, which men of great ſanctity were wont to feare, when ARSENIVS in the laſt point of life , was ſeen of his diſciples to weep and treble , they asked him why he feared death he anſwered. *Reuera filioli , metus hic quo me videtis affici nunquam omnino à me receſſit ex quo factus ſum Monachus.* Indeed my childrē the feare wherwith ye ſee me nowe afflicted , hath neuer quite left me from the time I was firſt made a Monke.

Then all the ſinnes of a mans former life come ruſhinge into his memory , repreſentinge themſelues vnto him , as it were in battaile aray, to deſtroy him , but eſpecially his greiuious ſinnes wherin he tooke greateſt delight , are continually preſent to his fancie , which doe ſo torment him that they driue him into a dangerous deſpaire of his ſaluation : and the remembrance of thoſe pleaſures , which before were gratefull , are now moſt bitter vnto him. That the wiſe man ſaieth true : *Ne intuaris vinum quando flaueſcit cum ſplenduerit in vitro color eius ingreditur blande, & in nouiſſimo mordebit vt coluber, & ſicut regulus venena diffundet :* Behold not wine when it waxeth yelowe, when the colour therof

Simon Metaph in vita eius to. 4. apud Surium.

Prouerb. 23.

therof shall shine in the glaffe : it goèth in pleafantly, but in the end, it will bite like a fnake and as a bafiliske it fpreads abrode his poifons.

Such a poifoned cup the enemie of mankinde prefenteth to the louers of the world to drinke. Such is the liquour of the outward gilded cup of *Babilon*.

VVicked man feinge himfelfe enuironed with fo many accufers, beginneth then to feare the fuccefs of his latter iudgement, and to bewaile himfelfe vvith bitter outcries, ô miferable and vnhappie man that haue liued thus longe in darknes, and vvalked in the footftepps of iniquitie, vvhat shall novve become of me ? if S. PAVLE faieth fuch as a man fovveth, fuch *Gal. 6.* he shall reap. I that haue fovved nothinge elfe but the vvorkes of the flesh, vvhat should I expect but corruption ?

If S. IOHN faieth, that no vncleane thinge shall enter into that heauenly cittie, vvhich is paued vvith burnished gold, vvhat part shall I haue therin, that am defiled vvith all kinde of luxurie.

Then follovve the Sacraments of the Church, Confeffiõ, Communion, extream Vnction, vvhich are the laft helps of our holy Mother the Catholique Church, to fuccour his dyinge foule.

From

From all these foresaid circumstances, thou maiest gather with what anxietie, a wicked man is oppressed at the hower of his departure. Then he will wish that he had led a better life, and what great austeritie he would vse, if longer time might be permitted to him. Then would he vehemently implore the diuine assistance, but the greatnes of his infirmity, and the panges of death approachinge will not suffer him, which will be so great that he shall scarce be able to tourne his thoughtes vpon God.

Behold after these, the Symtomes of this last infirmitie forrûners of death, and harbengers of thy last end, which certainly in themselues are horrible, and to the beholders terrible. The stomacke swelleth, the speech faileth, the feet beginne to die, the knees wax cold, the nostrells fall, the eies sinck, the face waxeth pale, the tongue can no longer performe its office, finally the striuinge of the soule goinge out of the body, disturbeth all the senses, and leaueth them wholly without vigour.

But who is able to expresse the anguish of the soule, which is farr greater? for then it is in a mighty agonie, both in regarde of the doubtfull euent of her saluation : and of the strict accoumpt she is presently to
                                    make

make of the deeds of her wholl life: as also
becaufe she naturally loueth the body, she
can not be feparated from it but with great
affliction, efpecially knowinge not what
shall become of her.

Hauinge well contemplated the foule
departinge the bodie, thou muft yet make
two iournies more: one in accompaninge
the body to the graue, the other in followinge the foule to the decidinge of her
caufe. And thou shalt fee the euent of both.
Marke therfore, the dead carcas how they
prepare a windinge sheete for it. What ex-
pedition they vfe to carry it out of the
houfe. Confider the folemnity and rites
wherwith it is carried to the graue. Howe
the bells ringe , and euery one inquire of
the dead. The office of the church alfo,
the prayers of the ftanders by, the dolefull
tune of the church, while the body is carried to the graue and buried. The teares of
freinds and kindred, and all thofe ceremo-
nies which are wont to be performed
about the dead.

Leauinge the bodie vnder the earth,
accompany the foule paffinge to a newe
and vnknowne region , where she expecteth the fentence of the eternall iudge.
Immagine with thy felfe that thou art prefent at this tribunall, and the wholl court
of

of heauen, waitinge with deepe filence, and great attention the euent and fentence of this iudgement, here muft be giuen a ftrict accompt of all receiuinges and disburf-mentes. I fay accompt, of thy life, of thy goods, of thy familie, of the diuine infpira-tions, of the meanes and occafions to liue well, and finally of the blood of IESVS CHRIST, and the vfe of his Sacraments, and accordinge as his accompt is, fo the fen-tence fhall be pronounced.

A Meditation for Thurfday.

THis day thou fhalt meditate vpō the latter iudgemēt, to the end that thou maieft ftirr vp in thy foule, two principall effects, which euery Chriftiā foule ought to haue, to witt, the feare of God and ha-tred of finne.

Place therfore firft before thine eies, ho-we terrible that day will be, wherin all the litigious caufes of the fonnes of *Adam* fhal-be decided, and a finall end put to the pro-ceffes of our wholl life, and what fhall be ordained of thofe for all eternitie, fhalbe publickly pronounced to the veiwe of the wholl world.

This day comprehendeth in it, all the dayes of all ages, paft, prefent, and to come. And exacteth a feuere accompt of all the
actions

actions of all men, powringe out all the fury vpon men, heaped vp together from forepaffed ages; becaufe then the torrent of God Almighties vengeance, shall ouerflowe beyonde its limits, rushinge with a greater violence, by howe much more it was the longer deteined, and at once shall ouerwhelme all Iniquity from the creation of the world.

Confider fecondly the dreadfull fignes which shall goe before this day. For our Sauiour faith: *Erunt figna in fole & luna &* Luc. 21. *ftellis.* And all creatures of heauen and earth shall tremble, vnderftãdinge their ruine to be at hande. Men alfo, as our Sauiour faith, worne and withered a way perceiuinge the horrible raginge of the fea: and they themfelues fcarce a heares breadth diftant from death. Seeinge alfo the mightie rifinges, and inundations of the water; and by thefe coniecturinge the calamities and miferie, thefe prodigious fignes threatẽ to the world: wilbe amazed with fuch a horrour, that they will be without life, without voyce, without colour, or human shape: they will be dead before they die, dreadinge their damnation before the fentence be pronounced, immagininge the future paine, by their prefent diftemper. Then euerie one out of exceedinge
feare,

feare, will be so solicitous of himselfe, that he will nothinge regard others whosoeuer they be, parents, or husbands, or wifs, or freinds or companions.

Imagine thirdly, the vniuersall deluge of fire, which shall goe before this iudgement: that dreadfull noise of the tumpett, which one of the Archangels shall blowe; wherwith all the people of the wholl world shalbe sommoned together, in one place makinge their appearance before the iudgment seat: and last of all that dreadfull Maiestie; the supreame iudge of the quick and dead, shall assume to him selfe vpon this tribunall.

Fourthly consider what exact accompt shall be required of euery one; Holy IOB saith: *Vere scio quod ita est quod non iustificetur homo compositus Deo. Si voluerit contendere cum eo, non poterit respondere vnum pro millé.* Indeed I knowe it is so, and that man cannot be iustified compared with God if he will contend with him he cannot answere him one for a thousand. What then shall become of man when God shall beginne to handle him accordinge to rigour of his iustice? when he shall speake to his conscience inwardly?

O wicked and peruerse man, what hast thou seene in me, that out of the height of
im-

impiety, defpifinge me , thou shouldeft
ioyne with my enemies ? I haue created
thee accordinge to mine owne Image and
likenes ; I haue illuminated thee with the
light of faith : I haue feafoned thee in the
Chriftian faith from thy infancy:I haue redeemed thee with my owne blood ; for
thy fake I haue fafted , watched , prayed,
vndergone tedious iournies , fweat blood,
and endured manie more miferies in the
courfe of my life ; for the loue of thee , I
haue fuffered perfecutions , iniuries, blaf-
phemies, and the verie Croffe it felfe. This
Croffe is my witnes , thefe nailes are my
witneffes,thefe woundes are my witneffes,
which thou feeft imprinted in my handes
and feete ; to conclude heauen and earth
that did behold my paffion are my witneffes. Howe I haue drawne thy foule. How
I haue redeemed thee with the ranfome
of my pretious blood.

Howe haft thou efteemed this pretious
margarite,bought by me with an ineftimable price. O generation of vipers , why
haft thou chofen to ferue my enemy with
a great deale of paine , and neglected thy
duetie towards me thy creatour and redeemer which thou mightft haue performed with a great deale of pleafure. I haue
called thee and thou wouldeft not anfwere

to my vocatiō : I haue knocked at the dore
of thy heart; and thou haſt refuſed me entrance. I haue ſtretched my armes vpon
the Croſſe, and thou haſt not regarded me,
thou deſpiſedſt my councells, promiſes and
theatninges. Pronounce therfore ô yee
Angels, the ſentence and be iudges betwixt
me and my vine. *Numquid amplius aliquid*

Iſai. 5.
facere potui vineæ meæ quod non feci ? What
could I doe any thinge more to my vine
that I haue not done?

   What will the reprobate and ſcoffers at
diuine miſteries anſwere ? they that haue
hiſhed at vertue, derided ſimplicitie, and
obſerued better the lawes of the world
then of God? they that haue ſtopped their
eares at the voyce of God ? they who haue
contemned his diuine inſpirations ? they
who haue bene rebellious againſt his comandements, and ingreatefull for his benefitts? What will thoſe libertins ſay, who
lettinge themſelues looſe to all vices, haue
liued as if there were no God at all, or
that he did not regarde the thinges that
are done belowe? What will thoſe ſay, who
haue followed their comodities, guſt and
pleaſure for a lawe. *Quid facietis in die viſita-*
tionis & calamitatis de longe venientis ? ad cuius
confugietis auxilium? & vbi derelinquetis gloriam
veſtram vt non incuruÿmine ſub vinculo & cum
                                                inter-

interfectis cadatis. VVhat will yee doe in the day of vifitation and of calamity cominge from farr ? to whofe help will ye flee, and where will yea leaue your glory, that ye be not bowed vnder the bond , and fall with the flaine.

Fiftly confider, that terrible fentence, which after iudgement, the fupreme iudge pronounceth againft the wicked, which he will thunder out with fuch a dreadfull noyfe, that at the found therof the eares of the ftanders by will ringe, as the Prophet ESAY faith : *Labia eius repleta funt indigna-* *tione, & lingua eius quafi ignis deuorans.* His lipps are filled with indignation, and his tongue as a deuouringe fire. For what flames can be fo ardent as thofe wordes: *Difce-* *dite à me maledicti in ignem æternum, qui para-* *tus eft Diabolo & Angelis eius.* Goe from me o yea curfed into euerlaftinge fire, prepared for the Diuill and his Angels. Euery word of which fentence is full of bitter torment. For who is able to comprehend what this feparation is, what curfe, what fire, what fociety , and finally what eternity to which the wicked are adiudged by force of this fentence?

*Efa.*30.

A Meditation for Fryday.

THis day thou shalt meditate vpō the torments of hell, that duely ponderinge them, thou maiest haue a more awe of God Almightie, and a greater hatred of sinne. S. BONAVENTVRE teacheth that these torments are to be considered accordinge to certaine similitudes sett downe by holy men, concerninge this matter. Wherfore it will not be beside our purpose (as the same Doctour in the same place saith) to imagine hell, a horrible confused CHAOS, a lake vnder the earth, a deepe fyery dungeon, or as a spacious citty, darke and terrible, burninge with obscure and fearfull fire; filled with waylinges, howlinges, weepinge for the inexplicable paines.

D. Bonau. in Fas. cap. 3.

In this miserable and vnhappie place are two kindes of torments, *pœna sensus, & pœna damni*, the punishment of sence, and the punishmēt of losse of God Almightie.

Consider that there is no outward, or inward sence of the damned, which is not afflicted with a proper torment; for as the damned in all their members and sences haue offended God, vsinge them as instruments and weapons wherby, neglectinge

&tinge the Society and lawe of God,
they ſerued ſinne. So the diuine iuſtice
hath ordained , that euery ſence accordinge to their deſert , should be tormented with a proper punishment , the
wanton and laſciuious eies , shalbe tor-
tured , with the hydious aſpect of diuils.
The eares which were open to lyes , de-
tractions , and other impurities ; shall
ringe with vnwonted clamours, out-cries
and blaſphemies. The noſes which were
delighted with ſweet odours, shalbe poyſ-
ned with an intollerable ſtinck. The taſt
which was glutted with dainty fare, shalbe tormented with intollerable hunger
and thirſt. The tongue which vttered de-
tractions and murmuringes , shall drinke the gall of dragons. The wanton
which gaue conſent to their brutish deſires shalbe frozen with extreame cold
and as holy IoB ſaith: *Ab aquis niuium tranſ-* Iob 24.
ibit ad colorem nimium : From the waters of
ſnowe they shall paſſe to the extremity of
heat.

The interiour ſences alſo shall not
want their torments , the imagination
shalbe tormented with the apprehenſion
of preſent paines , the memory with the
callinge to minde of fore-paſſed pleaſures , the vnderſtandinge with the feare of
futu-

future greifs , the will with an incredible hatred and raginge towards God.

In illa Euangil. ybi erit fletus & stridor dentium.

There as S. GREGORIE saith shalbe, in-tollerable cold vnquenchable fire, a neuer dyinge worme , a stinch which none is able to endure, horred darknes, greuious whippinges, vizards of diuils, confusion of sinners, and desperation of al good. Tell me I pray thee couldest thou endure on little moment the least part of al these tor-mentes? surely it would be very greuious, if not intollerable for thee. What the will it be to suffer this wholl inundation of euils, at one time in all thy members and fences, externall, and internall, not one or a thousand nights , but for all eternitie ? VVhat fence, what tongue, what minde of man is able to conceiue or expresse these thinges?

Neither are these the greatest torments the damned suffer. There remaineth yet a more greuious, which the diuines doe call the punishment of losse, which consisteth in the perpetuall priuation of the beatifi-call vision of God and his Saintes , and of all that glorious and blessed Societie. For that is the greatest torment, that depriueth man of the most excellent good. Seeinge therfore that God is that effectuall and cheefest good of all goods, to be depriued

of

of him, muſt needs be the greateſt of
all euils.

Theſe are the generall torments of the
damned; beſides theſe, there are other particular torments, wherwith euery one accordinge to their ſinnes are afflicted. The
proud, the enuious, the couetous, the luxu-
rious, and other vitious haue their peculiar
torments; the meaſure of paine there, ſhalbe proportionable to their pleaſure here,
confuſion there proportionable to their
glory and preſumption here : pouertie and
want, to plenty, hungér and thirſt, to gluttonie and to former delightes.

To all theſe aforeſaid torments , eternitie is yet to be added , which is as it were
the ſeale and key of all the reſt ; for if at
légth, they ſhould haue an end, they were
ſome way tollerable. That which is reſtrained to a certaine time can not be ſo vnſuf-
ferable, but this puniſhment is euerlaſtin-
ge , without ſolace , without relaxation,
without diminution ; where remaineth no
hope of an end of their torments , or tormentours, or themſelues that ſuffer them,
but is, as it were a perpetuall and irreuoca-
ble baniſhmét, neuer to be recalled, which
is a thinge of importance to be noted. That
the minde may be ſtirred vp therby, to that
ſauinge feare and loue of God.

C 3 From

From this eternitie of torments proceedeth that great hatred wherwith they are
incensed against God. Hence proceed those
horrible blasphemies and curses which
with their impure mouthes they raile at
God, sayinge. Cursed be God which hath
created vs, and hath condemned vs to an
euerlasting death, which doth so oppresse
and torments vs that notwithstandinge
neuer killeth. Cursed be his power, which
doth so greuiously afflict vs. Cursed be his
wisedome that hath laied open all our wickednes. Cursed be his iustice that hath
exacted eternall punishment for temporall
sins. Cursed be his Crosse which hath not
benefited vs. Cursed be his blood that was
shed, seeinge it requireth reuenge against
vs. Cursed be the Mother of God, who
although she be pious and propitious to
all, yet notwithstandinge hath shewed
herselfe to vs cruell and vnmercifull. Cursed be all the Saintes of God raigninge
with CHRIST, and reioyceinge at our miseries.

These are the hymnes, this is that harsh
melody, which the damned doe continually iarr, railinge at the almighty with dete-
sted blasphemies for all eternitie.

A Me-

A Meditation for Saterday.

THis day thou shalt meditate vpon the glory of the Saintes of God, which may more eagerly inflame thy foule, to contemne the vanities of this world, and afpire to that eternall felicitie.

To the end thou mayeft get a better knowledge and guft of this ineftimable glory. Confider thefe fiue thinges. Firft the excellency of the place. Secondly the ioy of that fociety. Thirdly the vifion of God. Forthly the glory of their bodies. Fifthly the compleat perfection of all aboundant good.

In the excellency of the place , take notice of the admirable and wonderfull fpacioufnes of it ; in approued authours thou readeft , that the leaft of the fixed ftarrs of heauen , is bigger then the wholl earth, and fome of them doe exceede the earth two or three hundred times in big-nes. Then caft vp thine cies to heauen and confider the innumerable multitude of them in the firmament, and thou shalt fee a great deale of void fpace, where many more may be placed, howe caft thou then but be aftonished at the greatnes of fo rare a fabricke ?

C 4   Then

Then consider the beutie of that place, which no tongue is able to expresse, for if God Almighty in this place of banishment and vale of miserie, hath made many thinges of admirable and comely hue: of what great beuty, and how much adorned dost thou thinke that place to be: which God would haue to be the ordinarie seat of his glory: the Pallace of his Maiestie: the mansion of the elect, and the Paradise of all pleasure?

After the beuty of the place, consider the Nobilitie of the Inhabitants, whose number, sanctity, riches, and glory, are farr beyound our imaginatiō. S. Iohn saith the multitude are so great that they are innumerable. S. Dionysivs affirmeth that the multitude of Angels doe farr exceed the nūber of sublunary creatures. Whom S. Thomas followinge thinketh, that as the heauens by many degrees exceed the bignes of the earth, beinge but as it were a point of them: so proportionably the glorious Spirits, therin conteined, doe surpasse all earthly thinges. VVhat can be thought more admirable? assuredly this well pondered would make a man loose himselfe in the abysse of God Almighties goodnes.

Yea without comparison euery one of these blessed Spirits is far more beutifull to
the

the eie then all this visible world. O what would it be to contemplate the incomprehensible number of so rare and glorious Spirits ? and to vnderstand their seuerall offices and perfections ? how the Angels bringe messages? how the Archangels Minister ? how the Principalities triumph? how the Powers reioyce ? how the Dominations bare sway? how the Vertues shine? how the Thrones doe glitter ? how the Cherubins doe illuminate ? how the Seraphins doe burne with loue ? and finally how all with one vnanimous consent doe prayse Almighty God.

If the conuersation and fellowship of good men be so delightfull, what pleasure will it be , to be assotiated to so great a multitude of Saintes ? to be conuersant with the Apostles ? to talke with the Prophets ? to discourse with Martyrs? and to enioy the blessed familiarity of all the elect ? O but what will it be to enioy his presence whome the morninge starrs doe magnifie? whose beutie the sun and moone admire ? before whome the holy Angels and all the celestiall Spirits doe prostrate themselues. That *sumum bonum* , that infinite good , which in it selfe comprehendeth all good whatsoeuer , ô what content will the heart of man feale to behold him,

him, who is one and all. Who although he be moſt ſimple without compoſition, yet conteineth in himſelfe the perfections of all thinges created. VVhat can the heart of man deſire greater?

If it were ſo much to ſee and heare Kinge SALOMON, that the Queene of SABA cominge from farr remote parts, moued with his great wiſedome, should ſay: 3.Reg.10. *Beati viri tui & beati ſerui tui, hi qui ſtant coram te ſemper & audiunt ſapientiam tuam:* Happy are thy men and happie are thy ſeruants, thoſe who ſtande before thee alwayes and heare thy wiſedome. VVhat would it be to behold that true SALO-MON? that eternall wiſedome? that immenſe maieſtie? that ineſtimable beutie? that infinite goodnes? and which is more to enioy him for all eter-nitie?

This is the eſſentiall and trueſt glory of the Saints: this is the laſt end and centre of all our wishes. Conſider more-ouer the glory of their bodies, which ſhalbe beuti-fied with theſe fowre giftes, ſubtilitie, agilitie, impaſſibilitie and claritie. VVhich will be ſo great, that euery one of the elect (as our bleſſed Sauiour ſaith) ſhall glitter like the ſun in the kingdome of his fa-ther.

If

If one only fun doth fo reioyce and illuminate this vniuerfe. VVhat doeft thou
thinke, fo many brighter funnes will doe
which fhall there fhine?

VVhat fhould I fpeake of other ioyes
which there fhalbe? health without infirmitie : libertie without violence : beutie
without deformity : immortalitie without corruption : aboundance without
want : reft without trouble : fecuritie
without feare : riches without pouerty : ioy without forrowe : honour without contradiction. There as S. AVGVSTI-
NE faith, fhalbe true glory when euery one
fhalbe comended without errour or flat-
tery. True honour fhal be denied to none
that is wortly of it, and it fhalbe giuen to
none vnworthy, neither fhall any vnworthy attempt it, there, where none
fhalbe permitted but the worthy. There
fhalbe true peace, where they fhall fuffer
no contradiction frō themfelues or others:
the reward of vertue fhalbe he which gaue
vertue. And he hath promifed to giue himfelfe. Then which, better or greater nothinge can be. For what other thinge is it
that he fpake by the Prophet : *Ero illorum
Deus, & ipfi erunt mihi plebs* : I will be their
God, and they fhalbe my people. If I doe
not who is it that can fatiate their foules?
I wil-

*D. Aug.
l. 22. de
ciuit. Dei
cap. 30.*

Leui. 26.

I wilbe that good which can possibly be desired of man. Their life, their peace, their honour. For so is that vnderstood which 1.Cor.13. the Apostle speaketh : *Vt sit Deus in omnibus*, That God be in all. He shalbe the end of all our desires, which shalbe contemplated without end , shalbe loued without tediousnes , shalbe praysed without ceasinge.

The place of the saints, if thou doest behold the spaciousnes of it , it shalbe most ample , if the beutie, most delicious , if the splendour, most exceeding bright. There shalbe admirable delightfull society, no vicissitude of times, the day shall not succeed the night , nor the night the day , but all time shalbe there a like. There shalbe one perpetuall springe, which the holy Ghost, with a wonderfull temper shall alwayes make greene and florishing, there shall all celebrate euerlastinge holy-dayes , reioyeing with vnspeakable gladnes , there shall all sound their instruments of musick and singe prayses to him, by whose power they liue and raigne for all eternity.

O celestiall citty, secure habitation, pallace flowinge with all delightes , people without murmuring, quiet Citizans , men without pouertie. O that I may at length enioy thee. O that the dayes of my banishment

ment were ended. VVhen will that ioyfull day come? VVhen shall I goe out of this mortallity? VVhen shall I come and appeare before thy face ô God.

A Meditation for Sunday.

THis day thou shalt spend, in recogitating God Almightie his benefitts, that thou mayest bee gratefull to him for the same, and thy heart inflamed with the loue of him, that hath heaped so manie fauours vpon thee. VVhich seeing they bee innumerable, thou shalt take fower of the cheifest to thy consideration, which are the benefitts of thy Creation, Preseruation, Redemption, and Vocation, besides particular benefitts specially bestowed vpon thee.

Touching the benefitt of thy creation, examine diligently what thou wert before, what God hath giuen thee when thou hadest no precedent meritts. Behold thy comely bodie well composed of its members and senses: Looke vpon thy noble soule, beutified with these excellent faculties, the vnderstanding, will, and memorie.

Remember that when he gaue thee thy soule, he gaue thee all thinges, seing there is
no

no perfection in any creature, which is not found more excellent in the soule of man. Hence it manifestly followeth, that when God bestowed this great benefitt vpon thee, he with it bestowed what els soeuer thou hast.

Concerninge the benefitt of thy conseruation and preseruation, consider that all thy being dependeth vpon the diuine prouidence and disposure, without which thou canst not moue a foote, or subsist the least moment of time. More-ouer for thy vse he hath created the wholl vniuersall world, and all thinges therin conteined; the earth, the sea, birds, fishes, beasts, plants; nay the verie Angels themselues he hath ordained to doe thee seruice. Consider thy health, the strength of limes, and thy verie life it selfe, which thou enioyest, to be the great benefitts of God Almightie, who, by dayly nourishment and other temporall helps, coserueth all these in their proper vigour. Obserue the miseries and tribulatiōs vnto which other mortall men are subiect; into which, as others thou hadst easily fallē, had not the diuine goodnes protected thee.

In the benefitt of thy Redemptiō: consider the aboundant good both in quantitie and qualitie, which he hath purchased to thee by it.

Then

Then call to minde the bitternes of his torments, which he suffered in soule and bodie to ease thee ; and that the acknowledgmēt of these fauours may take a greater impression in thee, in the mysterie of his passion take notice of these fower thinges. First, who it is that suffereth, secondly what he suffered, thirdly for whome he suffered, fourthly why he suffered.

He that suffered, was God, what he suffered, weare the most greuious torments, and such that neuer any mortall man did endure the like.

For whome ? for most ingratefull creatures, cursed and worthy of hell fyre.

VVhy? not for any comoditie or profitt of his owne, or that we had merited so much by our precedent meritts. But only moued to it by his infinite loue and bounty tovvards vs.

Cōcerninge the benefit of thy vocation, cōsider the grace he gaue thee, vvhē he infused into thee, the Christian faith, by the receiuing of Baptisme and other Sacraments: when he did enrolle thee in the booke of his eternitie, amongest faithsull soules. If after thy first vocatiō, vvhen by sinne thou hadest lost the innocencie of baptisme, he hath dravvne thee againe out of the mire of thy ovvne corrūptiō, restored thee to grace

and

and brought thee back againe into the
way of thy owne salutation : VVhat thankes giuinge oughteſt thou to render vnto
him, for ſo great a benefit ? How great was
his mercie to thee , that with longanimitie
he expected ſo manie yeares ? that he permitted thee to ſpend thy dayes in ſo great
impuritie of wickednes ? that he hath
often viſited thee with good and holy inſpirations? that he did not cutt of the thred
of thy peruerſe life , as he ſerued others in
the ſame place? To conclude, that he called
thee with ſuch efficacious grace, that he re-
ſtored thee from death to life, and opened
thine eies to contemplate his cleare light ?
How great was his clemécie towards thee,
that he ſupported thee with his grace, not
to returne back againe to thy former ſinns.
But to ouercome the enimies of mankind,
and conſtantly to perſeuere in a vertuous
courſe.

   Theſe are the comon benefits. Beſides
theſe, there are manie ſecret ons, known to
none but thoſe that receiue them , and
others , which indeed are not cleerly
known vnto themſelues , but only to him
that beſtowed them. How often for thy
prid , arrogancie , ingratitude and ſlouth
haſt thou deſerued to be left of God as
many for leſſer cauſes haue beene ? Yet not
with-

withstandinge he would not ? How often
hath God with his singulare prouidence,
exempted thee from euill, remoued occa-
sions of offending, broke the snare that the
enimie had laied for thy perdition ; hath
frustrated his expectation ; and would not
permit that his councells and machinations
should preuaile against thee ? hovv often
hath he done to vs as he did to S. PETER in
the Gospell : *Ecce Satanas expetiuit vos , vt* Luc.22.
cribaret sicut triticum. Ego autem rogaui pro te,
vt non deficiat fides tua : Behold Sattan hath
required to haue you for to sift as vvheat
but I haue praied for thee that thy faith
faile not. And vvho can knovv these secret
benefits but God alone ? benefits , vvhich
be palpable are easie to be seene , but those
vvhich be priuate consistinge in the vvor-
kinge of good or preuentinge of ill the
mind of man can not perfectly comprehend. Wherfore it is meet and conuenient
to reason, that vvee should render immor-
tall thankes to God , for all these benefits
and cofesse ingenuously, that vve haue receiued more, the vve are able to restore, and
that our obligations tovvards him , are so
great, that vvith any goods of ours vve
shall neuer liue to requite them, vvhen vve
cannot so much as number or comprehend them in our vnderstandinge.

D   CHAP.

Chap. III.

Of the time, and fruite of these Meditations.

BEHOVLD (Christian Reader) thou hast seauen former meditations, accomodated to euery day of the weeke, not so, that it is an offence to meditate vpon an other matter ; when as wee saied before , whatsoeuer inflameth the heart, to the loue and feare of God, and to the keepinge of his comandements , may profitably bee assumed for matter of meditation. VVe therfore out of so great a number haue selected these, both, for that they conteine the cheifest misteries of our faith , and that in them is force and efficacie , to rouse vp our souls to the loue and feare of God: as also to set before nouices, which haue need of a guide, prepared and as it were fore-chewed matter, least they confusedly wander vp and downe in this spacious feild, without any certaintie, now meditatig vpon one thinge and presently vpon an other.

More-ouer these meditatiõs, as wee haue
saied

saied elswhere, sute beſt with thoſe which doe begine to turne to God Almightie from their wicked courſes. For theſe had need, to be helped by the conſideration of theſe thinges, to the deteſtation and horrour of ſinne, the feare of God, the contempt of the world, which are as it were the firſt ſteps to the amendment of our former peruerſe life, therfore it is good that they ſhould ſometime inſiſt in them, that they may haue the better foundation for other enſuing vertues.

The former meditations to vvhome they properly belong.

OF SEAVEN OTHER
MEDITATIONS
OF
THE PASSION
OF
OVR LORD,

And the manner hovv it ought to
be meditated vpon.

CHAP. IV.

ERE followe seauen other
Meditations of the Passion
of CHRIST, his Resurrection
and Ascension into heauen,
to which others of his holy
life may well be added.

    But we must note, that in the Passion of
Six thin- our blessed Sauiour, six thinges cheefly are
ges cheif- to be meditated vpon. First, the bitternes
ly to be   of

of his forrowe, that we may compaffionate *confidered* with him. Secondly, the greatnes of our *in the paf-* finnes·, which were the caufe of his tor- *fion of* ments, that we may abhorr them. Third- *Chrift.* ly, the greatnes of the benefit, that we may be gratefull for it. Fourthly, the excel- lencie of the diuine charitie and bountie therin manifefted, that we may loue him more feruently. Fifthly, the conueniencie of the mifterie, that we may be drawne to admiration of it. Laftly, the multiplicitie of vertues of our bleffed Sauiour which did shine in this ftupendious mifterie, that we may partly immitate and partly admire them ; wherfore in the middeft of thefe meditations let vs fome time compaffio- nate with our bleffed Sauiour in the extre- mitie of his forrowes , extreame indeed, both by reafon of the tendernes of his bodie , as alfo for the great affection he bore vnto our foules. He did fuffer them without any manner of confolation , as we shall fpeake herafter in its proper place. Sometimes let vs ftirr vp in our felues compunction for our finnes, which were the caufe of thefe his fo great fuf- feringes. Sometimes let vs kindle in our fouls an ardent affection , confi- dering his great affection towards vs , which vpon the Croffe he declared and

D 3   mani-

manifested to the whole world. And the benefit which he beſtowed vpon vs in his paſſion, becauſe he bought vs with the ineſtimable price of his precious bloud , of which only we reape the fruite and commoditie. Sometimes let vs ruminate vpon the conueniencie of the manner , his eternall wiſdome would he pleaſed to chuſe, to cure our miſeries, to ſatisfie for our ſins, to releeue our neceſſities, to make vs partakers of his glorie , to repreſſe our prid , to induce vs to the loue and ioyfull ſufferinge of pouertie, iniuries , auſteritie , and all comendable laborious exercices. More-ouer it will not be beſids the matter , to looke into the admirable examples which did principally ſhine in the life and paſſion of our ſweet Sauiour, his meeknes , patience, obedience, mercie, pouertie, charitie , humilitie , bountie , modeſtie , and other his rare vertues , which in all his actions did glitter like ſtarrs in the firmament. And cheifly to this end, let vs meditate vpõ theſe thinges , that as neere as we can, we may imitate them. Let vs ſhake of ſlouth , and eleuate our ſouls , that as much as in our power lyeth with the help of his holy grace we may trace his ſacred foot-ſteps. This is the beſt and moſt profitable methode of meditatinge vpon our Bleſſed Sauiours

paſ-

paſſion, that is to ſay , that ther-by we be drawne to imitation, and ſo to be wholly transformed into our Bleſſed Sauiour, that each one may ſay with the Apoſtle: *Viuo autem iam non ego, viuit vero in me Chriſtus:* And nowe I liue but not I , but CHRIST in me. More-ouer in meditating our Bleſſed Sauiours paſſion , we muſt ſet him before the eies of our ſouls, imageninge that we ſee, as preſent the panges of his heauy ſufferinges; and we muſt not only inſiſt vpon the bare hiſtorie of his paſſion, but we muſt conſider other circumſtances , namely theſe fower , firſt , who it is that ſuffereth, ſecondly , for whome , thirdly , howe , fourthly , why. Firſt, he that ſuffereth is God, omnipotent, infinite, immenſe. For whome ? the moſt vngratefull creature in the world, and leſs regardinge his benefits. Howe ? with moſt profound humilitie, charitie, bountie, meeknes, mercie, patience, modeſtie, &c. VVhy? not for his owne commoditie, nor our merits ; but for his immenſe pietie, mercie, goodnes and loue towards vs.

Laſt of all, let vs not onely contemplate his outward, but his inward torments, for much more may be conſidered in the ſoule then in the bodie of CHRIST, both for the more ſenſible feelinge of his paſſion there,

as also for diuers other considerations
therin.

Thus hauing set downe this short pre-
face let vs proceed to the handlinge of the
misteries themselues of our blessed Sauiours passion.

Seauen other Meditations.

A Meditation for Munday.

THis day after thou hast seigned thy
selfe with the signe of the Crosse,
thou shalt meditate vpon the washinge of
the disciples feete, and institution of the
blessed Sacrament.

Consider, ô my soule, at this supper
sweet IESVS himselfe to be present, contemplate that inestimable example of humilitie, which he there proposed vnto thee
for imitation; when risinge from the table
where he sat with his disciples, hee would
be pleased to wash their feete: O sweete
IESVS, what is it that thou doest? O sweet
IESVS, why doth thy mightie Maiestie thus
diminish it selfe? O my soule, what woul-
dest thou haue thought to see God tum-
blinge at the feete of men, and prostrate
before IVDAS? O barbarous and cruel
man, could not so great humilitie molifie
thy

thy heart ? was not so great bountie and sweetnes able to penetrate thy entrals, and to reclaime thee from thy intended mischeife ? can it be that thou determineft to sell this meeke lambe for so small a price ? nay if it be so , how couldeft thou yet endure to behold so rare an example ? I wonder it did not wound thy guiltie soule with compunction for thy greuious crime ? O delicate hands, howe could you touch so filthie , sordide, and with sinne contaminated feete ? O pure and vnspotted hands , howe could you endure to wash those feete , that were fouled with goinge and cominge to make a sale of your precious bloud ? O thrice happie Apoftles , did you not tremble and ftand amazed at the sight of so great humilitie ? What doft thou doe PETER ? canft thou permitt the Lord of Maieftie to wash thy feete ? S. PETER wholly aftonished with the admiration of this spectacle , when he sawe our bleffed Sauiour fallinge downe at his feete , cryed out : *Domine tu mihi lauas pedes* ? Lord doeft thou wash my feete ? what, art not thou the Sonne of the euer-liuinge God ? art not thou the creatour of the whole world, the beutie of heauen, the Paradife of Angels , redeemer of mankind , splendour
of

of thy Fathers glorie, moſt deepe fountaine of the eternall wiſdome? and doeſt thou waſh my feet? howe cometh it to paſſe, that thou Lord of ſo great maieſtie and glorie ſhouldeſt thus debaſe thy ſelfe to ſo vile a ſeruice?

Thē cōſider, howe he waſhed all his diſciples feet one by one, and after waſhinge, wiped them with a linnen cloath wherwith he was girded, open the eies of thy mind to behold in theſe miſteries a repreſentation of our redemption. This linnen cloath ſo wiped their feet, that all the dirt which was vpon their feet did ſticke on the linnen cloath: not without miſterie.

For what more foule then mā conceiued in ſinne? What more pure thē CHRIST conceiued by the operation of the holy Ghoſt? *Dilectus meus candidus & rubicundus electus ex milibus*: My beloued ſaith the ſpouſe in the canticles is white and rudly choſen of thouſands. Yet not withſtandinge moſt pure, moſt beutifull CHRIST tooke vnto himſelfe all the ſpots of our ſoules: frō which that he might clēſe vs (as you may ſee him vpō the Croſſe) he would be pleaſed to defile himſelfe with the filth of our impuritie. Conſider laſtly with what words our Bleſſed Sauiour cloſed vp

        this

Cant. 5.

this humble action : *Exemplum dedi vobis vt*
quemadmodum ego feci vobis, ita & vos faciatis:
I haue giuen you an example that as I haue
done to you, you may doe the like. Which
words doe not only pertaine to this present action, and example of humilitie : but
likwise to all the actions of CHRIST
through-out his wholl life, vvhich is a most
absolute and perfect rule for vs to square
our actions by , especially of humilitie,
which is here to life represented vnto vs.

Of the institution of the blessed Sacrament.

HE that desireth to comprehend any
thinge of this noble misterie , must
certainly thinke, that no tounge is able to
expresse that immense loue , and ardent affection vvhervvith our blessed Sauiour
vvas inflamed tovvards his holy Church
and all faithfull soules, in institutinge this
stupendious misterie. For vvhen this brid- *The causes*
grome determined to depart out of this *vvhy*
mortall life, and to leaue the Church his *Christ in-*
beloued spouse ; least this is departure *stituted*
should be any occasion to her of forget- *this Sa-*
tinge her redeemer; he gaue her this Sacra- *crament.*
ment vvherin he himselfe is present , as a *The first.*
pledge and memoriall of his perpetuall
loue.

Then

The second   Then seinge he was to be longe absent; least his spouse should remaine solitarie alone, he, for her consolation, would leaue himselfe for her companion in this holy Sacrament.

The third.   When our blessed Sauiour was to suffer death for the redemption of his spouse, to enrich her with his most pretious bloud, and to purge her from sinnes : least she should be defrauded of so great a treasure, he would giue her a key in this Sacrament wherby she might at her pleasure enioy these riches: for as S. CHRYSOSTOME saith, we must thinke as often as we come to this Sacrament we put our mouth to the bleedinge side of CHRIST , and from thence drinke his most precious blood whose merits we participate.

The fourth   More-ouer this celestiall bridgrome, did desire to be tenderly beloued of his spouse , and for this cause would leaue her this misticall meat, consecrated with most efficatious words, and therin so great vertue , that whosoeuer receiues it worthily shall presently be strooke with the dartes of loue.

The fifth.   He would likewise bestowe vpon his spouse some sure pledge therby to make her secure of the certaine succession of future glorie, that in hope of so great a good,
he

he might temper the laborious difficultie
and make the tedious bitternes of this
prefent life, to be more tollerable ; wherfore that the fpoufe might certainly beleeue , that she shall at length attaine
to thefe vnfpeakable goods , he hath
giuen her for a pawne , this ineſtimable treafure , vvhich is as much
vvorth as that vvhich is expeſted hereafter, that she should not doubt but that
God vvill giue her himfelfe in glorie
vvhere he liueth in fpirit , that vvould
be pleafed to giue her himfelfe in this
vale of teares , vvhere he liueth in
flesh.

He vvould more-ouer vvhen he dyed *The fixth.*
make his laſt vvill and teſtament , vvherin he left to his fpoufe a fingular man-
na to cure all her infirmities , a gift then
vvhich , nothinge can be more foue-
raigne , nothinge more pretious , feeing the deity it felfe is therin conteined.

Laſtly , he defired to feede our foules *The fe-*
with fome heauenly foode , feinge they *uenth.*
need no leſſe nourishment that they might
liue fpiritually , then the body needeth
corporall fuſtinence that she might liue
corporally. Wherfore this fpirituall phy-
fition whē he had diligently examined and
felt

felt the pulſe of our fragilitie , inſtituted
this holy Sacrament which he exhibited
vnto vs vnder the ſpecies or forme of
bread, that he might declare what effect it
should worke in vs, that is to ſay, that it is
as neceſſarie for our ſoules, as bread for
the bodie.

A *Meditation for Tvveſday.*

THis day thou shalt meditate of the
prayer CHRIST made in the garden,
the methode therof, and the contumelies
he ſuffered in the howſe of ANNAS.

Conſider therfore , howe CHRIST our
Lord, after the conſummation of his myſticall body with his diſciples, before he
entred into the tragedie of his paſſion,
went to make his prayer vpon the mount
Oliuet, wherby he would inſtruct vs, that
in all aduerſities and tribulations. of this
preſent life, we fly to prayer, as to a holy
anchore ; the power of which is ſo great,
that it either beateth back the forces of
tribulations, or (which is of greater excel-
lencie) miniſtreth ſufficient ſtrength to endure them, with a conſtant and willinge
mind.

He tooke for companions in his iourny
three of his diſciples , whome he loued
aboue

aboue the reſt, S. Peter, S. Iames, and
S. Iohn. Which as they were eie-witt-
neſſes of his transfiguration, ſo likwiſe they
ſhould be preſent in his agonie, to behold
him for the loue of man now transformed
into a farr more different shape ; then he
was, when he manifeſted himſelfe vnto
them, in a glorious and glitteringe forme.

That alſo he might open vnto them, his
inward greiſe, to be much greater then appeared outwardly; He ſaith vnto them :
Triſtis eſt anima mea vſque ad mortem. Suſti-
nete hic & vigilate mecum: My ſoule is heauy
vnto death. Stay heere and vvatch vvith
me. O vvordes full of compaſſion ! Then
departinge from his diſciples a ſtones caſt,
vvith great ſubmiſſion and reuerence he
praied his Father: *Pater ſi fieri poteſt tranſeat à*
me Calix iſte, verumtamen non mea voluntas
ſed tua fiat : Father if it be poſſible let this
Chalice paſſe from me, but not my vvill,
but thine be done. Which prayer vvhen he
had repeated thrice, he fell into ſuch an
agonie, that he ſvveat drops of blood,
trickling dovvne the earth, from his precious body.

Conſider that, partly the foreſeeinge of
the moſt vnſpeakable torments that euer
any mortall man ſuffered, prepared for his
most

most tender body : partly the distinct representatiō of the sins of the whole world, for the expiatinge of which he was nowe to suffer death vpon the Crosse : partly the remembrance of the ingratitude of many, which would not esteeme , or reape any profit from this great benefitt, strock such a deepe impression into his soule , that it filled it with sad and incredible anxiety, so troubled his senses and tender flesh, that all the elements of his body beeinge weakened , the opened pores on euery side swett out drops of blood. If the flesh , which properly suffered not this anguish, but only through a simple immagination , was thus afflicted, what did his soule feale ; to whome properly these sorrowes did appertaine ?

His prayer beinge ended , that counterfait freind of CHRIST *Iudas* the traitour, came attēded with a hellish band; he I say which renounced his apostleship , to be head and Captaine of a troope of hellhounds , behold in the fore-front of that wicked multitude, impudently cominge to his master whome before he had solde, betraying him with a kisse of peace and freindship.

In that hower saied IESVS to the company, which came to apprehend him:

You

You haue come out as to a theefe to apprehend me vvith svvordes and staues ? I satt euery day vvith you teachinge in the temple , and you laied not hould on me. But this is your hovver and the povver of darkenes.

This misterie is worthy of admiration, for what thinge can be more admirable and stupendious , then to see the only be-gotten Sonne of God , not only in the forme of sinfull man, but in the shape of a condemned man : *Hæc est hora vestra, & po-testas tenebrarum :* This is your hower and the power of darkenes. From which wordes, is gathered that this innocēt lambe, was left to the diabolicall cruelty of the princes of darkenes, who by their vice-ge-rentes and ministers powred all the malice and mischeife they were able to conceiue against him. Consider, how much for thy sake the supreme Maiestie of God is hum-bled , to endure all the extremitie of tor-métes that euer any suffered in this present life , not to die for his owne faults but for thy sins , but he did vndergoe this of his owne accord, to free thee from the power of Sattan.

He had skarce spoken these wordes, when that wholl rabble of hunger-starued wolues, gapinge after their prey , rushed vpon this meeke and innocent lambe , ha-

E   linge,

linge, tearinge and afflictinge him with as
much cruelty as euer they could. O barbarous and inhumane proceedinges ? ô
cruell and sauage blowes, contumelious
violences, wherwith they tormented him?
they insulted after a horred manner no
otherwise, the conquerers retourne loaden
with spoiles after they haue put to flight
their enemies, or hunters when they haue
caught their prey. The handes which a
little before were exercised in workinge
miracles, they were nowe bound with
ropes so cruelly, that they rased the skin,
and besmeared them with blood. Thus
they led him through the publick streetes
of *Ierusalem*, followinge him with contumelies and blowes : behould him in this
iournie goinge alone, left by all his disciples, compassed with a multitude of his
enemies, forced to make such hast, that he
was wholly out of breath, his colour
changed, his face blushinge, and his wholl
body weakened and wearied by reason of
the intollerable present difficultie.

Although our blessed Sauiour was
barbarously and most cruelly handled by
that blood-suckinge multitude: yet neuer
the less thou mightst haue seene in his
countenance a pleasant sweetnes, in his
eies a comely grauitie, in his manners a diuine

uine grace , which all the torments of the
wholl world could not so much as diminish in the least degree.

After this goe with our blessed Sauiour
into the House of A N N A s the high
Preist, that there thou maiest take notice
what fauour he reaped for his mild ans-
wer, when A N N A s examined him of his,
and his disciples doctrine : which vvas,
that one of the Officers gaue him a cruell
blovve vpon his cheeke sayinge: *Sic respon-*
des Pontifici ? Doest thou ansvver the high
Preist so ? to him C H R I S T replied : *Si*
male locutus sum, testimonium perhibe de malo: Ioan. 18.
si autem bene, quid me cædis ? If I haue spoken euill bringe testimony of it , but if
vvel, vvhy doest thou beate me ?

Behould, ô my soule, not only the mild
ansvver, but the print of the Officers hand
in his tender cheeke, his countenance notvvithstandinge quiet and amiable , not a
vvhitt moued at the shame of so great an
affront , because he invvardly thought so
lovve and humbly of himselfe, that he had
tourned the other side vvithout delay , if
the rascald had desired it.

A Meditation for VVeddensday.

THis day thou shalt consider, how CHRIST our Lord was offered vp to CAYPHAS the high Preist: what torments he endured there all that night: how S. PETER denied him : and last of all how cruelly he was scourged.

Consider first of all, how he was led from the house of ANNAS to CAYPHAS his house, it is worth thy paines to followe him thether. For there thou shalt see the mighty sun of iustice ecclypsed: there thou shalt behould, the diuine face vpon which the Angels themselues delight to gaze , to be deformed with the filthie spittinges of the Iewes. For our blessed Sauiour standinge in the middest of them, was coniured by the high Preist in the name of his Father , to speake out, what he was. He answered as beseeming himselfe : but they who were vnworthy of such an answere , blinded with the splendour of this great light , like mad dogges rushed vpon him, vometing vp the bitter gaule of their wholl malice against him.

They began whole troupes of them to buffet him, to beate and kick him, they spit
vpon

vpon his diuine face,and threwe the verie
snot of their filthy noses vpon it. Others
hood-winked his eies with a dirty linnen
cloath, smiteinge him vpō the cheeke, and
would in mokerie haue him prophecy
who it was that strooke him. O admirable and vn-heard of patience, and humilitie of the only begotten Sonne of God.
O the face which the Angels of heauen
doe contemplate with incredible ioy, besmeared with their sordid and filthy spittinges.

Men, when they spit, comonly tourne
themselues to some foule place, some what
remote from the sight of others. In this
pallace was there no place found more
contemptible therin to cast their spit and
filthy dryuell, then the sacred face of
CHRIST IESVS? O man that art but
dust and ashes, canst thou choose but be
stirred vp to humility, and contempt of
thy selfe at so rare an example?

Consider more-ouer, what tormentes
our blessed Sauiour suffered all that night,
how the Officers that kept him, that
sleepe should not close his eies, afflicted
him, derided the supreme Maiestie of
God, and loaded him with many iniurious
contumelies.

Waigh

Waighe with thy selfe, my soule, that now thy spouse is made the white and mark, receiuing vpõ him selfe all the dartes of iniurious contumelies that the mischeiuous Iewes could shute at him. O cruell night, o vnquiet night, in which thou blessed I E s v s couldest rest no more by reason of anguish and affliction, then others who tooke pleasure to torment the. The night was ordained for the rest of all creatures, that the mẽbers and senses wearied with the labour of the day before, might then take some repose. But the wicked Soldiers that kept thee, spent it in tormentinge of thy senses, they did bind thy bodie, vexed thy soule, fettered thy hands and feete with manicles, buffeted thy cheekes, spit vpon thy face, blinded thine eies, so that all thy senses when they should haue beene refreshed were afflicted.

O! howe farre did these mattins differ from those, which at the same time the blessed Angels did singe in heauen? they cried holy, holy: and the Iewes cried he is guiltie of death, crucifie, crucifie him. O angelicall spirits which vnderstood both cries, what could you imagine or thinke whẽ you sawe the inhumane crueltie wherwith he was handled in earth, whome in heauen you adored with so

great

great submission and reuerence ? did you not wonder to see him suffer all these extreame tormentes for to expiate the sins of those, who inflicted them vpon him? who hath euer heard of such immense charitie, that for this reason one should suffer death, to heale the greife and cure the woundes of his murtherers ?

The fall of S. P E T E R, that great pillar, did not a little increase the anxietie of this tedious night; that he, whome he enteirely loued amongst the rest whome he chose to be present at his glorious transfiguration, to whome he committed the primacie of his holy Church, whome he ordained to be head and Prince of the Apostles, that he I say, should before his face, and in his presence denie him, not once but thrice, addinge blasphemies and oathes, that he knewe not the man. Tell me P E T E R, did this man seeme to thee so vngodly and wicked, that in future times thou dideft feare, it would bee a disgrace vnto thee to confess him now? dideft thou not consider that thou didst first pronounce the sentence of condemnation against him, before he was adiudged by the high Preifts, when thou dideft not esteeme him so much as worthy of thy acknowledgment ? couldeft thou doe a greater iniury to CHRIST IESVS?

But CHRIST forrowfull for this great
fault of S. PETER turned himfelfe, and
caft his eies vpon him , that with his gratious countenance he might reduce this
wandering sheepe into the sheepfold of
his mercies. O admirable afpect, fecret indeed , but full of fignification , which
S. PETER knewe right vvell, and vvell
vnderftood of vvhat force and efficacy it
vvas. The crovvinge of the cock had little
auailed to his compunction and conuer-
fiō, had not the countenance of CHRIST
our Sauiour bene adioyned. Whofe eies
did fpeake and vvorke that ftupendious
chaunge, the certainty of vvhich, not only
the flovving teares of S. PETER, but of
our bleffed Sauiour himfelfe did fufficient-
ly teftifie.

After all thefe iniuries confider, vvhat
CHRIST did fuffer, vvhen he vvas bound
to be fcourged at the pillar, for the iudge
vvhen he favve, that be could not pacifie
the fury of thofe infernall monfters , he
thought good to aduife thē, to beate him
vvith roddes and vvhippes. Wherby his
vvholl bodie might be torne, hoping that
vvay to molifie their obftinate and obdurate hearts : that vvhen they favve him fo
torne and mangeled , they vvould ceafe
                                            fur-

further to defire his cruell death.

Enter novve my foule in fpirit, into the houfe of P i l a t e , and haue teares in readines , for thou vvilt haue neede of them , if thou shalt diligently confider, vvhat vvas done there.

Behould hovv inhumanely thefe abiect and infamous roagues fpovled our bleffed Sauiour of his garmetes. Marke the humility of C h r i s t , hovv he fuffered himfelfe to be ftripped , not fo much as opening his mouth , nor vtteringe any vvord againft their iniurious behauiour. See his facred body bound to the pillar vvith many ropes, in fuch a faffion that on euery fide they might haue rome to torture him.

Confider , hovv our Lord of Angels ftood alone in the middeft of his cruell enemies , vvithout any Aduocates or Procuratours that vvould defend his caufe, yea altogether vvithout any one man, vvho at leaftvvife a farr of, vvould fo much as copaffionate the bitternes of his tormetes. Doeft thou not heare the noife of roddes and vvhippes wherwith they loaded, teared and rent the delicate fleshe of I e s v s, addinge ftroke vpo ftroke, and vvound to vvound ? doeft thou not fee his vvholl body in one short moment of time , vvith the

the vehemency and often iteratinge the blowes , to be couered as it were with one vlcer , his skin to be dravvne from the flesh , and blood from his vvholl body , from the crovvne of his head to the soles of his feete , to flovve dovvne vpon the earth ? especially , is it not dreadfull for thee to behould the place betvvixt the shoulders , vvherupon almost the vvholl force of all the blovves did light?

Consider hovv C H R I S T the Sauiour of the vvorld , after that extreame cruelty of his tormentours , vvent vp and dovvne the Pallace all torne and cutt, seekinge and gathering vp his garmentes , not findinge one amongst those inhumane rascalls, that vvould shevv vnto him the least act of humanity , in vvashinge or refreshing his vvoundes , or lend their hand to help him to putt on his cloaths. All these thinges are vvorthy of our diligent consideration, that therby vve might stirr vp our soules to due compassion of his miseries.

A Meditation for Thursday.

THis day thou shalt meditate , hovv
CHRIST vvas crovvned vvith
thornes , his prefentation before all the
people, his condemnation, his bringinge
out to the place of execution , and laft of
all his caryinge of his Croffe.

The Spoufe in the Canticles inuited vs
to the confideratiō of thefe tormētes, when
she faide:*Egredimini filiæ* Sion *& videte Regem* Cant. 3.
SALOMONEM *in Diademate , quo coro-*
nauit eum Mater fua in die defponfationis eius, &
*in die lætitiæ cordis eius:*Goe forth yea daugh-
ters of *Sion* and fee Kinge SALOMON in
the Diademe vvhervvith his Mother hath
crovvned him , in the day of his defpou-
finge,and in the day of the ioy of his heart.

What doeft thou doe?vvhat doeft thou
thinke my foule?my tounge vvhy art thou
filēt?O fweet Sauiour whē I opē mine eies,
and behould this forrowfull fpectacle, my
heart is rēt vvith greife. What,Lord,vvere
not thy former tormētes.imminētdeath,and
aboundāce of thy blood already shed,fuffi-
ciēt for the redēptiō of mankinde?but thou
muft yet be crovvned vvith sharp thornes?

My foule that thou Maieft the better vn-
derftād this fadd fpectacle,fett before thine
eies our bleffed Sauiour,in his former beutie
be-

before he suffered these tormentes? Then behould him on the contrary in this miserable state. If in the first, thou doest rightly veiwe him, thou shalt see him more beutifull then the sun. In his eies a comely grauity, in his speech a gratious facillity: in his actions singular modesty:in the gesture of his wholl body profound humility, ioyned with reuerent Maiesty.

Then after thou hast satiated thy soule with pleasure,in behouldingthis rare peece of admirable perfection,then tourne thine eies againe, and looke vpon him, as he is in this present miserable state. Ridiculously cloathed in purple, bearinge in his hand a reede for a Kingely Sceptre, and vpon his head a Crowne of sharpe thornes, in steade of a regall Diademe,his eies were dimmed, his face pall and wan,fouled and couered with the filthy spittles of the Iewes: behould him within,and without: his heart consumed with greife: his body torne with woūdes and blowes,forsaken of his disciples, hastened to vndergoe death of his enemies, mocked of the Soldiars: despised of rhe highe Preifts: reiected as a wicked Kinge arrogantly assuming this title: vniustly accused, and destitute of all humane aide.

Doe

Doe not confider thefe thinges as done
and paft many yeares fince, but imagine
with thy felfe, that at this prefent they be
in actinge before thy face ; nor as an other
mans forrowes,but as thine owne afflictiõs,
fett thy felfe in his place and coniecture
what tormétes thou shouldeft fuffer,if thy
head were boared to the skull and thy
brain-pan pearced with sharp thornes?
But what doe I fay thornes , when thou
canft skearce endure the prick of a fmall
needle? howe great then was the paine,
his tender head fuffered , with this newe
and vn-heard-of torment.

The Coronatiõ of our bleffed Sauiour,
with many mockes and fcornes being ended the iudge produced him before the
people, faying: *Ecce homo:*Behould the mã.
If yea thirft after the death of the man,
behould him fcarce a heares bredth diftãt
from it, yea he is brought to that pafs,that
he deferueth rather commiferation, then
your enuy , if yea feare that he will make
himfelfe a Kinge, behould he is fo deformed,that he fcarce reteineth the shape of a
mã: doe yea feare any violence from thefe
hands that are fo ftraightly manicled? doe
yea dreade any harme frõ a mã that is caft
into fuch a miferable and deiected ftate,
whofe body is fo mãgeled and weakened?
Con-

Cõsider, ô my soule, in what state thy Sauiour was, when the very iudge himselfe, did thinke with this aspect, would moue his bloody enemies to compassion : from vvhich vve may gather, vvhat a miserable thinge it is, to see a Christian of such an obdurate heart, vvhich can or vvill not condole the passions of our Sauiour, vvhen they vvere such ; that the very iudge did thinke them sufficient, to molifie the malice of his enemies. But P I L A T E seeinge vvith thees exceedinge tormentes, he could no vvay temper or asvvage their fury, vvent into his Pallace satt in the iudgment seat to pronounce the deffinitiue sentéce against C H R I S T. Novve the Cross vvas prepared at the dore and the fatall standard vvhich thretned ruine to our blessed Sauiour ; vvas novve in a readines.

The sentence beinge pronounced vvith the addition of more tormentes, they loaded his vvearied shoulders vvith a heauy Crosse, to carry to the place of his execution.

But our meeke Lord, not only not reiected it, but out of that immense charity tovvards vs, vvhervvith he suffered for our sins, obediently and vvillingly embraced it.

Novv

Now the innocent I s a a c with his weake shoulders, supported the intollerable burthen of the Croffe to the place of facrifice. The fimple people and deuout women, followed him weepinge. For who was able to conteine teares,to fee the Lord and Kinge of Angels goinge thus on foote,with the extremity of tormentes,his knees quiueriuge, his body ftoopinge, his eies blinded , his face befmeared with blood , his head crowned with thornes, and his eares deafened with the noife of droomes and trumpetts ?

Leaue a while,ô my foule,this horred fpe ctacle,& with wateringe eies, with fobbes, and figthes goe to the bleffed Virgine, and fay to her. Lady of Angels , Queene of heauê,Gate of Paradife, Aduocate of the world, Sanctuary of finners, Health of the iuft,Ioy of the Saintes,Miftreffe of vertue, Mirrour of purity , Symboll of chaftity, Patterne of patience,and Rule of all perfection. O me miferable and vnfortunate, what haue I feene with the eies of faith ? Howe could I liue to behould fo inhumane vfage, interrupting fighes will not permitt me fcarce to fpeake , howe I left thy only begôttê Sône,loadê vvith a mighty Croffe, to vvhich he vvas prefently to be nayled, and carryinge it to the place of execution.
What

What heart, what minde, what soule, is able to comprehend the dolour, the blessed Virgine M A R I E then did suffer? her heart fainted, and a dead sweate with extreame anguish possessed her wholl body, and presently she had giuen vp the ghost, had not the diuine dispensation reserued her, till better times, for her greater merite, and more aboundant reward.

The blessed Virgine, with speed followeth the steps of her beloued Sonne, that ardent desire wherwith she was inflamed to see him, added vigour to her, of which sorrowe had bereaued her : she heard a farr of the noise of armes, the concourse of people, and the sound of trumpets, on euery side publishing the passion of C H R I S T, after that she sawe the glitteringe of launces and holbeards: in the way she found his footsteps sprincked with drops of blood, by which without any guid or leader she might easily find the way. Approachinge to her Sonne, she lifted vp her eies swelled with teares, to behould him, whome she esteemed dearer then her owne soule.

O what strife was there in the soule of this blessed Virgine, betwixt feare and loue ? she did vehemently desire to see her Sonne, but on the other side she durst not
                                                                              cast

caſt her eies vpon him in this lamentable
and afflicted ſtate. At length when ſhe
drew neerer, theſe two celeſtiall lights beheld eatch other, their eies pearced eatch
others ſoule, but greiſe enforced their
tongues to ſilence, notwithſtanding their
heartes did mutually diſcourſe, and the
Sonne vnto the Mother ſaid: Sweet Mother, why comeſt thou hether ony loue,
my doue? thy ſorrowe reneweth my miſeries, and my tormētes crucifieth thy ſoule?
retourne, retourne againe into thy houſe.
This defiled company of theeues and
murtherers beſeemeth not thy virginall
purity. Theſe and the like words they inwardly vttered ; all the way vntill they
came to the place of execution.

A Meditation for Fryday.

THis day thou ſhalt meditate vpon the
miſterie of the Croſſe, and the ſeauen
wordes which C H R I S T ſpake vpon it:
Rouze vp my ſoule and duely ponder this
great miſtery of the Croſſe, which
brought fourth the fruite of ſatisfactiō, to
expiate that great loſſe, which all mankind
ſuffered by a tree.

Conſider how, before our bleſſed Sauiour came to the Mount of *Caluarie* (to
make his death more ignominious) his
F   cruell

cruell tormenters ſtripped him of all his cloathes, except his coate, which was without ſeame , behould howe patiently this meeke lambe ſuffereth his garmentes to be taken from him, not ſo much as openinge his mouth or ſpeakinge one worde againſt their barbarous dealinge. He permitted theſe thinges willingly , but with a great ſtraine to modeſty. He was ſtripped naked that we might receiue a better garment, to couer the nakednes of our ſins , then that of A D A M the firſt parent of all mankind, made of the leaues of fig-trees to couer the nakednes of his body.

Some Doctours thinke that the crowne of thornes was taken of, to pull with more facillitie his vnſeamed garment ouer his eares and after to be faſtened on againe, which could not be without a vehement paine, the ſharp thornes did a freſh wound his ſacred head with vnſpeakable torment. And ſurely this is not vnlike , ſeeing in the wholl time of his paſſion they ſpared him in nothinge ; but the bittereſt tormentes they could deuiſe, they heaped vpon him, eſpecially when the Euangeliſt ſaith , they did to him whatſoeuer they would. This coate did ſo cleaue to the woundes of his ſacred body, by reaſon of the congealed blood, that when the barbarous hangemen
                                    drewe

drewe it of with exceeding violence, they
renewed againe the woundes of I E S V S,
they pulled of with it many particles of
flesh, so that the wholl body of CHRIST,
in euery part fleyed and bloody, from the
head to the foote seemed to be but one
entire and continuate wound.

Weigh well with thy selfe (my soule) the
immense goodnes and mercy of God, manifested in these tormentes, behould he
that spreadeth the heauens with cloudes,
vesteth the greene and pleasant feilds with
flowers , and he that liberally bestoweth
clothinge vpon euery creature , behould
him I say starke naked. Consider what
cold, this pretious body, beinge wounded,
suffered, when they had not only spoyled
him of his garmentes, but his very skin was
not enteire , neither were his woundes
bound vp, but exposed to the iniury of the
aire.

If S. P E T E R, being well clothed could
not ouercome the cold of the fore-passed
night: What cold doest thou thinke this
delicate body suffered being in euery
place wounded and all naked?

Then consider how CHRIST was
fastened to the Crosse, and what torment
he suffered, when the sharp nayles pearced
the most sensible parts of his tender body;

Weigh

Weigh with thy selfe that the blessed Virgine, which beheld these thinges with her eies, and hearing, the frequent blowes of the mallet, which they iterated in driuinge the nayles into the handes and feet of her Sonne, was not vnsensible, but the heart of the Mother was pearced with the handes and feete of the Sonne.

When CHRIST was made fast vpon the Crosse, presently they lifted it vp, and put it into a hole there before prepared, behold how these wicked torterours of innocēt IESVS pricked forward with their owne malice, lett the heauy Crosse fall into the hole with such a violence, that it so much strained his body hanginge only by the nayles, and rent wider the woundes of his handes and feete.

Sweet Sauiour cā there befound a heart so hard and steely, which is not molified at such a spectacle, when the very stones did cleaue in sunder, as sensible of thy cruell tormentes?

O Lord, the dolours of death compassed thee round about, the stormes and waues of the raginge sea enuirouned thee on euery side. The waters entred into thy soule, thou didest descend to the deepe abysse, where thou couldst find no footinge. When thy heauenly Father did forsake

fake thee, Lord, what couldft thou expect
thine enemies would doe? they cried out
againft thee, and thy freindes did wound
thy heart, thy foule was fad and heauy, nei
ther was there any that would cõfort thee.

Lord, from thefe vnheard-of tormẽtes,
and aboundãt fatisfactiõ which thou haft
made for my fins, I cannot but acknowledge with all humility the greiuioufnes of
my heinous tranfgreffion, which were the
occafions of all thy miferies. I fee thee my
King and God faftned vpon a wodden
Croffe, with two yron nayles; thy pretious
and tender flesh to be ftretched without
any manner of refpite. If thou wouldeft a
little eafe thy felfe vpon thy feete, the
weight of thy wholl body enlargeth their
woũdes: if thou wouldeft leaue the burthẽ
to thy hãds, the weight of it doth likewife
rend their woundes; thy facred head could
find no reft becaufe thou hadeft no other
pillowe thẽ the fharpe crowne of thornes.

O virgine Mother howe willingly
wouldeft thou haue embraced him in
thine armes, therõ to eafe and reft himfelfe
a little. But the armes of the Croffe would
not permitt the, vpon which, if he would
repofe the fharp thornes ftrooke deeper
into his head: the troubles of the Sonne
were much augmented by the prefence

F 3 of

of the Mother ; which no leſſe crucified his ſoule then the Ievves his body to the Croſſe.

O ſvveet I E S V, in one day thou dideſt carry a double croſſe, the one vpon thy body, the other in thy ſoule , the one of paſſion , the other of compaſſion , the one pearced thy body vvith nayles of iron, the other thy ſoule vvith nayles of ſorrovve. What tonge is able to expreſſe , vvhat thou dideſt ſuffer to ſee the anguiſh of thy Deare Mother ? vvhoſe ſoule thou dideſt certainly knovve to be crucified together vvith thee ? vvhen thou didſt behould her heauy heart , pearced vvith the ſvvord of ſorrovve : vvhen vvith bloody eies thou didſt looke vpon her beutifull face , pale and vvan: and didſt heare the ſightes of her dyinge ſoule , lamentinge that ſhe could not dye. What didſt thou ſuffer to ſee pure fountaines of teares guſhinge from her eies, and to heare her pittifull complaintes ſhe made in ſorrovvinge for thy ſufferinges.

Thē conſider the ſeauē vvordes vvhich C H R I S T ſpake vpon the Croſſe , to his heauenly Father, ſayinge : *Pater ignoſce illis quia neſciunt quid faciunt :* Father forgiue them for they knovv not vvhat they doe. To the Theefe : This day thou ſhalt be vvith

vvith me in Paradife ; To his Mother:
Woman behould thy Sonne. To the people he faid : I thirft. And to God againe:
My God, my God , vvhy haft thou far fa-
ken me. *Confummatum eft* : It is confum-
mate. In to thy hands I commande my
fpirit.

Ruminate, my foule, vvith vvhat exceedinge charitie, he made interceffion to his
heauenly Father, for his enemies and per-
fecutours. With vvhat piety and mercy he
receiued the penitent Theefe into his fauour. With vvhat affection he committed
his Mother to the protection of his beloued difciple : vvith vvhat ardour he tefti-
fied himfelfe vehemently to thirft after the
faluation of mankind. With vvhat cla-
mour he thundered out his prayer, expref-
finge to the diuine Maieftie the greiuioufnes of his tribulations. Hovve perfectly he
fulfilled the obedience, enioyned to hime
by his heauely Father. And laftly hovve he
yealded his foule into his bleffed handes.

Euery one of vvhich vvordes doe afford vs a great deale of matter for our in-
ftruction. In the firft, vve are taught , to
loue our enemies : in the fecond, mercy tovvardes finners : in the 3. piety tovvardes
our parents : in the fourth, to thirft after
our neighbours faluatio: in the fift, vvhen

F 4　　　vve

we are oppressed with tribulations , and seeminge as it were to be left of God, to fly to prayer : in the sixth, the vertue of obedience and perseuerance : in the seauenth, perfect resignation into the handes of God , which is the sume of all perfection.

A Meditation for Saterday.

THis day thou shalt meditate vpon the pearcinge of our blessed Sauiours side with a speare : the takinge downe of CHRIST from the Crosse: the lamentations of the women : and other thinges which did occurr about his buriall.

First take notice, how that CHRIST, after he gaue vp the ghost vpō the Crosse, his enemies much reioyced at his death. But yet there was not an end of their insatiate cruelty , but still their encreasinge malice raged against him being dead. They diuided and cast lotts for his garmētes, and with a speare pearced his pretious side.

O barbarous caitifes ! ô adamantine heartes! did you thinke those tormentes he suffered before his death were not sufficient , that you would not vouchsafe to spare him beinge dead ? what madnes did possesse your soules ? lift vp your eies and
be-

behold his dead face, his eies funck, his hanginge head, and his wholl body beinge wan and pale. Although your heartes be harder then adamant, yet let this pittifull afpect molifie them.

Behould the centurian ftroock â launce into his facred fide vvith fuch violéce, that the very Croffe did tremble, out of whofe fide did gush aboundance of blood and water, for the redemption of all mankind. O riuer of paradife rūninge forth to water the wholl earth! O pretious wound which rather the loue thou dideft bare to vs finfull men, then the enemies weapon did inflict! O gate of heauen, windowe of paradife, place of reft, tower of fortitude, fanctuary of the iuft, neaft of doues, tombe of pilgrimes, flourishinge bed of the fpoufe! Haile facred woūd, which pearceft deuout heartes, haile rofe of incredible beauty, haile pretious ftone of ineftimable valour, haile dore, through which, lieth open a free paffage to the heart of C H R I S T, an argument of his loue, and pledge of eternall felicity.

Confider that in the eueninge, I O-S E P H and N I C O D E M V S came with ladders to loofe and take downe the body of our Sauiour : but the bleffed Virgine after all thefe tormentes, perceiuinge her
Son-

Sonne to be taken from the Crosse , and disposed for the graue , she tooke him whē he was let downe, in her armes, humbly beseechinge that holy company , that they would suffer her to come neere his body , and to bestowe her last kisse and embracinges vpon him, which vpon the Crosse she could not doe. Which they would not , nor could deny. For if her freinds had depriued her of him dead, which her enemies did her of him liuinge, they had redoubled the anguish of her soule.

When she sawe her Sonne in this case, what greife , what dolours can we immagine she then did suffer ? Angels of peace come and lament with this blessed Virgine, lament heauen, lament starres, lament all creatures of the vvorld. She embraced the mangeled body of her beloued Sonne, she hugged him in her armes (for loue administred this strēgth) she thrust her face amongst the thornes to come to kisse his mouth , vvherby she vvounded her face vvith the sharp pricks vvhich she vvashed vvith flovvinge teares ;

O svveet Mother , is this thy beloued Sonne ? is this he vvhome thou didest conceiue vvith great glorie, and bringe fourth vvith great ioy? is this that bright mirrour in vvhich thou vvert vvont to see thy selfe?

all

all that were present did likewise mourne, the other MARIES, which were there mourned, the noble-men lamented, heauen and earth with all creatures mourned with the blessed Virgine.

That holy Euangelist lamented, who often embracinge the body of his deare Master, said: O my good Lord and Master, who shall hereafter teach and instruct me? with whome nowe shall I consult in doubtfull occasiõs? vpon whose lapp shall I now rest my selfe? who shall now reueale vnto me celestiall secretes? what suddaine change is this? yeasterday I rested vpon thy sacred brest, where thou didst communicate to me the ioyes and glory of euerlastinge life, and nowe in recompence of that benefit I embrace thee dead in my armes? is this that countenance which I beheld glorious and transfigurated vpon the mount of Thabor? is this that face which I sawe brighter and more glitteringe then the sun?

And that blessed sinner S. MARY MAGDALEN lamented, who often kissinge the feete of her Sauiour, said: O the true light of mine eies, the only remedie and solace of my soule. If I sinne againe, who shall hereafter receiue me into fauour? who shall defend me from the ca-

lumlūnies of the Pharisies ? O how altered are these feete from those I washed with my teares? O beloued of my heart, why doe I not dye with thee ? O life of my soule, how can I say, I loue thee, when I liuinge, see thee dead before me ?

Thus this blessed cōpany did mourne, and lament , wateringe with aboundant teares the body of I E S V S. The sepulchre beinge ready they spiced his holy body with sweet spices, they wrapped it vp in a fine linnen cloth , bound his head with a handkercher, laied it vpon a beere, carried it to the place of buriall and put it into a newe monument.

The monument was couered with a stone, and the face of M A R I E obscured with a cloud of sorrowe. When there againe she bad her Sonne adue , she then began to be more and more sensible of her solitude. For then she savve her selfe, to be depriued of the greatest good. But her heart remained buried vvith her trea-sure in the graue.

A Meditation for Sunday.

THis day thou shalt confider and meditate of the defcent of C H R I S T to *lymbus Patrum:* his refurrection: diuers apparitions to the bleffed Virgine M A R I E; S. M A R I E M A G D A L E N E , and his other difciples: and laft of all his glorious afcenfion into heauen.

Take notice therfore of the incredible ioy, the Fathers, vvhich vvere deteined *in lymbus,* felt at they cominge of the redeeme vvho came to free them from the darke prifon, vvherin they vvere shutt for many thoufand yeares. W hat prayfes, vvhat giuinge of thankes did they render to him, vvho had brought them to the longe defired hauen of their faluation? they vvhich retourne from the eaft *Indies,* are vvont to fay, that they thinke all their forepaffed labours vvell beftovved, only for that ioy they finde, the firft day of their arriuall into their country. If the banishment of a yeare or tvvo, and the tedioufnes of a little trouble fome iourny, can breed fuch ioy in men, vvhat vvill the abfence of three or fovvre thoufand yeares doe frō that pleafaūt and celeftiall country. W hat ioy therfore doe vve thinke, thofe holy Fathers had, vvhen they tooke poffeffion of it ?

Then

Then confider the exceffiue ioy of the bleffed Virgine, when she fawe her Sonne rifen from death, when it is moft certaine, and vndoubted, that she felt the greateft forrowe and affliction at his ignominious death and paffion that could be, her ioy muft needs excell the reft, in his triumphāt refurrectiō. How great doeft thou thinke was her content and pleafure to fee her Sonne, whome she greuioufly lamented before his death, liuinge, glorious, and attended with a ioyfull troop of holy Patriarches, whome he brought a longe with him? What faid she? what did she? with what kiffes did she falute him? with what affection did she embrace him? what pleafant riuers of teares diftilled from her eies? how earneftly did she defire to followe her Sonne, had it been permitted to her?

More-ouer take notice, of the ioy of the holy MARIES, particularly of her which ftood weepinge, at the Sepulcre of CHRIST, then, when she fawe him whome her foule loued : without doubt she caft her felfe at his feete, when she beheld him liuinge, whome she fought amongft the dead.

After his Mother, he therfore appeared to her, who loued him moft ardently, and, aboue

aboue others, fought him moft diligently and perfeuerantly, to inftruct vs that when we looke for God , vve muft feeke him vvith teares and diligence.

Confider that after this, he appeared to his difciples going vnto *Emaus*, in the habit of a Pilgrime; behould, hovv curteoufly he ioyned himfelfe a companion to them: hovve familiarly he conuerfed vvith them: hovve handfomely he diffembled his perfon: and after, vvith vvhat affection he manifefted himfelfe vnto them, and laft of all hovv he left their tounges and lippes filled vvith the delightfull difcourfe of his Maieftie. Let thy difcourfe and talke, be like thefe difciples, as they trauailed in the vvay, of the loue and paffion of our bleffed Sauiour; and I dare be bould to fay , that he vvill not deny vnto thee his facred prefence.

In the myftery of our bleffed Sauiours afcenfion, firft confider that he deferred it for forty dayes , that in the meane time often appearinge to his difciples, he might inftruct them, and vvith them difcourfe of the kingdome of heauen. For he vvould not forfake them by afcendinge into heauen, before he had difpofed their mindes to afcende vvith him fpiritually.

Hence

Hence vve may note, that those are often depriued of the corporall presence of CHRIST, and of sensible deuotion, vvho vvith the vvinges of contemplation fly vp to heauen and feare no danger. Wherin the diuine prouidence, vvhervvith it curbeth & gouerneth the elect, doth vvonderfully manifest it selfe, hovve it strégthneth the vveake, exerciseth the stronge, giueth milke to little ones, prepareth stronger meat for great ones, comforteth some, afflicteth others, and to conclude accomodates himselfe to all accordinge to their seuerall degrees in their spirituall profitt. Wherfore he that is roborated by diuine comfort, ought therfore not to presume of him selfe, seeinge this sensible consolation, is but the meat for infirme ones, and a great signe of vveaknes: nor he that is exercised by affliction, ought therfore to be deiected, seeinge temptation is for the most part, a testimony of a valiant minde.

CHRIST ascended vp to heauen, in the preséce of his disciples, that they might be vvittnesses of this mystery, of vvhich they vvere eie-beholders, none can giue better testimony of God almighties deedes, then he vvhich hath learned them by experience : vvherfore he that vvould certainly

tainly knowe , how good, howe sweet, and mercifull he is towardes his, and what is the force and efficacy of his diuine grace,loue,prouidence,and spirituall consolatiõs: lett him aske those,which indeed haue had experience of them,for they,and only they, will giue him the best instructions and satisfaction.

More-ouer C H R I S T would ascend, his disciples lookinge vpon him,that they might prosecute him with their eies and spirit , that they might haue a cordiall fealinge of his departure : that in his absence, they might feare to remaine alone, and that they might the better dispose themselues to receiue his holy grace. The Prophet H E L I S E V S , when H E- 4. *Reg.* 2. L I A S was to be taken and separated from him,desired that he would giue him his spirit , H E L I A S made answere: *Rem quidem difficilem postulasti , attamen si videris me, quando tollar à te , erit tibi quod petisti ; Si autem non videris,non erit.* Thou hast asked a hard thing: neuer the lesse if thou see me when I shall be taken from thee, thou shalt haue what thou hast asked : but if thou see me not, thou shalt not haue it.

In like manner they shall be heires of the spirit of C H R I S T, whome loue

G doth

doth cause to mourne, for his departure: to whome his absence doth seeme greuious, who earnestly whilst they liue in this banishment, desire his holy presence. Such a Sainct was he that saied: thou art gon my comfortour, without any care of me , at thy departure thou didest blesse thine, and I sawe it not ; the Angels promised, that thou shouldest retourne againe , and I heard them not. Who is able to expresse or vnderstand the solitude, trouble, cries and teares of the blessed Virgine, of his beloued disciple , S. MARIE MAGDA-LEN, and the other Apostles: when they sawe CHRIST to be pulled from them, who together with him carried vp their affectionate heartes? and yet notwithstandinge it is saied of them , that they retourned with great ioy into *Hierusalem* : the same loue and affection which made them bewaile the visible losse of their beloued Lord and Master, did likewise cause that they congratulated eatch other ; much reioycinge at his glory, for it is the nature of true loue, not so much to seeke the comoditie of it selfe, as the honour and comodity of the person that is beloued.

Last of all to close vp this meditation, it is left to vs to consider, with what glory, with what ioy, this noble conquerour was

brought

brought into that heauenly citty: what so-
lemnities were then instituted in the glorious Paradise, howe magnificently was he
entertained by those celestiall citizens?
what a delightfull spectacle was it, to see
men accompanied with Angels, to goe in
procession, and to sett vpon those seates,
which for many thousand yeares, were va-
cant. But a most rauishinge ioy it was, to
behold, the sacred humanity of C H R I S T
I E S V S, farr transcending al others, to sett
at the right hand of his eternall Father.

All these thinges are worthy of thy attentiue consideration, that thou maiest
learne, that the labours thou doest vndergoe for the loue of God, are not spent in
vaine, therfore he that humbled himselfe
vnder all creatures, it was requisite that he
should be exalted aboue all; that the louers
of true glory may trace this path, they
must expect if they desire to be aboue all,
that first they be subiect to all, euen their
inferiours.

CHAP. V.

Of six thinges necessary to prayer.

T HESE are the exercises and meditations (Christian Reader)
wherwith euery day thou Maiest
feed thy soule, which if thou doest rightly vse , thou wilt neuer want matter , to
Six partes buesy thy minde deuoutly. But thou must
necessary note, that meditation, if it be well perfor-
for medi- med, ought to consist of six partes. Some
tation. of which goe before, others followe mentall prayer.

Prepara- First before we apply our selues to me-
tion. ditation , it is necessarie , that our minde
and soule be diligently prepared to this
holy exercice. As the stringes of an instrument , except they be before-hand well
tuned , will neuer make a pleasant melody.

Reading. After preparation ought to followe the
readinge of some holy mystery , accordinge to the distribution of dayes in the
weeke , which in younge beginners is
cheifely necessary vntill with continuall

vse

vſe and cuſtome , matter of meditation
offereth it ſelfe vnto their memories. Then
inſiſt vpon the matter to be meditated
vpon. To meditation we muſt ioyne de- *Medita-*
uout and ſyncere giuinge of thankes to *tion.*
God for all his benefits : then a generall *Giuinge*
oblation of all the life of C H R I S T , for *of than-*
recompence of any benefit, and our owne *oblation.*
workes to the honour and glory of God.
Laſt of all, petition , which is cheifely cal- *Petition.*
led prayer, wherin we deſire all things neceſſarie for our owne ſaluation , of our
neighbours, and the good of the wholl
Church.

Theſe ſix partes are required to mentall
prayer , which beſides other comodities
they miniſter aboundant matter of meditation , ſeeing they ſett before vs diuers
ſortes of meates, that if one will not reliſh
our ſpirituall taſt , we may fall vpon an
other : if we be deficient in one ; in an
other we may employ our mindes , and
kindle our deuotion.

But in euery meditation , neither all
theſe partes nor order is alwayes neceſſary:
although, as I ſaid before, to younge beginners, it is. That they ſhould haue a certaine methode, accordinge to which they
are to guide them ſelues, wherfore in that
which hath, or ſhall be ſaid, my intention

is not to fett downe a generall rule , or immutable perpetuall lawes , the violatinge of which fhould be a fault , but my meaninge is, to introduce , and bringe in younge beginners and nouices into the right way, and methode of meditation: which when they are once in vfe , experience , but efpecially the holy Ghoft will better informe them.

CHAP.

CHAP. VI.

Of the preparation neceſſarie to prayer.

IT will not be beſids our purpoſe to hādle all theſe partes ſeuerally, we will therfore firſt beginne with preparation which we did put firſt.

He therfore which goeth about to meditate, after he hath placed his body after a decent manner, either kneelinge, or ſtandinge, or compoſinge himſelfe in manner of a Croſſe, or proſtratinge himſelfe vpon the ground, or ſittinge, if infirmitie or neceſſitie doth ſo require, lett him firſt ſigne himſelfe with the ſigne of the Croſſe, then let him recollect the diſperſed powers of his ſoule, eſpecially the imagination, and ſequeſter it from all temporall and tranſitorie thinges. Lett him eleuate his vnderſtandinge to God, conſideringe his diuine preſence, with that due reuerence and attention as is requiſite, and lett him imagine God Almightie himſelfe to be preſente in his ſoule, as in verie deed hee is.

G 4 If

If it be the morninge meditation, after a generall act of contritiō, for his sins, let him make to God a generall confessiō: if in the eueninge let him examine his conscience, concerninge all his thoughtes, wordes, and workes, of that day: of the forgetfulnes of God Almightie his benefits , and of the sinnes of his former life, humbly prostratinge himselfe in the sight of the diuine Maiestie in whose presence, he now is after a particular māner, sayinge the wordes of the Patriarch A B R A H A M : *Loquar ad*

Gen. 18. *Dominum meum, cum sim puluis & cinis:* Shall I speake to my Lord, seeinge I am but dust and ashes. And singinge this Psalme.

122. To thee haue I lifted vp mine eies, vvhich dvvellest in the heauens. Behould as the eies of seruantes, are on the handes of their masters. As the eies of the handmaide on the handes of her mistresse : so are our eies vnto our Lord God vntil he haue mercie on vs. Haue mercie on vs, ô Lord, haue mercie on vs: Glorie be to the Father, &c.

Cor. 2. And because we are not able of our selues to thinke any good, but all our sufficiencie is from God, and because none can say Lord I E S V S, that is to say, call vpon the name of I E S V S , without the holy Ghost, to thee therfore, ô holy Ghost, doe I turne my selfe , with teares imploringe

thy

thy affiftance: *Come holy Ghoft fend fourth from heauen the glitteringe beames of thy true light: Come Father of the poore, come giuer of revvardes, come light of our heartes, fvveet comforter, fvveet gueft of the foule, fvveet refreshinge, reft in labour, temperature in heat, in mourninge a gratefull folace, ô bleffed light, replenish the heartes of the faithfull.* Then followeth the prayer. *Deus qui corda fideliū, &c.* Thefe beinge faid, he fhall pray to God to beftowe vpō him his diuine grace, to affift at this holy exercife, with that attentiō, due recollection, feare and reuerence, befeeminge fo great a Maieftie, hūbly befeechinge him, fo to paffe ouer this time of holy prayer, that he may retourne from thence fortified with new feruour, to execute what foeuer fhall belonge to his holy feruice, for prayer which beareth not this fruite, is luke-warme, imperfect and of no moment before God.

CHAP.

CHAP. VII.

Of Readinge.

AFTER a due preparation, followeth readinge of those thinges which are to be meditated vpon. Which must not be too hasty but mature, serious and quiet, to which the vnderstandinge must not only be attentiue, to vnderstand those thinges which are red: but also, and cheifely the will: that those thinges which are vnderstood may giue a spirituall gust and fealinge. When he falleth vpon any place, which much moueth his affection, lett him there pause a while, that in his heart it may cause a greater impressiõ. He must also beware not to spend too much time in readinge therby to hinder meditation, it being a more fruitefull exercise, for-asmuch as thinges attentiuely considered pearce more inwardly, and produce greater effects. If peraduenture some time it happeneth the mind so to be dispersed, that it cannot settle it selfe to prayer, then it is better to insist a while longer in readinge, or to ioyne readinge to meditation, or after the readinge of one point

VVhat to doe vvhẽ the mind is distracted.

point

point to pauſe vpon that a while, then after the ſame manner to proceed to the others. Although the vnderſtandinge tyed to certaine wordes which are red , cannot ſo freely be carried into diuerſe affections , as when it is free from this bond.

It is oftentimes very profitable for a man to vſe ſome violence to himſelfe , to expell his vaine and triflinge fancies after the example of the Patriarch I A C O B, manfully to wraſtle againſt them, perſeueringe vnto the end, after which fight , the victorie beinge obteined , God doth for the moſt part, giue greater deuotion , or more pure contemplation , or ſome other ſupernaturall gift, which he neuer denieth, to thoſe who faithfully fight in his cauſe.

Its putting out of vnprofitable thoughts violence is to be vſed

C H A P.

Chap. VIII.

Of Meditation.

AFTER readinge followeth meditation. Which is some times of such thinges as can be represented to our immaginatio̅: as the life and passion of our blessed Sauiour : the latter iudgment, hell, and the Kingedome of heauen. Sometimes of such thinges as are subiect rather to the vnderstandinge, then immagination, as the consideration of God Almighties benefits, his bounty, clemency and other perfections which are in God.

These meditations are called, the one intellectuall, the other immaginarie. Both which in these exercises are to be vsed after a different manner, as occasion requireth. When the meditatio̅ is immaginarie, so that the thinge meditated vpon, hath, or euer had, any actuall existance or beinge, vve must so frame and represent it to our fancie, as though vve vvere present in the same place, and savve vvith our eies those thinges, vvhich there vvere done. This representation vvill make the consideration

of

of these thinges, more viuacious, and cause a greater impression in our soules. For if our immaginatiō can comprehend wholl citties and countryes, with lesse difficulty, can it comprehende one mysterie. This helpeth much to the recollection of the minde: this will retaine the same busied in it selfe, as a bee in the hyue, where she worketh and disposeth all things diligently. But in these thinges a moderatiō must be vsed, for to run with a violent immagination to *Hierusalem*, to frame to the fancie those thinges which are to be meditated there, doth oftentimes hurt the head. Wherfore it is good to abstaine from immoderate immaginations, least nature oppressed with too violent apprehensions, becomes infirme and weake.

CHAP.

CHAP. IX.

Of giuinge of thankes.

AFTER meditation followeth giuinge of thankes, the occasion of
which must be taken from the
matter meditated vpon; for example if
the meditation be of the passion of our
Sauiour , we must giue thankes vnto
him that , he hath redeemed vs from so
great tormentes. If of sinnes: that, with
longanimity he hath expected vs to doe
pennance. If of the miseries of this life:
that he hath preserued vs from the greatest part of them. If of death : that hetherto he hath defended vs from the pe-
rills of sodaine death, and hath fauou-
rably granted vs time of penance. If of
the glory of Paradise ; that he hath
created vs to that end , that after the stormes and troubles of this present life , we
should enioy eternall felicity , after this
manner, we are to proceed in other meditations,

To

To these benefits , we may ioyne the others which we handled before , to witt, the benefits of our creation , conferuation, redemption and vocation. As much as in vs lieth , lett vs giue him thankes that he hath created vs after his owne image and likenes , that he hath giuen vs a memorie to remember him , an vnderstandinge to know him , and a will to loue him. That he hath comitted vs to the custodie of Angels , that by the help of our Angel Guardian, he hath exempted vs from many daungers, preserued vs from many mortall sinns, defended vs from death and malice of the deuill , while we were in this cafe (which was no lesse, then to free vs from euerlastinge death , to which by sinn we were obnoxious.) That he would vouchsafe to assume our nature vpon him, and for our fakes suffer a most ignominious death. That we were borne of Christian parentes; that we were regenerated by Baptisme : that in this present life he hath promised grace, and vnspeakable glory in the world to come : that he hath adopted vs for his Sonnes : that in the Sacrament of confirmation , he hath fortified vs with stronge weapons to fight against the world,

the

the flesh, and the deuill; that he hath giuen himselfe to vs in the Sacrament of the aulter: that he hath left vnto vs the Sacramēt of penance , to recouer that grace which was lost by mortall sin. That he hath visited vs dayly with good and holy inspirations: that he hath giuen vs grace to perseuer in holy and pious exercises.

After the same methode we must proceed in accountinge other God Almighties benefites, as well generall as particular, and for all publicke or priuate , manifest or secret, giue him thankes: and we must inuite all creatures celestiall and terrestiall to bare vs company in this holy exercise: singinge the songe of the three children : *Benedicite omnia opera Domini Domino : lauda-* *te & superexaltate eum in secula, &c.* And the Psalme : *Benedic anima mea Domino : &* *omnia que intra me sunt, nomini sancto eius.* *Benedic anima mea Domino : & noli obliuisci* *omnes retributiones eius. Qui propitiatur omni-* *bus iniquitatibus tuis : qui sanat omnes infirmi-* *tates tuas. Qui redimit de interitu vitam tuam:* *qui coronat te in misericordia & miserationibus.* My soule blesse thou our Lord : and all thinges , that are with in me , his holie name. My soule blesse thou our Lord: and forget not all his retributions. Who is propitious to all thine iniquities: who healeth all

all thine infirmities. Who redeemeth thy life from deadly falling : who crowneth thee in mercie and commiserations.

CHAP. X.

Of Oblation.

CORDIALL thākes beinge giuen to God , presently the heart breaketh naturally into that affection, which the Kingly Prophet DAVID felt in himselfe when he said : *Quid retribuam* Psal. 115. *Domino pro omnibus quæ retribuit mihi?* What shall I render to our Lord: for al thinges that he hath rendred to me? Which desire we shall in some sort satisfie, if we offer to God whatsoeuer we haue. First therfore we must offer to God our selues , for his perpetuall seruātes, wholly resigninge our selues to his holy will, howsoeuer he shall please to dispose of vs. We must likwise direct, all our thoughtes, wordes and workes, whatsoeuer we shall doe or suffer, to the supreme honour and glorie of his sacred Name. Then we must offer to God the Father , all the merits of his only be-

H   gotten

gotten Sonne, all the labours and sorrowes he did vndergoe in this miserable world, to fulfill the will of his heauenly Father, beginninge from his natiuitie, and hard manger, to his contumelious crucifyinge and giuinge vp the ghost : for as much as these are all the goods and meanes, wherof in the newe Testamēt, he hath left vs heires; wherfore, as that is no lesse our owne, which is giuen vs freely, then that we get with our industrie : so the meritts of C H R I S T, which he hath freely bestowed vpon vs, are no lesse our owne, then if we had got them with our sweat and labour.

Hence euery man may offer this sacred oblation, as the first, numbringe one by one all the labours and vertues of the life of C H R I S T, his obedience, patience, humilitie, charitie, and his other vertues, seeinge these are the most excellent of all oblations, that we can offer to God.

C H A P.

CHAP. XI.

Of Petition.

THIS noble oblation beinge well performed, we may securely and confidētly proceed to the askinge of any gifts and graces. First therfore God Almightie is to be prayed vnto, with inflamed charitie and ardent Zeale of his diuine honour, for the conuersion of all nations, that all people may be illuminated with the knowledge of him, prayfinge and adoringe him as the only true and liuinge God. To this end from the bottome of our heartes we may vtter the wordes of the Kingely Prophet: *Confiteantur tibi populi Deus: confiteantur tibi populi omnes:* Let people, ô God, confeffe to thee: let all people confeffe to thee. Pfal. 66.

Then we muft pray to God for the Prelates of the Church, the supreme Paftour, Cardinalls, Archbishops, Bishops and other Prelates, that he would be pleafed fo to gouerne and illuminate them with the light of his heauenly grace, that they may be able to bring all men to the knowledge and obedience of their creatour.

We

We muſt alſo pray to God for Kinges and Princes (as S. Pavle admonisheth) and for all men placed in dignitie, that by their diligent care, their ſubiects may liue à quiet life , well inſtructed with honeſt manners, for this is gratefull to God, that willeth all should be ſaued , and come to the knowledge of his truth.

Then for all the members of his myſticall bodie , for the iuſt that he would be pleaſed to conſerue them in their ſanctitie. For ſinners, to conuert them, from their wicked courſes, to the amendment of their liues. For the dead, that he would free them from the expiatinge tormētes wherin they are deteined , and bringe them to their eternall reſt.

We muſt pray to God, for the poore infirme captiues , band-ſlaues or others in whatſoeuer tribulation , that for the merits of his Deare Sonne , he would vouchſafe to help, and free them from all their miſeries.

After we haue prayed for the good of our neighbours, let vs at length intreat for our owne neceſſities, which diſcretion will teach euery one in particular (if he be not altogether ignorant of himſelfe) what they are. But that we may ſet doune a methode for beginners , we will lead them into
this

this path way. First therfore we must pray to God, that for the merits and passion of his only begotten Sonne; he would pardon our sins, giue vs grace to auoide them, and to expiate them with good workes worthy of penance; but especially to implore for help and assistance against those euill inclinations and vices to which we are most propence, layinge open to our heauenly physition all the woundes of our diseased soules, that with the oyntment of holy grace, he would heale them.

Then let vs aske, for the most excellent vertues wherin the wholl perfection of a Christian man consisteth, for example, faith, hope, charitie, feare, humilitie, patience, obedience, fortitude in aduersitie, pouertie of spirit, contempt of the world, true discretion, puritie of intention, and others like to these, which are placed in the supreme top of a spirituall buildinge. Faith is the prime roote and foundation of a Christian: hope is a staffe to defend vs from all tribulations of this present life: charitie the end of all perfection: feare of God, the beginninge of true wisedome: humilitie is the *Basis* and ground-worke of all vertues: patience is the strongest armour against the fury of our enemies:

H 3   obe-

obedience is the moſt gratefull oblation to God, wherin man offereth himſelfe for a ſacrifice, diſcretion is the eie of the ſoule, fortitude the hand therof, wherwith it bringeth all her workes vnto perfection: purity of intentiō directeth all her actions vnto God. We muſt after pray for other vertues, which may help vs forward in the way of perfection: as, ſobriety in meate and drinke, moderation of the tongue, cuſtody of the ſenſes, modeſty and compoſition of the outward mā, ſweetnes in giuing good example to our neighbours, rigour and ſeuerity towardes our ſelues, and the like.

Laſt of all we muſt conclude this petition, with a feruent imploringe of the diuine loue, and heere to pauſe a while, ſo that the cheifeſt part of time be ſpent in an earneſt deſiringe of this grace and fauour, ſeeinge in the diuine loue all our felicitie doth conſiſt, to that end this prayer followinge will not be vnprofitable.

A prayer for the obteininge of diuine loue.

G Rant I beſeech thee, ô Lord, that I may loue thee with all my ſoule, with all my heart, with all my ſtrength, ô my only hope, my perfect glorie, my refuge and

and solace. O my dearest of all freindes,
sweet spouse, flowrishinge spouse, sweeter
then any hony. Delight of my heart, life
of my soule, ioy of my spirit. O bright day
of eternitie, cleare light of my bowels, paradise of my heart, originall of all my good,
ô my cheifest strength, prepare, ô Lord in
my soule a delicious bed, that accordinge
to thy promise, there thou maiest dwell,
and make thy mansion. Mortifie in me
whatsoeuer is displeasinge to thee, and
make me a man accordinge to thine owne
heart. Pearce the marrowe of my soule.
Wound my heart with the dartes of deare
affection, and inebriate me with the wine
of loue.

When shall I perfectly please thee in
all thinges? when shall I cast from me all
thinges contrary to thee? when shall I be
wholly thine? when shall I leaue to be
mine owne? when shall nothinge liue in
me, but what is thine? when shall I embrace thee with ardent affection? when
wilt thou inflame, and consume me with
the flames of loue? when wilt thou pearce
and replenish me on euery side, with thy
sweetnes? whē wilt thou lay open and manifest to my pouerty, that pretious Kingedome which is within me, that is to say,
thy sacred selfe with all thy riches? when

H 4   wilt

wilt thou vnite me perfectly vnto thee?
when wilt thou transforme and swallowe
me vp wholly in thee , that from thee I
may neuer depart ? when wilt thou remoue from me all obstacles, which hinder
me that am not one spirite with thee. O beloued of my soule! O delight of my heart!
Looke downe vpon me and heare me, not
for my owne merits, but out of thy infinite
goodnes : instruct, illuminate, direct, and
help me in all, and through all , that I neither speake or doe any thinge , but that
which I shall knowe to be gratefull before
thy sight,

O my God, my loue, my ioy, my pleasure, my fortresse and my life ! why doest
thou not help the poore and needy , imploringe thy assistance ? thou which fillest
heaue and earth, why doest thou suffer my
heart to be empty ? thou which cloathest
the flowers and lilies of the feildes with
beauty : thou which nourishest the birdes
of the aire : thou which susteinest the least
creature of the earth : why art thou vn-
mindfull of me, that forgetteth all thinges
for the loue of thee. O immense goodnes!
I had knowledge of thee too late , that I
loued thee no sooner. O newe and ancient
beauty ! O miserable was my state when I
liue.l without thy loue ! O wretched was
my

my condition, when I knewe thee not ! ô
intollerable blindneſſe of my heart vvhen
I ſavv thee not ! I ſought thee farr abrood,
vvhē thou vvert vvithin me. Yet at length,
though late, I haue found thee, let not thy
mercy ſuffer me, ô Lord, that euer I forſake or leaue thee againe.

And becauſe to haue eies to ſee thee is
one of the cheefeſt thinges that pleaſeth
thee, Lord, giue me the eies of a ſolitarie
turtle, to contemplate thee, giue me chaſt
eies full of modeſtie : humble and amo-
rous: ſanctified and vveepinge: attent and
diſcreet eies vvhich may vnderſtand and
performe thy vvill. Lord giue me grace
to behold thee vvith ſuch eies , as thou
maieſt looke vpon me againe , as thou dideſt vpon Peter, vvhen he denied thee,
and dideſt moue him to bitter compunction for his ſins. Looke vpon me as thou
dideſt vpon the prodigall childe , vvhen
thou dideſt runn to imbrace and kiſſe
him: Or as vpon the Publican, not daring
to lift vp his eies to heauen. Behold me
vvith thoſe eies that thou dideſt inuite
Marie Magdalene to penan-
ce, and to vvaſh thy feete vvith teares. Or
vvith thoſe eies vvhervvith the Spouſe in
the Canticles incited thee to her loue
vvhen thou ſaydeſt: *Quam pulchra es amica* Cant. 4.
mea,

mea, quam pulchra es! oculi tui columbarum!
Hovv beautifull art thou my loue, hovv
beautifull art thou! thine eies as it vvere of
doues.

That my aspect be pleasinge, and that
the beautie of my soule be gratefull vnto
thee, doe thou I beseech thee bestovve the
gift of vertues and graces vpon me, to
deck and trim my selfe, wherby I may liue
to glorifie thy holy name for euer and
euer.

O mercifull and holy Trinitie! Father,
Sonne, and holy Ghost, one only true
God, teach, direct and help me in all.
O Father omnipotent, I beseech thee by
the greatnes of thy immense povver, to
confirme and strengthen my memory in
thee only, and to replenish it vvith holy
and pious cogitations. O Sonne most
vvise, illuminate my small vnderstandinge
vvith thy eternall vvisedome, to knovv
thy euerlastinge truth, and my ovvne misery. O holy Ghost loue of the Father and
the Sonne, vvith thy incomprehensible
goodnes make my vvill conformable to
thy diuine pleasure, inflame it vvith such a
fire of thy holy loue, that no waters which
rise from the turbulent feare of euill sug-
gestions, may be able to extinguish it.
O holy Trinitie and one God, I would to
God

God I could doe nothinge elſe but prayſe and loue thee, and as much as all thy holy Saintes. I would to God I had the loue of all creatures in me alone , I would with a willinge minde trāsferrand tourne it to the loue of thee, although this were nothinge, in reſpect of what thou deſerueſt. Only thou thy ſelfe , canſt worthily loue and praiſe thy ſelfe. Becauſe none elſe beſides thee , is able to vnderſtand thy incomprehenſible goodnes , and therfore the iuſt poiſe of loue reſideth only in thy ſacred breſt.

O bleſſed Virgine Marie , Mother of God , Queene of heauen , Lady of the world, Manſion of the holy Ghoſt , Lilly of purity , Roſe of patience , Paradiſe of pleaſure , Mirrour of chaſtity, Veſſell of innocency, intercede for me miſerable baniſhed wretch , and beſtowe vpon me a portion of thy aboundant charity.

O all yea Saintes of God, and yea angelicall Spirits, which burne with a vehement affection of your Creatour, eſpecially yea Seraphins, who inflame both heauen and earth with loue, doe not forſake my miſerable ſoule , but purifie it as you did the lippes of Esay from all vice and vncleancs, and ſet it on fire with the flames of your ardent loue, that I may loue and ſeeke our
Lord

Lord God, restinge and remaininge in him
for euer and euer.   Amen.

Chap. XII.

Certaine documentes to be obserued about Meditation.

HETHERTO we haue only set
downe plentifull matter for meditation, which for the present is
verie necessarie, because the greatest part
of men, either neglect or disdaine this
exercise, because they want sufficient matter to consider vpon; nowe we will briefly
handle those thinges which pertaine to
the forme and methode of meditation, of
which, though the holy Ghost be the
principall master, neuer-the-lesse experience teacheth vs, that certaine documétes are
likewise necessary, because the way to
heauen is cragged and full of difficulties,
wherfore ther is need of a guide, without
which, many haue gone astray a longe
time from the right path, or at leastwise,
haue not attained to their desired end, so
soon as they expected.

The

The first Document.

THe first Documēt therfore is, that we doe not so adheare to those thinges, which aboue we haue digested into seuerall pointes, and times, as that we should thinke it a fault, to fall vpon other thinges, wherin the minde may reape more aboundant fruit, for seeing deuotion is the end of all those exercises, that which cometh nearest to this scope, is alwayes to be accompted best. Which ought not lightly vpon euery occasion to be done, but with a cleare and manifest profit.

The second Document.

WE must be wary of too many speculations in this exercise, and vse rather efficatious affections of the will, then curious discourses of the vnderstandinge: wherfore they goe not in the right vvay that meditatē of diuine mysteries, as though they were to preach them to the people in a sermon: which is rather to dissipate, then recollect the spirit. And to wander abrood, thē to be busied in their owne home. Therfore he that will meditate with fruit to his soule, must come to it, like an humble simple creature, bringinge rather

awill

a will difpofed to taft thefe holy myfteries profitably, then acrimony of vnderftandinge to difcuffe them learnedly. For this is proper to thofe who giue themfelues to ftuddies , not to thofe who confecrate themfelues vnto deuotion.

The third Document.

IN the precedent Document we declared , how the vnderftandinge is to be moderated and fubiected to the will, nowe we will prefix fome limits to the will , out of which she cannot ftraggle without a fault. That therfore she be not too immoderate in her exercife, we muft knowe, that deuotion is neuer to be expreffed with the violence of our armes, as fome doe thinke, who with côftrained forrowe doe wringe out teares and commiferation, while they confider the tormentes of CHRIST IE-SVS: for this doth rather dry the heart, thẽ make it capable of diuine vifitations (as CASSIANVS doth excellently teach) more-ouer this extraordinarie force, doth often hurt the body, and by reafon of the burthen, which this violéce bringeth with it, the mind is left fo naufeous that it feareth to retourne againe to thefe exercifes: when experiéce teacheth, that it is the caufe of fo

much

much trouble, he therfore that will fruit-
fully meditate vpō the paſſion of CHRIST,
let him not be too anxious for ſenſible cō-
miſeration, but let it ſuffice, that he exhibi-
teth himſelfe preſent to his ſufferinges, be-
holdinge them with a ſimple and quiet eie,
and conſideringe them with a tender com-
paſſiue heart, rather diſpoſed to entertaine
that affection which God almightiesmer-
cy ſhall ſuggeſt , then that which ſhalbe
wronge out with violence. Which when
he hath done, let him not be ſolicitous nor
ſorrowfull, what other ;thinges God doth
deny or will not giue.

The fourth Document.

HEnce we may gather what attentiō,
is to be obſerued in prayer , wherfore the heart muſt not be languiſhinge,
remiſſe or deiected ; but quicke, attentiue
and eleuated to heauenly thinges. And as
it is neceſſarie to come to God with ſuch
attention, eleuation of the minde, and ab-
ſtraction from ſenſible thinges ; ſo it is no
leſſe neceſſarie to temper ſweetly this attention , that it be neither hurtfull to bo-
dily health , nor impediment to extinguiſh
deuotion. For when any be ſo intenſiue
to the matter they meditate vpon , without any reſpect to their infirme nature,

ture, doe oftentimes so dull their braines, that they be vnapt for other exercises. On the contrarie, there are some, to auoid this danger are so remisse and lasy in their attentiō, that easily they suffer their mindes to be distracted with other idle thoughtes

These two extreames, that they may be both auoided, such moderatiō is necessarie, that the head be not weakened with too violent attention, nor the thoughtes permitted carelessly to wander out of supine negligence, in which thinge, we must immitate a good rider vpon an vntovvard horse, vvhich neither holdeth him in too hard, nor looseth the raines vpon his neck, but guideth him equally, that he giueth not back, nor goeth forvvard too speedily. So vve must striue in meditation that attention be moderate, diligently resistinge euill thoughtes, but not violent vvith anxietie.

We must note also, that, these thinges vve here speake of attention, are cheefly to be taken heed of in the beginninge of meditation: for it often happeneth, that, those vvhich are too violent in the beginninge, doe founder in the middest of meditation. As trauailers makinge too much speed in their settinge forth, are tired in the middest of their iourny.

The

The fifth Document.

A Mongſt all documentes this is cheifly to be obſerued, that when in
meditation we cannot preſently perceiue
that ſweetnes of deuotion we expect, not
therfore to wax puſillanimous, or leaue of
from the exerciſe begun, but patiently
with longanimity expect the cominge of
our lord : ſeeinge it beſeemeth the excellency of the diuine Maieſtie: the vility and
baſenes of mans condition, the importance
of the buſines we haue in hand, to ſtay a
while before the gates of his ſacred pallace:
If he cometh preſently after a little expectation, with many thankes let vs with
gratitude entertaine this vndeſerued fauour: If he maketh longer delaies, let vs
humble our ſelues before him, and confeſſe
that we doe not deſerue this grace : If he
vouchſafeth not to come at all, let vs bare
it patienthy with a quiete mind, and content our ſelues, that we haue offered our
ſelues, with all we haue vnto him for a
gratefull ſacrifice: that we haue denied our
owne proper wills, reſigninge thé vnto his
Power: that we haue crucified all our inordinate appetites : that we haue fought
againſt our paſsions and vices. And finally

        I   that

that we haue performed whatfoeuer was in our power to be done. And althongh we haue not worshiped him with fenfible deuotion. Yet let it fuffice vs, if that we haue worshiped him *inspirit and truth*, as he requireth.

Laft of all, let vs perfwade our felues, that this is the moft dangerous and cheifeft to be feared rocke of this prefent nauigation, and place, wher in the true and faithfull feruantes of God are tried, and diftinguished from infidells, from which if we shall depart in fafety, in all others, we shall haue a profperous fucceffe.

The fixth Document.

THis document not much differeth from the former, which not withftandinge is equally neceffarie, and this it is, that the feruant of god muft not content himfelfe, that he hath felt a little fenfible guft from meditation; as many doe, when they haue shed a little dry teare, or felt a little molifyinge of the heart, that they haue attained to the fcope and end of this exercife.

But they are farr deceiued, for euen as to make the earth fruitfull one little shewer
which

which alaieth the dust, is not sufficient, but it must haue a great deale of
raine throughly foke into the rootes of
the plantes, before it can giue any hopes of
a fruitfull yeare: fo the aboundance of celeftiall waters, are neceffarie to our foules
for to make them bringe fourth the fruit
of good workes. Wherfore we are not
with out caufe admonifhed by fpirituall
men, that we should fpend as much time
as poffible we can in this holy exercife, and
it is better to infift fome longe time together, then by fitts. For when the time is
short, it wilbe almoft all confumed, in quie-
tinge the immagination, and recollecting
the heart. and it often happeneth, that
whilft we should reape the fruit of ourfor-
mer trouble, meditation is quite broke of.

Concerninge the prefixed time for
meditation, it feemeth to me, what foeuer
is lefs the two howers, or an hower and
halfe, is to little for this exercife, becaufe almoft one hower is fpent in tuninge the
inftrument of our foules, repreffinge idle
and vnprofitable thoughts, and recolle-
ctinge the minde from temporall thinges:
and fome time alfo is neceffarie to fpend in
reapinge the fruit of our prayer in the latter end.

Although I cannot deny, but after fome
I 2   pious

pious action the mind is better difposed
for meditation: for as dried wood quickly
burneth, fo the mind that is well difpofed,
is fooner kindled with this celeftiall fire.

The morninge alfo is the beft time for
meditation, becaufe the mind is then moft
free from fancies, and therfore can with
better facillitie apply it felf to this holy
exercife. But who by reafon of the multi-
plicity of outward affaires, cannot fpend fo
much time, yet at leaftwife let them, with
the poore widdowe in the ghofpell, offerr
vp to god the fmall mite of their fyncere
affection. And no doubt but he who pro-
uideth for all creatures accordinge to their
feuerall neceffities, will gracioufly accept
it, if their culpable negligence doth not de-
ferue the contrarie.

The

The seauenth Document.

THE seauenth document is, that he, that is visited with diuine consolations in, or, out of prayer, ought to haue a speciall care to spend that time ; aboue other, with fruite vnto his soule, for whilest this prosperous gale doth blowe, he will goe further in his iourny towardes heauen in one hower, then other wise, he hath, or shall doe in many dayes. So did the holy Father S. FRANCIS doe of whom S. BONAVENTVRE writeth that he had such a solicitous care of diuine visitations, that whensoeuer vpon the way he was recreated with them, he would either goe before, or stay behind his companion a while, vntill he had digested this diuine morsell sent vnto him from heauen. They which are negligent and carlesse to answere diuine visitations, are comonly chastised with this punishment from God , that when they seeke, they will hardly find them.

The

The eighth Document.

THE last Document and of greatest
moment is, in this exercise of prayer
we must ioyne meditation to contemplation, seeinge one is, as it were a ladder vnto
the other: wherfore it is the part of meditation, with diligent attention to consider
and ponderate celestiall thinges, first one,
then an other, that at last some pious affection may be stirred vp in the soule, like
him that with a steele striketh fire out of a
flint: but it is the property of contemplation which followeth meditation, to enioy
this kindled fire, that is to say, to embrace
that affection, which with much labour
he hath sought and found, in deep silence
and tranquillitie of spirit, not with many
discourses and speculations of the vnderstandinge, but with a pure simple relation
and eie to veritie, hence a certaine doctour
saith, that medition doth discouse with labour and small profit, but contemplation
without any trouble, and with much fruit:
the one doth seeke, and the other findeth:
the one doth chewe, and the other eateth
the meate: the one doth reason and consider, the other contemplateth those thinges
she loues and tasteth, and in fine the one is
the

the meanes, the other is the end : the one is the way and motion, the other the tearme of the way and end of the action. From these thinges which we haue said, that rule or axiome is very frequent amongst spirituall Masters, which fewe of their schollers doe rightly vnderstand. That is, *fine adepto media omnia cessare.* The end beinge atteined vnto, all meanes doe cease. For example, the mariner resteth when he hath ariued to his desired hauen. So he that meditates, when by the meanes of meditation he shall come to the rest and sweet gust of contemplation, ought to leaue the cragged way of reasoninge and discourse, contentinge him selfe, with the memorie of godalmightie alone, whome he may behold as present to his soule, and quietly enioy that sweet affection, which he shall vouchsafe to bestowe vpon him, whether it be of loue, admiration, ioy, or the like, and the reason is, because the end of this busines consisteth rather in loue, and affection of the will, then in speculations of the vnderstandinge. When therfore the will hath captiuated the one, and atteined to the other affection : all reasoninge and speculations of the vnderstandinge are to be left: that the soule may bend all her forces to it, without a confused wanderinge to the actions of the other powers. Therfore a certaine doctour giueth this counsell to those who perceiue the selues to be inflamed with the fire of diuine loue, that they should quite abolish all other thoughtes and speculations, though neuer so sublime and subtile, not that they are euill, but becaufe for the prefent they hinder a greater good. And this is no other, then after we haue come to the end, to leaue meditation for the loue of contemplation.

Which we may doe (to fpeake particularly of this matter) in the end of euery exercife (that is to fay) after the petition of diuine loue, as aboue faid: and that for too reafons, firft becaufe it is fuppofed that the labour of the finifhed exercife hath produced fome fruite of deuotiõ towardes God almighty, as the wifeman faith, *melius eft finis orationis, quam principium*. Better is the end of prayer, then the beginninge. Secõdly it is expedient, that, after labour in prayer, the vnderftandinge reft a while, and recreate it felfe in the armes of contemplation.

Heere let euery one refift what foeuer immaginations shall prefent them felues vnto his minde, fet him ftill his vnderftandinge, let him faften his memorie ftrongly
vpon

vpon god, consideringe that he is placed
in his holy preséce. But let him not adheare
to any particular contemplation of God,
but only content himselfe with that knowledge, which faith hath ministred vnto
him: and to this let him add his will and affection, seeinge this is only that which em-
braceth God, and in which the wholl
fruite of meditation consisteth. The weake
vnderstandinge is little able to conceiue, or
comprehend any thinge of God, but the
will can loue him verie much.

Let him therfore rouze vp himselfe from
téporall thinges, and let him recollect himselfe with in himselfe (that is to say) to the
centre of his soule, where is the liuely image of god, here let him harken attentiuely
as though he heard God almightie speakinge from a high tutret, or as though he
held him fast being present in his soule: or
as though there were no other persons in
the world, besides God and him-selfe.

Nay I say more, let him quite forget
him selfe, and those thinges which he
doeth: for as one of the ancient holy Fathers saith, prayer is then euery way compleat, when he that prayeth doth not consider that he is before God in prayer. And
this is to be done not only in the end of the
exercise, but in the middest and in euerie

part of meditation. For as often at this spirituall sleepe shall sweetly oppresse any one (that is to say) when the vnderstādinge is drowned as it were in a sleepe, (but the will watchinge) let him quietly enioy this delicate meate as longe as it shall last.

But when it is digested, let him retourne againe to meditation, in which we must behaue our selues like a gardiner, who, when he wattereth a bedd of his garden, after he hath once sprincled it with water expecteth a while, vntill it be drunke in, then sprincleth againe, that at last it may throughly wett the earth, That it may become more fruitefull. But what the soule cast into this heauenly sleepe, and illuminated with the splendour of this eternall light, doth enioy! what sacietie, what charitie, what internall peace! no tongue is able to expresse: this is that peace which exceedeth all vnderstandinge, this is that felicitie, a greater then which cannot be immagined in this vale of miserie: there are many so inflamed with this fire of diuine loue, that their interiours, at the verie memory of this blessed name without any meditation at all before, doe rest in ioy.

These need no more consideration or discourses, to loue god, then a mother needes

des motiues to loue her child, or the bride her husband. Others there are so absorped in God, not only in prayer, but also in outward busines, that they wholly forget thē selues, and all creatures for the loue of him. neither are these effects of diuine loue to be admired, seeinge worldly loue causeth often times greater matters in the mindes of men, that it makes them madd. What shall we attribute lesse efficacie to grace then vnto nature and sin? When therfore the soule shall feale this operation of diuine loue, in what part of prayer soeuer it happeneth, let him neuer refuse it, although he spend all the time of this exercise in it without any manner of consideration at all of that point, he purposed to meditate vpō (except he be specially obliged vnto it.) For as saint AVGVSTINE saith vocall prayer ought to be left, if it hurteth deuotion, so meditation ought to be differred if it hurteth contemplatioū. But as it is necessarie to leaue meditation for this affection, and to ascend from the lesser to the greater: so often times this contemplation is to be left for meditation, when it is so vehement, that the corporall health, receiueth some domage therby. This oftentimes happeneth to those who taken with the pleasure of this diuine sweetnes, giue them selues

too

too indiscreetly to these exercises, and vse
them too immoderately, to whome (as a
certaine Doctour saith) this vvilbe the
best remedy , that they desist from con-
templatiō, tourninge their mindes to some
other good affection, as of compassion in
meditatinge of the sufferinges of our Sauiour. Or about the sinns and miseries of
this world, to exonerate the hearte, diuer-
tinge it from that too much intension.

THE SECOND PART.

OF
DEVOTION
AND OF
THOSE THINGS
WHICH THERVNTO
BELONGE.

CHAP. I.

VVhat is deuotion.

AMONGST all the troublsome difficulties, to which they who frequent the exercises of prayer and meditatiō, are subiect, none is greater, then that which they suffer from the defect of deuotion, which often felt in prayer.

Deuotion maketh all thinges easy. prayer. For if they haue this, nothinge is more sweet, nothinge more pleasant, nothinge more easie, then to insist to prayer and meditation. But if that be wantinge, nothinge more hard, nothinge more difficult, nothinge more burthensome then to pray. Wherfore seeing we haue already spoken of prayer, meditation, and the methode to performe it. Nowe it will not be besides our purpose to treate of those thinges which partly promote, and partly hinder and extinguish deuotion in the mind of man. As also to lay open the temptations which are obuious to those who frequent these pious exercises, and last of all to annex some certaine documentes, vvhich may not a little auaile to the vvell performance of this busines. We vvill therfore beginne from the definition of deuotion : that it may manifestly appeare vvhat a pretious margarite it is, for vvhich vve vvarr.

Deuotion, as S. T H O M A S saith, is a vertue vvhich maketh a man prompt and readie to euerie vertuous deed, and stirringe him vp to doe vvell. vvhich definition euidently shevveth the necessitie and vtilitie of this vertue, as conteininge more in it, then any man can immagine.

For

For the better vnderstandinge of this,
vve muft knovve, that the cheifeft impediment that hindereth vs from leadinge a
vertuous life, is the corruption of humane
nature, proceedinge from finne, vvhich
bringes vvith it a veh ement inclination to
vice, and a great difficultie to doe vvell;
this make the vvay of vertue cragged and
troublefome, although in it felfe confidered, nothinge in this vvorld, is fo fvveet, fo
louely, fo beautifull.

The diuine wifedome hath ordeined
the help of deuotion, as a moft conveni-
nient remedie to ouer-come this difficultie:
for as the north wind diffipateth clouds,
and maketh a cleare skey, fo true deuotion
expelleth from the mind, the tedioufnes
of this way, and maketh vs with alacritie
prompt to pious actions. This vertue doth
fo farr forth obteine the name of vertue,
that likevvife it a fpeciall gift of the holy
ghoft; a heauenly devve, an affiftance obteined by prayer, vvhofe property is to
remoue all difficulties happeninge in
prayer and meditation : to expell tepiditie: to minifter alacritie in the diuine feruice, to inftruct the vnderftandinge: to roborate the vvill: to kindle in our heartes
heauenly loue: to extinguish the flames of
vnlavvfull defires: to ingendre a hatred
and

and loathinge of sinne and all transitorie
thinges:and last of all to him that possesseth
it, to infuse a newe feruour, a newe spirit,
a newe mind,and newe desires to doe well.
For as S A M P S O N as longe as he had his
haire,did exceede all men in strength : but
when that was cutt he was as weake as
others. So the soule of euerie Christian recreated with the help of deuotiō,is stronge
and valiant. But when it is depriued of it, it
becometh infirme and weake.

But aboue all the prayses, which can be
heaped vpō this vertue,this is the cheifest,
that although it be but one only vertue,
yet it is a prick and motiue to all:they therfore that desire,to walke in a vertuous way
must get this for a spurr, for without it, he
will neuer be able to rule his rebellious
flesh.

Hence it manifestly appeareth, in what
the true essence of deuotion doth consist,
not in tendernes of heart, or abundance
of consolations wherwith they which me-
In vvhat ditate are often recreated,except a prompt
deuotion alacritie of the mind to doe well be ther-
consisteth. vnto adioyned: especially seeinge it some
times happeneth, the one to be foūd with-
out the other,God almightie so disposinge
for the triall of his seruātes. Though I can
not denie. But that these consolations doe
often

often proceed from deuotiō and promptitude of the minde to doe well, and on the
contrarie, that true deuotion is not a little
augmented by the same consolations and
spirituall gusts. And therfore the seruantes
of God may lawfully desire and aske thē,
not for the delight they bringe with them,
but because they doe greatly increase deuotion which maketh vs with alacritie to
apply our selues to vertuous actiōs, which
the Kingly Prophet testifieth of himselfe sayinge : *Viam mandatorum tuorum cu-
curri, cum dilatasti cor meum* : I haue runne
the wayes of thy commandementes when
thou hast enlarged my heart, that is, when
thou hast recreated me with the sweetnes
of thy consolations which are the cause of
this my readines.

Now let vs treat of the meanes, wherby
this vertue is to be atteined vnto , which
will bringe no small profit with it, for seeinge it is the spurr to all other vertues , to
set downe the meanes , wherby it is to be
obteined, is no other thinge then to pre-
sribe the meanes to get all other vertues.

K   CHAP.

CHAP. II.

Nine meanes or helpes vvherby this vertue of deuotion may be atteined vnto, vvith the least difficultie.

*Conti-
nuance of
exercife
helpeth
deuotion.*

THE thinges which promote deuotion are many, of which we will handle a fewe.

First, it helpeth much deuotion: if those exercifes be vndertaken with a generous refolution, ready to vndergoe what difficulty foeuer shall occurr, for the obteininge of this pretious margarite. For it is certaine, that nothinge is excellent which is not difficult, of which kind is deuotion, efpecially in beginninges.

*Cuftodie
of the
heare.*

Secondly, a diligent cuftodie of the heart from euery vaine and vnprofitable cogitation, from affections, ftrange loue, and turbulent motions, doth much promote deuotion. For it is euident, that euerie one of these, is no little hindrance, feeinge this vertue cheifly requireth a quiete heart, free from all inordinate affection, and fo well compofed as the ftringes of a well tuned inftrument.

Thirdly,

Thirdly, custodie of the senses : espe- *Custody* cially the eies, tongue, and eares, seeinge by *of the* these the heart is much distracted. For *senses.* those thinges which enter in through the eies and eares, doe straine the minde with diuers imaginatiōs, and cōsequētly disturbe and trouble the peace and tranquility of the soule. Wherfore one not without cause saied , that he that meditateth must be deafe, blind, and dumbe. For by how much lesse he wādereth abroade, with greater re- collection, will he reioyce at home.

Forthly , solitude helpeth deuotion *solitude.* much, for it doth not only remoue the oc- casions of sinne, and take away the causes which cheifly disturb the heart and senses, but it maketh a solitary man , to rouze vp himselfe from temporall thinges , to be present to himselfe and conuerse incessant- ly with God. To which the opportunity of the place doth admonish, which admit- teth no other societie.

Fifthly , the readinge of spirituall *Readinge* bookes doth not a little nourish deuotion, *of spiri-* becaufe it adminiſtreth matter of confide- *tuall* ration , abſtracteth the minde from all *bookes.* thinges created, ſtirreth vp deuotion , and cauſeth that a mā doth ſooner adheare to the conſideration of thoſe thinges , which in readinge offered him a more pleaſant
K 2   taſt,

taft, that, that wherwith the heart aboundeth may oftner occurr to his memorie.

Continuall memory of God.

Sixthly, continuall memory of God almightie, and dayly immagination of his sacred prefence, that alwayes thou art in his fight, with a frequent vfe of afpirations which S. Avgvstine calleth iaculatorie prayers. For thefe doe guard the pallace of the mind, conferuinge deuotion in her feruour: that a man is alwayes willinge to pious actions, and ready to holy prayer: this document is one of the principall inftrumentes of a fpirituall life, and the only remedy for thofe, who haue neither time nor place with opportunity, to infift to longer prayer and meditation, and they which doe thus beftowe their labour to frequent afpirations, will in a short time profit much.

Perfeuerance.

Seauenthly, perfcuerance in good exercifes, that fo times and places be duely obferued, efpecially morninge and eueninge, as fitteft times for prayer.

Corporall aufterities.

Eighthly, corporall abftinence and aufterities doe much help deuotion: faftinge from meate: a frugall table: a hard bed: haire cloth: difcipline, and the like. As they originally proceed frõ deuotiõ of the minde: fo they doe not a little cherish, conferue and nourish the roote from whence they fpringe,

fpringe , which is deuotion.

Laft.y , workes of mercy are a great *Workes* fpurr vnto deuotion, becaufe they increafe *of mercy.* the confidence we haue to appeare before God, and to be prefented before his facred Maieftie: they doe accōpanie our prayers: and finally they merite that they be fooner heard of God, efpecially feeinge they pro-ceed from a mercifull heart.

K 3   CHAP.

Chap. III.

Nine impedementes of deuotion.

AS there be nine thinges which doe promote deuotion, so likwise there be nine impedimentes that doe hinder the same.

Veniall sinns. The first impediment of deuotion is, sinnes not only mortall, but also veniall, for these although they doe not quite abolish charitie, yet at leastwise they diminish the feruour of it, and consequently make vs lesse apt vnto deuotion. Wherfore with all diligence they are to be auoided, not only for the euill they bringe with them, but also for the good which they hinder.

Remorse of conscience. Secondly, remorse of conscience proceedinge from sins, when it is in extreames becaufe it doth disquiete the minde, weakeneth the heade, and maketh a man vnfit for factes of vertue.

Anxiety of heart. Thirdly, anxietie of heart and inordinate sadnes, for with these, the delight of a good conscience and spirituall ioy of the inward minde, can hardly sute and agree.

Fourthly, too many cares which doe dis-

disquiete the mind, like the Egiptian pre- *Cares of*
fects who did oppreſſe the children of *the mind.*
I S R A E L with too immoderate labours:
nor will euer ſuffer them to take that ſpirituall repoſe, which they should haue often
had in prayer. Yea at that time aboue
others they diſturbe the mind, endeauo-
ringe to ſeduce her from her ſpirituall
exerciſe.

Fiftly, a multitude of affaires, which *Affaires.*
take vp our whole time, ſuffocates the
ſpirit, ſcarce leauinge for a man a moment
to employ in Godalmightie his ſeruice.

Sixthly, delightes and pleaſures of the *Delights*
ſenſes, for theſe make ſpirituall exerciſes *of the*
vnſauoury, and a man vnworthy to be *ſenſes.*
recreated with heauenly conſolations, for
as ſaint B E R N A R D ſaith, he is not worthy
of the viſitations of the holy ghoſt that
ſeeketh after worldly ſolace.

Seauethly inordinate delighte in eatinge *Inordi-*
and drinkinge : eſpecially longe and *nate de-*
ſumpteous ſuppers, which make a man *light in*
vnapt to ſpirituall exerciſes. For when the *eatinge*
body is oppreſſed with too much meate, *and drin-*
the ſpirit cannot ſo freely eleuate it ſelfe to *kinge.*
God.

Eighthly curioſitie of the ſenſes and *Curioſity*
vnderſtandinge, as to ſee ſightes and heare *of the*
newe rumoirs, becauſe theſe doe ſpend *ſenſes.*

K 4   pre-

pretious time, disturbe and ouerthrough the tranquilitie of the minde distractinge it with many impertinences, which can be no small hinderance to deuotion.

Intermission of exercises.

Lastly, an intermission of our wonted exercises, except when they are not omitted or differred for a pious cause or iust necessitie. For the spirit of deuotion is delicate: which when it is gone it hardly retourneth againe, at least with great difficultie. For as trees and plantes must be watered in due season otherwise they wither away and perish: so deuotion, except it be watred with the waters of holy meditation, doth easily vanish.

These thinges we haue set downe breifly, that they may be the better remembred, vse and experience of them will afford a longer explication.

CHAP.

CHAP. IV.

*Of the common temptations vvhich for
the moſt part aſſault thoſe, vvho
giue themſelues to meditations : as
alſo of the remedies againſt them.*

NOw let vs ſee with what temptations they which frequent , the
exerciſe of prayer and meditation
are moleſted : that we may prouide conuenient remedies for them. Which be theſe.

1. The want of ſpirituall conſolations.
2. A multitude of vnprofitable thoughtes.
3. Thoughtes of infidelitie and blaſphemy.
4. Fancies in the night. 5. Sleepineſſe and
drowſineſſe. 6. Diffidence of goinge forward. 7. Too much preſumption of their
owne ſanctitie. 8. Inordinate deſire of learninge. 9. And indiſcreet zeale.

Theſe are the common temptations
which doe trouble thoſe which would
leade a vertuous life.

Of

Of the first temptation, and the remedie therof.

TO him that wanteth spirituall cõsola-
tions, this is the remedie, that therfore
he omitteth not his customarie exercises of
prayer, although they seeme vnsauourie
and of no fruite, but let him set him selfe in
the presence of God, cominge before him
as guilty of many greeuious sins, let him
search diligently, the corners of his owne
conscience, and consider whether or no
through his owne default, he hath lost this
grace, if so, let him beseech God almighty
to pardon him for this sinne, admiringe
the inestimable riches of his diuine patience in toleratinge vs so longe.

By this meanes he will reape no small
fruite from his aridity of spirit, takinge
from thence occasion of profounder humilitie when he considereth his owne malice and peruersnes in heapinge vp of sin,
or of more ardent affection when he seeth
God almighties goodnes in pardoninge
the same. And although he enioyeth no
pleasure at all in his exercises, let him not
therfore absteine from the continuation of
them, for it is not alwayes necessary, that it
should be sweet and sauoury to the present

sent taft, which wilbe hereafter profitable. *There-*
Especially when it is often feen by expe- *vvard of*
rience that thofe who conftantly perfeuer *thofe*
in their intended exercifes , not giuing *vvho in*
ouer in the time of this aridity , but conti- *the time*
nue them with what care and diligence *of drineffe*
poffibly they are able, that thefe I fay, de- *of fpirit,*
part from this table recreated with many *ther*
heauenly confolations, and much fpirituall *vvonted*
ioy, feinge they find nothinge to be omit- *exercifes.*
ted on their partes. It is but a fmall matter
to protract prayer for a longe fpace when
it floweth with confolations , but when
thefe are taken away, not to defift , is an
admirable act of vertue: for in this humility shineth , patience is eminent , and true
perfeuerance in good workes , is manifefted.

But it is neceffary in the time, of aridity,
to haue a greater care of himfelfe, watchinge ouer himfelfe with greater diligence,
to difcuffe his confcience more fincerely,
and to obferue all his wordes and actions
more accurately. For then when alacrity
and fpirituall ioy (which is the principall
oare of this nauigation) is abfent , with
greater vigilance the defect of grace is to
be fupplied.

When thou findeft thy felfe to be in
this ftate, thou oughteft to thinke , as S.
B E R-

BERNARD admonisheth, that the sentinells which did watch thee, are a sleepe, that the walls that did defend thee, are broken downe, and therfore the only hope of safegard to consist in armes, when all is gone which did otherwise protect thee, safety is to be sought with an armed hand. O what deserued glory followeth such a soule, which winneth the triumphant lawrell after such a manner, she fighteth a combate with the enemie without either sword or buckler, is valient without helpe, who although she be alone susteineth the wholl battaile, with as much courage, as though she were compassed round about with troopes of auxiliatorie forces.

This is the cheifest proofe, wherby the syncerity, and goodnes of the freindes of God is knowne, wherby the true are seuered from false seruantes.

A remedie for the second temptation.

VVhat to doe vvhē vve haue vnprofitable thoughtes.

AGainst the temptation of importune and vnprofitable cogitations which are wont to vex those that pray, and disquiet them with no small molestation, this is the remedie. To resist them manfully, prouided alwayes, that resistance be not
ioy-

ioyned with too much violence and anxietie of fpirit. Seeinge this worke dependeth not fo much of our ftrength, as
God almighties grace and profound humilitie. Wherfore when any one is befett
with thefe temptatiõs, let him confidently
tourne himfelfe to God without any fcru-
ple or anxietie of mind, (feeinge this is no
fault or at leaft a very fmall one)with great
fubmiffion and deuotion of heart, fayinge,
behould Lord, behould what I am? what
other thinge can be looked for frõ this or-
dure but fuch filthy fauours? What other
ftuite can be expected from this earth
which thou dideft curfe in the beginninge
of the world, but thornes and thiftles?
What good cã it bringe forth, except thou
lord doeft purge it from all corruptiõ? this
beinge faid, let him retourne to cõtinue his
meditations with patience expectinge the
vifitation of our lord, who is neuer wantinge to the humble of fpirit. If yet the
tumoult of thefe troublefome fancies doth
not ceafe, neuerthelefs let him ftill refift
conftantly; repellinge the force of them to
the vttermoft of his power. From this per-
feuerant battaile (beleeue me)he will reape
more gaine and merite, then if he had
enioyed the greateft confolations in his
meditation.

A re-

A remedy for the third temptation.

TO ouercome the temptation of blasphomous thoughtes, we muſt knowe as there is no temptation ſo troubleſome to a pious mind. So likwiſe there is none leſs dangerous. Therfore the beſt remedie is to contemne them. For ſeeinge ſinne conſiſteth not in ſenſe, but delight of thoſe thinges we thinke of. But in theſe there is no pleaſure, but rather tortour. Therfore they may chalinge the name of puniſhment rather then of ſinne. And the more vexatiō is in them, the further of we are from conſentinge vnto any ſinne, therfore it is beſt not to feare, but contemne them: ſeeinge feare maketh them more ſtronge and violent.

Temptations of thoughtes of blaſphemy ought to be contemned.

A remedie for the fourth temptation.

AGainſt the temptations of infidelitie, he who is vexed with ſuch cogitations, on the one ſide let him conſider the imbecilitie of mans condition, on the other ſid the greatnes of the diuine power, to whome nothinge is impoſible: thoſe thinges which God hath commanded let him alwayes bare in mind; for others let him
neuer

neuer busy himselfe in searchinge curi-
ously the workes of supreme maiestie,
seeing the least of them doe farr transcend
humane capacity. Wherfore he that desireth to enter in to this sainctuary of Gods
workes, let him enter with profound
humility and reuerence, endued with the
eies of a simple doue, not of a subtile ser-
pent:and let him bare the mind of a meeke
disciple,and not of a temerarious iudge,let
him put on the shape of a child for such our
lord maketh partakers of his diuine secretes, let him not minde to search or knowe
the causes of Gods workes, let him shutt
the eies of naturall reason, and open the
eies of faith.For these are the hades wherwith Gods workes ought to be handled.
Humane vnderstandinge is able to comprehende the workes of men, but not of
God, seeinge they are not capable of so
much light.

In conside-ring Gods vvorkes good heed ought to be taken.

    This temptation seeinge it is one of the
greatest,which doth assault men,and bringeth none,or small delight with it, is to be
cured with the remedy of the precedent
temptation.That is,to make slight of it,for
it cannot staine the soule with any great
blemish, because where the will is contrarie there is no daunger of any sinne.

                           A re-

A remedy for the fifth temptation.

THere are some who are troubled with many feares and fancies when they goe to pray in solitary places, remote from the company of men, against which temptation, there is no more efficatious remedie then for a mā to arme himselfe with a curragious mind, perseueringe in his exercise, for this feare is ouercome with fightinge, not with flyinge: moreouer let him consider, that the deuill nor any other thinge what soeuer else can hurt vs, except God permitts. Let him also consider, that we are compassed about with a custody of Angels, which doe guard vs, as well in, as out of prayer, they assist vs carryinge vp our prayers to heauen, they help vs to bringe to nothinge the deuises of our crafty enemie, and to confound all his mischeiuous plottes.

Feare is ouercome vvith fightinge not vvith flyinge.

A remedie for the sixth temptation.

TO ouercome sleepe, wherwith some, that meditate are often molested: we must consider, that sometime it proceedeth from mere necessity , and then it is not to be denied the body what is its due , least it hindreth what is our right. Some times it proceedeth out of infirmitie, then he must take heede not to vex himselfe too much, seeinge herein is no sinne at all : but moderately as much as strength suffereth , resistinge it: nowe vsinge some industry, then some small violéce, that prayer doth not altogether perish, without which, nothinge in this life cã be had secure, butwhen it cõmeth out of slouth, or from the deuill, then there is no better remedy then to absteine from wine, and not to vse water in aboundance, but as much as quencheth his thirst, to pray vpon his knees , or after some other painefull gesture of the body , let him vse discipline or other corporall austerity to driue sleepe from his eies. To conclude, the remedy of this, and all others is , instantly to implore his assistance, who is ready to giue it to all, so they aske it feruently and constantly.

Drovvsi-nes in prayer arriseth from a threfold cause.

L   *A re-*

A remedie for the seauenth temptation.

AGainst the temptations of diffidéce and presumption, seeinge they in them selues be contrary, it is requisite to apply diuers remedies. Against diffidence: let him consider, that we doe not rest vp-on our owne merits, but vpon God almighties grace, who is so much the more willinge to assist man, by how much the more he is diffident of his owne forces, placinge a firme hope in the goodnes of God, to whome nothinge is impossible: the remedy for presumption is, to consider, that the most euident and certaine argument is, that a man is yet furthest from true sanctitie, when he thinketh himselfe to be neerest.

Man ought cheifly to rely vpon Gods grace not his ovvne merits.

More-ouer let him looke vpõ himselfe in the liues of saintes, who nowe raigne with C H R I S T, or liue yet in this mortall life, as in a lookiinge glasse, to which of these he doth compare himselfe, he will see, that he is no more then a dwarfe in respect of a giant, which consideration will not a little suppress his pride.

A re-

A remedie for the eighth temptation.

AGainſt the inordinate deſire of ſtu-
die and learninge: it is good to conſider how farr vertue exceedeth ſcience:
and how much the knowledge of God
excelleth humane wiſedome. Hence a man
may learne how neceſſarie it is, to beſtowe
more labour vpon one, then vpon the
other. More-ouer the world hath all the
excellence that can be deſired, but cannot
auoyd this miſery, that it muſt end with
life. What then more miſerable then to
ſeeke after that with ſo much labour, and
expence which ſo quickly periſheth? If all
thinges in the world could be knowne,
they are but as nothinge, and therfore it is
much better to exerciſe our ſelues in the
loue of God, the fruite wherof remaineth
for euer, and in whome we ſee and knowe,
all thinges. Laſt of all, in the day of iudgment, we ſhall not be asked what we
haue read, but what we haue done, not
how eloquently we haue ſpoken, but how
well we haue liued.

The diuine vviſdome doth infi-nitly ex-ceed hu-mane pru-dence.

L 2   A re-

A remedie for the ninth temptation.

THe cheifest remedie againft indifcreet zeale of helpinge others, is, fo to attéde to the good of our neighbours, that we hurte not our felues : and fo to haue a care of the confciences of others , that we neglect not our owne, but in affiftinge thé it is good to referue fo much time, as is fufficient to conferue the heart in deuotion and recollection. And this is, as S. PAVLE faith: *Ambulare in fpiritu* : to walke in fpirit, that is to fay that a man be more in God then in himfelfe. Seeinge therfore that the prime roote of all our good vpon this dependeth, we muft ftriue, that our prayer be fo profounde and longe , as may conferue the foule in deuotion , which euery fhort meditation is not able to doe , but deuoute and longe.

The fal-uation of our nei-bour is fo to be re-garded that vve doe not negle⌈ our vvne foules.

CHAP.

Chap. V.

Other certaine admonitions necessarie for spirituall persons.

THE thinge that affordeth greatest difficulty in this spirituall iournie, is , to knowe how to come to God, and to conuerse with him familiarly. Let therfore none dare to enter into this way without a good guide , and well instructed with necessarie admonitions and documentes , of which we will sett downe a fewe, accordinge to our wounted breuitie.

The first is, wherby we are taught what end we must aime at in these our spirituall exercises. We must therfore knowe that since to communicate with God almightie of it selfe is most delightfull , hauinge no bitternes mixed with it, as the wise man testifieth : hence it cometh to passe that many allured with the pleasure of this admirable and vnused sweetnes (which is greater then can be comprehended) come to God and frequent these spirituall actions , as readinge, prayer, meditation, vse of the Sacra- *The errour and abuse of some.*

L 3 ment,

ment, for the great contēt and delight they take in them, so that for the principall end wherwith they are moued, is this admirable sweetnes which they vehemently desire. This is a great errour and many are plunged in it , for seeinge to loue and seeke God should be the cheifest end of all our actions, these loue and seeke themselues , that is to say, their owne gust and sensible delight, rather then God , which was the scope of the contemplatiue Philosophie of the gentills. Especially as a certaine Doctour saieth, that this is a kind of auarice, luxurie, and spirituall gluttonie, no less pernicious then carnall. From this errour springeth an other braunch. (To wit) that many iudge themselues, and others accordinge to the ebbinge , and flovvinge of consolations, so farr that they are persvvaded, that a man is more, or lesse perfect by howe much more or lesse, he is visited with diuine consolatiōs. This is a great mistake.

Vvhat shouldbe the endof spirituall exercises. Against both these temptations this generall doctrine is a remedy: that euerie one must knowe that the scope of all these exer cises, and the cheife end of a spirituall life, is the obseruinge of Gods cōmaundemētes, and a perfect fullfillinge of his diuine vvill: to this it is necessarie that our ovvne vvill be mortified, that the vvill of God may the
bet-

better liue and raigne in vs. Seeinge both thefe are directly contrarie the one to the other. But this noble victorie feeing it cannot be obteined vvithout fpeciall fauour and allurementes of God , therfore vve ought to frequent the exercife of prayer, the better by it (and indeed the only meanes) to obteine this grace , and to bringe this ferious bufines of our foules perfection to a good and defired end. With this intention vve may confidently defire of God internall confolations , as vve haue faied before. This did the Prophet DAVID vvhen he faied : *Redde mihi Domine lætitiam falutaris tui , & fpiritu priucipali confirma me:* Giue me,ô Lord, the ioy of thy faluation, and confirme me with thy principall fpirit.

Hence it is manifeft , what end euerie one ought to prefix to himfelfe in thefe exercifes, and howe they fhould efteeme and meafure their owne and others profitt : not accordinge to the multitude of flowinge confolations. But accordinge to thofe thinges they haue conftantly fuffered for God,partly in fulfillinge his diuine pleafure,partly in renouncinge their owne proper wills.

And that this ought to be the end of all our prayer and readinge it appeareth by that one Pfalme of the Prophet DAVID

L 4   which

which beginneth : *Beati immaculati in via,
qui ambulant in lege Domini :* Blessed are the
immaculate in the way , which walke in
the lawe of our Lord. Which is the longest
Psalme in the Psalter , notwithstandinge
there is not one verse in it , in which there
is not mention of the lawe of God, and
keepinge his comaundemetes. Which the
holy Ghost hath so ordeined, that me may
learne to direct all prayer, and readinge to
this end and scope. From which they that
doe decline, doe cast themselues into the secret snares of the eneiny, who with his suttle
craft perswadeth them that, that is some
great matter which indeed is nothinge ,
and for this cause men most exercised in
spirituall matters doe affirme, the only
touchstone of true vertue to be , not that
sensible delight which is founde in prayer:
but patience in affliction , abnegation of
ones owne selfe, a syncere and enteire fullfillinge of the diuine will , and finally in a
diligent obseruinge of God almighties
lawes and comaundemetes, though I must
confess that prayer it selfe, and the frequet
consolatios that are founde therin, doe not
a little conduce and help to the better ef-
fectinge of these thinges fore mentioned.

They which are desirous to knowe
how much progresse they haue made in
the

the way of God, let them examine how
much they haue increased in interiour and
exteriour humility : how willingly they
haue put vp iniuries, with what minde
they haue borne with others infirmities:
how they haue compationated the imperfections of their neighbours: what confidence they haue had in God in the tedious
time of tribulation:how they haue bridled
their tongues: how they haue kept their
heart: how they haue mortified their flesh
with all vnlawfull delightes, and made it
subiect to the spirit. With what moderation they haue behaued them selues in
prosperitie and aduersitie; With what
grauitie and discretion they haue gouer-
ned all their actions: and aboue all how
dead they haue beene to the world, with
all its pleasures, honours, and dignities:
and accordingly as they haue profited in
these vertues let them measure their perfection, and not accordinge to the consolations wherwith God hath visited them,
wherfore let euerie cne be sure to beare
one hande and the cheifest ouer himselfe in
mortification ; the other in prayer,seeinge
the one can not be atteined vnto without
the other.

The signes by vvhich vve may coniecture hovve much vve haue profited in the vvay of perfe-
ction.

The second Admonition.

AS it is not lawfull to desire consolations and spirituall comforts, to that end, that in them we should sett vp our rest, but only as they affist vs in our spirituall progresse, much lesse is it lawfull to wish for visions, reuelations and the like, which to those who are not well grounded in humility, may be a great cause of their vtter ruine, neither is there any reason to feare, that those who refuse or reiect the should be disobedient to God, because when it shall please God to reueale any thinge, he will doe it after such a fashion, that he to whome such thinges shall be reuealed, shalbe so certaine of them, that he will haue no reason either to feare or doubt, though he should himselfe neuer so much striue against them.

The third Admonition.

WE must haue a speciall care, not to speake to others, those sensible consolations, which God almightie hath bene pleased to recreate vs with all. Except it be to our spirituall directour. Hence it is that, that mellifluous Doctour was wont

to

to aduife euery one to haue thefe wordes
written in great letters in his chamber :
MY SECRET TO MY SELFE : MY
SECRET TO MY SELFE.

The fovvrth Admonition.

MOreouer we muft alwayes take
good heede to deale with God
with much humilitie and reuerence, neuer
to efteeme our felues fo high in his fauour,
as we neglect to caft downe our eies vpon
our owne bafenes, and to fhrowd our
winges in the prefence of fo great a maieftie, as holy S. AVGVSTINE was wont
to doe, of whome it is written, that he had
learned to reioyce before God with feare
and tremblinge.

Vve must al. vvaies remaine in humili-ty.

The fifth Admonition.

WE haue heretofore counfailed the
feruant of God, that he côfecrateth
fome certaine time of the day to recol-
lectiõ. But now befids the ordinarie courfe,
we fay, that he muft fome times fequefter
himfelfe from all bufines, and emploimêts,
as much as is poffible , and giue himfelfe
wholly ouer to deuotion, the better to fatt
his foule with the aboundance of fpirituall
dainties, recoueringe his dayly loffes , and
get-

gettinge newe force to goe forward in his
fpirituall iourny. Which although it be
not amiffe to doe at all times , yet more
fpecially , vpon the principall feafts of the
yeare : in the time of temptation : after a
longe iourny : after troublefome bufines,
which gaue matter of much diftraction,
that then we exclude from our foules all
exteriour thinges, and call our felues back
againe to the point from whence we did
digreffe.

The fixth Admonition.

THere be many which be not difcreet
in their fpirituall exercifes, when they
enioy heauenly confolations, and it oftentimes falleth out, that this profperitie doth
expofe them to manifeft perill , for when
God almightie shewreth downe , more
aboundantly this celeftiall dewe, vpō their
foules, they are fo rauished with the fweet-
nes of it, that they addict themfelues without meafure to this only exercife : to this
end they prolonge the time of prayer, ma-
cerate themfelues with watchinge and
other corporall aufterities, fo that nature it
felfe at length is conftrained to finke vnder
the burthen of fuch indifcreet mortification. Hence it cometh to paffe, that many
ab-

abhorre spirituall exercises, and some are not only made by this meanes vnfitt for corporall , but also dull for spirituall labours of prayer and meditation. Wherfore in all these , there is great neede of discretion, especially in the beginninge , when spirituall consolations be more feruent, and commonly whē discretion is least. For we must so order our diet that we doe not faint in the middest of our iourny. On the contrary there be some so slouthfull and vndeuout, that vnder the colour of discretiō, immoderatly make much of theselues, refusinge the least labour, or trouble. This although it be dangerous to all , but especially to beginners. For as S. BERNARD saith , it is impossible that he should perseuer longe in a spirituall course, who is discreet at first. That whē he is a nouice esteemeth himselfe wise, and when he is younge gouerneth himselfe like an old man. Neither can I easily iudge which of these , be more dangerous. Except, as THOMAS A KEMPIS saith , the first is more incurable, for whilst the body is stronge and sounde, there may be hopes to cure tepiditie: but when it is once weakened through indiscretion, it scarce euer can be brought to its former feruour.

The

The seauenth Admonition.

THere is yet an other daunger, more pernicious then the former, which is, that some hauing experience of this inestimable vertue of prayer, that all the fruite of a spirituall life doth depend vpon it. Hence they perswade themselues, that in it all is conteined. And that only, that vertue doth suffice for our saluation, which makes them to neglect other vertues, which are likewise the foundations and proppes which doe vphold a spirituall buildinge, which beinge taken away the wholl fabrick falleth to ruine ; wherfore they that seeke after this one only vertue with such indiscreet auiditie, the more they labour the lesse fuite they reape. But the seruant of God that expecteth merit and comfort in the way of perfection must not fix his eies so much vpon one only vertue, although it be neuer so rare and excellent, but generally attend to all, as one stringe vpon an instrument maketh no musique, except we strike the rest: so one vertue cannot make a spirituall harmonie in our soules, if the other be

wan-

wantinge , not vnlike a clock , which
if there be but a fault in one whele , the
others will ſtand . So it is in a ſpirituall
clock , if one vertue be deficient.

The eighth Document.

THeſe thinges which we haue hetherto ſaied , which doe help to
deuotion. Are ſo to be taken as prepa-
ratories, wherwith a man doth diſpoſe
himſelfe to God almightie his grace , and
behaue himſelfe manfully in his holy ſeruice , with this caution, that we ſhould
not put our confidence in them, but in
God.

This I ſay becauſe, there are ſome which
labour to reduce all rules into art, think-
inge that they haue atteined to the perfection of that exerciſe, if they obſerue
exactly the rules therof. But they which
put good principalls into practice , vvill
quicky atteine vnto their deſired end,
vvhich doinge, they care not to reduce
grace into art , nor to attribute that to humane rules, vvhich is the gift of God. Hēce
vve ſay that it is not neceſſarie to follovve
theſe rules, and documentes as dependinge
of art, but as inſtrumentes of grace. Becauſe

a man

a man vvill learne thus to knovve, that the principall meanes, vvhich one ought to feeke after, is profound humilitie, vvith the confideration of our ovvne bafenes, and a great confidence in God almighties mercie. To the end that vve may come to the knovvledge of the one and the other, let vs povvre out teares vvithout intermiffion, and continually pray, that as vve expect at the gate of humilitie, fo vve may obteine by it, all our defires, and perfeuere in humble thankefgiuinge to the diuine bountie, vvithout any truft to our ovvne vvorkes or any thinge that is ours.

AD HONOREM DEI.

FINIS.

THE TABLE.

M   the

THE TABLE.

THE TABLE.

THe second Part, of deuotion and of those thinges vvhich thervnto belonge. 141. Of nine helpes vvherby the vertue of deuotion may be atteined vnto vvith the least difficultie. 1. Continuall exercise. 2. Custodie of the heart. 3. Custodie of the senses. 4. Solitude. 5. Readinge of spirituall bookes. 6. Continuall memorie of God. 7. Perseuerance. 8. Corporall austeritie. 9. VVorkes of mercie. Fol. 146. 147. 148. 149.

Of nine impedimentes of deuotion. 1. Veniall sinnes. 2. Remorse of conscience. 3. Anxitie of heart. 4. Cares of the minde. 5. A multitude of affaires. 6. Delight of the senses. 7. Inordinate delight in eatinge and drinkinge. 8. Curiositie of the senses. 9. In-

THE TABLE.

F I N I S.

Ordo Baptizandi
1636

ORDO
BAPTIZANDI

ALIAQVE SACRA-
menta administrandi, &
Officia quædam Ecclesia-
stica ritè peragendi.

EX RITVALI ROMANO,
iussu Pauli Quinti edito,
extractus.

Pro Anglia , Hibernia , &
Scotia.

PARISIIS,
M. DC. XXXVI.

DE BAPTISMO.

BENEDICTIO FON-
tis Baptismi, extra Sabba-
tum Paschæ & Penteco-
stes, vbi aqua consecrata
non habetur.

PRIMVM lauatur
& mūdatur vas Ba-
ptisterij, deinde a-
quâ limpidâ reple-
tur. Tum Sacerdos superpelliceo, vel Alba, & stola indutus, cum alijs Clericis, vel e-
tiam Sacerdotibus si adsint,
Cruce, & duobus cereis præ-
cedentibus, ac Thuribulo &
incenso, & cū vasculo Chris-

A ij

matis & Olei Cathecumeno-
rum, vadit ad Fontem , & ibi
(vel ante Altare Baptisterij ,
si modò fuerit) dicat Litanias
ordinarias, prout habentur in
Breuiario, post Psalmos Pœnitentiales, &c.

Et ante vers. Vt nos exau-
dire digneris , dicat, & secun-
dò repetat sequentem versú.

Vt Fontem istum ad rege-
nerandam tibi nouam prolem
bene † dicere, & consecrare
† digneris: Te rogamus audi
nos.

Vt fontem istum ad regene-
randam tibi nouam prolem
bene † dicere, & consecrare
† digneris ; Te rogamus audi nos,

Potest etiam dici Latinia
breuior, vt in Missali in Sab-

bato sancto : & dicto vltimo
Kyrie eleison, Sacerdos dicat Pater noster, & Credo in
Deum &c. omnia clara voce:
quibus initis dicat. ℣. Apud
te Domine est fons vitæ ℞. Et
in lumine tuo videbimus lu-
men. ℣. Domine exaudi orationem meam. ℞. Et clamor
meus ad te veniat. ℣. Dominus vobiscum. ℞. Et cū spiritu tuo.   Oremus.

OMnipotens sempiterne
Deus adesto magnæ pie-
tatis tuæ mysterijs, adesto Sa-
cramentis , & ad recreandos
nouos populos, quos tibi Fons
Baptismatis parturit, spiritum
adoptionis emitte : vt quod
nostræ humilitatis gerendum
est ministerio, virtutis tuæ im-
pleatur effectu. Per Dominū

A iij

noſtrum Ieſum Chriſtum filium tuum, qui tecum viuit·&
regnat in vnitate Spiritus ſancti Deus, per omnia ſæcula ſæculorum. ℟. Amen.

    Exorciſmus aquæ.

EXorcizo te creatura a-
  quę, per Deum †viuum,
per Deum †verum, per Deũ
† ſanctum, per Deum qui te
in principio, verbo ſeparauit
ab arida, cuius ſuper te ſpiritus ferebatur: qui te de paradi-
ſo manare iuſſit,

    Hic manu aquam diuidat,
& deinde de ea effundat extra
marginem Fontis, verſus qua-
tuor Orbis partes, proſequés.

    Et in quatuor fluminibus
totam terram rigare pręcepit:
qui te in deſerto amaram per
lignum dulcem fecit atq; po-

tabilē; quite de petra produxit, vt populum, quem ex Æ-
gypto liberauerat, ſiti fatigatū
recrearet. Exorcizo te, & per
Iᴇsᴠᴍ Chriſtum Filium eius
vnicum, Dominum noſtrum,
qui te in Cana Galilææ ſigno
admirabili ſua potentiâ con-
uertit in vinum; qui ſuper te
pedibus ambulauit, & à Ioan-
ne in Iordane in te Baptizatus
eſt : qui te vnâ cum ſanguine
de latere ſuo produxit, & diſ-
cipulis ſuis iuſſit vt credentes
baptizarent in te, dicens : Ite,
docete omnes gentes , bapti-
zantes eos in nomine Patris,
& Filij, & Spiritus ſanᓗi; vt
efficiaris aqua ſanᓗa, aqua
benediᓗa, aqua quælauat ſor-
des, & mundat peccata. Tibi
igitur præcipio omnis ſpiritus

immunde, omne phantasma,
omne mendacium, eradicare
& effugare ab hac creatura a-
quæ, vt qui in ipsa baptizandi
erunt, fiat eis fons aquæ saliē-
tis in vitam æternam, & rege-
nerans eos Deo Patri, & Filio,
& Spiritui sancto, in nomine
eiusdem Domini nostri IESV
Christi, qui venturus est iudicare viuos & mortuos, & sæculum per ignem. ℟. Amen.
O remus.

DOmine sancte Pater
omnipotens, æterne
Deus, aquarum spiritualium
sanctificator, te suppliciter
deprecamur, vt ad hoc mini-
sterium humilitatis nostræ respicere digneris, & super has
aquas abluendis & purifican-
dis hominibus præparatas,

Angelum sanctitatis emittas,
quò peccatis vitæ prioris ab-
lutis, reatúque deterso, purum
sancto Spiritui habitaculum
regenerati effici mereantur.
Per Dominum nostrum Ie-
sum Christum filium tuũ, qui
tecum viuit & regnat, in vnitate, eiusdem Spiritus sancti
Deus, per omnia sæcula sæculorum, ℞. Amen.

Tunc sufflet ter in aquam
versus tres partes secundùm
hanc figuram Y. deinde imponit incensum in Thuribulo,
& Fontem incensat. Postea
infundens de Oleo Cathecu-
menorum in aquam in modũ
Crucis, clara voce dicat:

Sanctificetur, & fœcunde-
tur Fons iste oleo salutis re-
nascentibus ex eo in vitam æ-

ternam, in nomine † Patris,
& † Filij, & Spiritus † sancti. ℟. Amen.

Deinde infundat de Chris-
mate, modo quo supra, dicés:
Infusio Chrismatis Domini
Iesu Christi, & Spiritus sancti
Paracliti, fiat in nomine san-
ctæ Trinitatis. ℟. Amen.

Postea accipit ambas am-
pullas dicti Olei sācti & Chrismatis, & de vtroque simul
in modum Crucis infunden-
do, dicat:

Commixtio Chrismatis san-
ctificationis, & Olei vnctio-
nis, & aquæ Baptismatis pariter fiat in nomine † Patris, &
† Filij, & Spiritus † sancti. ℟.
Amen.

Tú deposita ampulla, dex-
terâ manu Oleum sanctum &

Chrisma infusum miscet cum
aqua, & spargit per totum Fō-
tem. Deinde medulla panis
manum tergit, & si quis bapti-
zandus est, eum baptizat, vt
inferius. Quòd si neminem
baptizat, statim man⁹ abluat,
& ablutio effundatur in Sacrarium.

ORDO

MINISTRANDI

SACRAMENTVM BAP-
tismi Paruulorum.

Cùm Infans delatus fuerit ante fores Ecclesiæ, colloca-
tus super brachium dexte-
rum deferentis ; Sacerdos
indutus superpelliceo (vel
Alba) cum stola, accepto
nomine baptizandi, stans
dicat.

N. Quid petis ab Eccle-
siâ Dei? Patrinus res-
pondet. Fidem. Sacerdos.
Fides quid tibi præstat ? Patrinus respondet. Vitam æternam. Sacerdos. Si igitur vis

ad vitam ingredi, serua mandata : Diliges Dominum Deum tuum ex toto corde tuo , & ex tota anima tua, & ex tota mente tua, & Proximum sicut teipsum. Deinde ter exsufflet leniter in faciem Infantis, & dicat semel : Exi ab eo (vel ab ea) immunde spiritus, & da locum Spiritui Sancto paraclito. Postea pollice faciat signum Crucis in fronte,& in pectore Infantis, dicens : Accipe signum Crucis tam in † fronte, quam in † corde; sume fidem cælestiú præceptorum ; & talis esto moribus, vt templum Dei iam esse possis.

O remus.

PReces nostras, quæsumus Domine, clementer exau-

di : & hunc (vel hanc) ele-
ctum tuum N. Crucis Domi-
nicæ impressione signatum,
perpetua virtute custodi, vt
magnitudinis gloriæ tuæ rudimenta seruans, per custodiã
mandatorum tuorum ad regenerationis gloriam peruenire
mereatur. Per Christum &c.
℞ Amen.

Deinde imponat manum
super caput Infantis, ac dicat :

Oremus.

OMnipotens sempiterne
Deus, Pater Domini
nostri Iesu Christi, respicere
dignare super hunc (vel hãc)
famulum tuum N. quem ad
rudimenta fidei vocare dignatus es, omnem cæcitatem cordis ab eo expelle : disrumpe
omnes laqueos Satanæ, qui-

bus fuerat colligatus : aperi ei
Domine ianuam pietatis tuæ,
vt ſigno ſapientiæ tuæ imbutus, omnium cupiditatum fœtoribus careat, & ad ſuauem
odorem præceptorum tuorum
lætus tibi in Ecclesia tua de-
ſeruiat, & proficiat de die in
diem. Per eundem Chriſtum
Dominũ noſtrum. ℞. Amen.

Deinde Sacerdos benedi-
cat ſalem, qui ſemel benedictus, aliâs ad eumdem vſũ de-
ſeruire poteſt. Benedictio
ſalis.

Exorcizo te creatura ſalis,
in nomine Dei Patris †
omnipotentis, & in charitate
Domini noſtri Ieſu † Chriſti,
& in virtute Spiritus † ſancti.
Exorcizo te per Deum † viuũ,
per Deum † verum, per Deũ

✝ sanctum, per Deum ✝ qui
te ad tutelam humani generis
procreauit,& populo venien-
ti ad credulitatem per seruos
suos consecrari præcepit,vt in
nomine sanctæ Trinitatis efficiaris salutare Sacramentum
ad effugandum inimicum.
Proinde rogamus te, Domi-
ne Deus noster,vt hanc crea-
turã salis sanctificando ✝ san-
ctifices , & benedicendo ✝
benedicas,vt fiat omnibus ac-
cipientibus perfecta medici-
na, permanens in visceribus
eorum, in nomine eiusdē Domini nostri Iesu Christi, qui
venturus est iudicare viuos &
mortuos, & sæculum per
ignem. ℞. Amen.

Deinde immitat modicum
salis benedicti in os Infantis,
dicens :

dicens : N. Accipe salem sapientiæ: propitiatio sit tibi in
vitam æternam. ℞. Amen.
Sacerdos. Pax tecum. ℞. Et
cum spiritu tuo.

Oremus.

DEus patrum nostrorum,
vniuersæ Conditor ve-
ritatis, te supplices exoramus,
vt hunc (vel hanc) famulum
tuum, N. respicere digneris
propitius, & hoc primum pa-
bulum salis gustantem, non
diutiùs esurire permittas, quò
minùs cibo expleatur cælesti,
quatenus sit semper spiritu feruens, spe gaudens, tuo semper
nomini seruiens. Perduc eum
Domine quæsumus, ad nouæ
regenerationis lauacrum, vt
cum fidelibus tuis promissionum tuarum æterna præmia

B

conſequi mereatur. Per Chriſtum Dominum noſtrum. ℞.
Amen.

Exorcizo te immunde ſpiritus in nomine † Patris, & Filij † , & Spiritus † ſancti, vt
exeas & recedas ab hoc famulo Dei N. Ipſe enim tibi imperat, maledicte damnate, qui
pedibus ſuper mare ambulauit, & Petro mergenti dexteram porrexit.

Ergo, maledicte Diabole,
recognoſce ſententiam tuam,
& da honorem Deo viuo &
vero, da honorem Ieſu Chriſto Filio eius , & Spiritui ſancto, & recede ab hoc famulo
Dei N. quia iſtum ſibi Deus
& Domin⁹ noſter Ieſus Chriſtus ad ſuam ſãctam gratiam,
& benedictionem, Fontem-

que Baptifmatis vocare dignatus eft.

Hic pollice in fronte fignat
Infantem, dicens :

Et hoc fignum fanctæ Cru-
cis † quod nos fronti eius damus, tu maledicte Diabole nũ-
quã audeas violare. Per eumdem Dominum noftrum. ℞.
Amen.

Mox imponit manum fuper
caput Infantis, & dicat:

O remus.

ÆTernam ac iuftiffimam
pietatem tuam depre-
cor , Domine fancte, Pater
omnipotens, æterne Deus, auctor luminis & veritatis, fuper
hũc (vel hanc) famulum tuũ
N. vt digneris illum illumi-
nare lumine intelligētiæ tuæ:
munda eum , & fanctifica: da

B ij

ei scientiam veram, vt dignus
gratia Baptismi tui effectus,
teneat firmam spem, consiliũ
rectum, & doctrinam sanctã.
Per Christum Dominum no-
strum. ℟. Amen.

Postea Sacerdos imponit
extremam partem Stolæ super
Infantem & introducit eum
in Ecclesia, dicens : N. Ingredere in templum Dei, vt
habeas partem cũ Christo in
vitam æternam. ℟. Amen.

Cum fuerint Ecclesiam in-
gressi, Sacerdos procedens ad
Fontem cum Susceptoribus
coniunctim, clara voce dicat:

CRedo in Deum, Patrem
omnipotentem, Creato-
rem cæli & terræ. Et in Iesum
Christum Filium eius vnicũ,
Dominum nostrum. Qui con-

ceptus est de Spiritu sancto, natus ex Maria Virgine, Passus sub Pontio Pilato crucifixus, mortuus, & sepultus. Descendit ad inferos, tertia die resurrexit à mortuis. Ascendit ad Cælos, sedet ad dexteram Dei Patris omnipotentis. Inde venturus est iudicare viuos & mortuos. Credo in Spiritum sanctum, Sanctam Ecclesiam Catholicam, Sanctorum Communionem, Remissionē peccatorum, Carnis resurrectionem, & Vitam æternam. Amen.

P Ater noster, qui es in cælis, sanctificetur nomen tuum: adueniat regnum tuum: fiat voluntas tua, sicut in cælo, & in terra. Panem nostrū quotidianum da nobis hodie:

& dimitte nobis debita nostra, sicut & nos dimittimus
debitoribus nostris. Et ne nos
inducas in tentationem: sed libera nos à malo. Amen.

Ac deinde antequam acce-
dat ad Baptisterium, dicat.
Exorcismus.

EXorcizo te omnis spiritus
immunde, in nomine Dei
Patris † omnipotentis, & in
nomine Iesu Christi Filij eius
† Domini & Iudicis nostri,
& in virtute Spiritus † sancti,
vt discedas ab hoc plasmate
Dei N. quod Dominus noster
ad templú sanctum suum vocare dignatus est, vt fiat templum Dei viui, & Spiritus
sanctus habitet in eo. Per eú-
dem Christum Dominum no-
strum, qui venturus est iudi-

care viuos & mortuos, & sæculum per ignem, ℞. Amen.

Postea Sacerdos digito ac-
cipiat de saliua oris sui, & tangat aures, & nares infantis:
tangendo verò aurem dexteram & sinistram dicat:

Ephpheta, quod est adape-
rire: Deinde tangat nares dicens: In odorem suauitatis.
Tu autem effugare diabole
appropinquat enim iudicium
Dei.

Postea interrogabit baptizandum nominatim dicens:
N. Abrenuntias Satanæ?
Respondet Patrinus: Abre-
nuntio. Et ab omnibus operi-
bus eius? ℞. Abrenuntio. Et
omnibus pōpis eius ℞. Abrenuntio.

Deinde Sacerdos intingit
B iiij

pollicé in Oleo Cathecume-
norum, & Infantem vngit in
pectore, & inter fcapulas in
modum Crucis dicens : **Ego
te linio** † Oleo falutis in Chrifto Iefu Domino noftro , vt
habeas vitam æternam. ℟.
Amen.

Subinde pollicem & inuncta
loca abftergit bombacio, vel
re fimili , & interrrogat ex-
preffo nomine baptizandum,
Patrino refpondente. **Credis
in Deum Patrem omnipoten-
tem, Creatorem Cæli & Terræ?** ℟. **Credo. Credis in Ie-
fum Chriftum Filium eius v-
nicum Dominum noftrum,
natum, & paffum ?** ℟. **Credo.
Credis in Spiritum fanctum,
Sanctam Ecclefiam Catholi-
cam, Sanctorum communio-**

nem, Remiſſionem peccato-
rum, carnis Reſurrectionem,
vitam æternam? ℟. Credo.

Subinde expreſſo nomine
baptizãdi Sacerdos dicat: N.
Vis baptizari? Reſpõdet Patrinus: Volo.

Tunc Patrino, vel Matri-
na, vel vtroque (ſi ambo ad-
mittantur) Infantem tenente, Sacerdos de vaſculo, ſeu
vrceolo accipit aquam Bap-
tiſmalem, & de ea ter fundit
ſuper caput Infantis in modũ
Crucis; & ſimul verba profe-
rens, ſemel tantùm diſtinctè,
& attentè dicat: N. Ego te
baptizo in nomine † Patris,
fundit primò & † Filij, fundit ſecundò, & Spiritus † sã-
cti, fundit tertio.

¶ Vbi autem eſt conſuetu-

do baptizandi per immerfio-
nem , Sacerdos accipit Infantem & aduertens ne lædatur,
cautè immergit, & trina mér-
fione baptizat, & femel tantû
dicat : N. Ego te baptizo , in
nomine† Patris , † & Filij,&
Spiritus † fanĉti.

Mox Patrinus , vel Matri-
na, vel vterque fimul Infantē
de facro fonte leuat, fufcipiēs
illum de manu Sacerdotis.

¶ Si vero dubitatur, an Infans fuerit baptizatus , vtatur
hac forma. Si non es baptizatus, Ego te baptizo in nomine
† Patris,& † Filij, & Spiritus
† fanĉti. Amen.

Deinde intingit pollicem in
facro Chrifmate, & vngit Infantem in fummitate capitis,
in modum Crucis, dicens.

Deus omnipotens, Pater Dñi nostri Iesu Christi, qui te regenerauit ex aqua & Spiritu sancto, quique dedit tibi remissionem omniú peccatorum (hic inungit) ipse te liniat Chrismate salutis † in eodem Christo Iesu Domino nostro in vitam æternam. ℞. Amen.

Sacerdos. Pax tibi. ℞. Et cũ spiritu tuo.

Tum bombacio; aut re simili abstergit pollicem suum, & locum inunctum, & imponit capiti eius linteolum candidũ loco vestis albæ, dicens: Accipe vestem candidam, quam immaculatam perferas ante tribunal Domini nostri Iesu Christi, vt habeas vitam æternam. ℞. Amen.

Postea dat ei, vel Patrino, candelam accensam, dicens: Accipe lampadem ardentem, & irreprehensibilis custodi Baptismum tuum : serua Dei mandata, vt cum Dominus venerit ad nuptias, possis occurrere ei vna cum omnibus Sanctis in aula cælesti, habeasque vitam æternam, & viuas in sæcula sæculorū. ℟. Amen.

Postremo dicit : N. Vade in pace, & Dominus sit tecū. ℟. Amen.

¶ Si infans ægrotus adeo grauiter laboret, vt periculum immineat ne pereat, antequā Baptismus perficiatur, Sacerdos omissis, quæ baptismum præcedunt; eum baptizet, ter, vel semel infundens aquam super caput eius in modum

Crucis, dicens. Ego te Baptizo in nomine † Patris, &c.

¶ Si non habetur aqua Bap-
tiſmalis, & periculum im-
pendeat, Sacerdos vtatur aqua
ſimplici.

¶ Deinde ſi habeat Chriſma
liniat eum in vertice, dicens:
Deus omnipotens, Pater Domini noſtri Ieſu Chriſti, &c.
vt ſuprà.

Poſtea dat ei linteolum can-
didum, dicens: Accipe ve-
ſtem, &c.

Ac demum det ei ceream
candelam accenſam, dicens:
Accipe lampadem, vt ſupra.
Si ſuperuixerit, ſuppleātur alij
ritus omiſſi.

¶ Admonendi ſunt Suſce-
ptores de ſpirituali cognatio-
ne, quam contraxerunt cum

baptizato, baptizatíque Patre & Matre; quæ cognatio impedit matrimonium, ac dirimit.

¶ Curet Sacerdos parentes Infantis admoneri, ne in lecto secum ipsi, vel Nutrices paruulum habeant, propter oppressionis periculum: sed eum diligenter custodiant, & opportunè ad Christianam disciplinam instituant.

ORDO SVPPLENDI
omissa super bapti-
zatum.

CVm vrgente mortis pe-
riculo, vel alia cogente
necessitate, siue paruulus, siue adultus, sacris precibus
ac ceremoniis prætermissis,
fuerit baptizatus, vbi conua-
luerit, vel cessauerit periculú,
& ad Ecclesiam delatus fuerit, omissa omnia suppleantur:
idemque ordo ac ritus seruetur qui in Baptismo paruulo-
rum præscriptus est: Excepto
quod interrogatio, **An velit
baptizari,** formáque Baptismi, & ablutio prætermittun-
tur, & quædam Orationes, &

Exorcismi suo quique loco immutati, vt infrà dicuntur.

Sacerdos igitur antequam immitat salem in os baptizati, manum super caput eius imponens dicat:

Oremus.

OMnipotens sempiterne Deus, Pater Domini nostri Iesu Christi, respicere dignare super hunc (vel hâc) famulum tuum N. quem dudum ad rudimenta fidei vocare dignatus es, omnem cæcitatem cordis ab eo expelle, disrumpe omnes laqueos Satanæ, quibus fuerat colligatus: aperi ei Domine, ianuam pietatis tuæ, vt signo Sapientiæ tuæ imbutus, omnium cupiditatum fœtoribus careat, & ad suauem odorem præceptorum

ceptorum tuorum lætus tibi
in Ecclesia tua deseruiat, &
proficiat de die in diē, vt ido-
neus sit frui gratiâ Baptismi
tui, quem suscepit, salis per-
cepta medicinâ. Per eundem
Christum Dominū. ℞. Amē.

Deinde posteaquam modi-
cum salis immisit in os baptizati, dicens: Accipe salem sapientiæ, propitiatio sit tibi in
vitam æternam. ℞. Amen.
dicat: Oremus.

DEus Patrum nostrorum,
Deus vniuersæ Condi-
tor veritatis, te supplices exoramus, vt hunc (vel hāc) famulum tuum N. respicere digneris propitius, vt hoc pa-
bulum salis gustantem non
diutiùs esurire permittas, quò
minùs cibo expleatur cælesti,

C

quatenus sit semper spiritu
feruens, spe gaudens, tuo semper nomini seruiens, & quem
ad nouæ regenerationis lauacrum perduxisti : quæsumus
Domine, vt cum fidelibus tuis
promissionum tuarum æterna
præmia consequi mereatur.
Per Christum Dominum no-
strum. ℞. Amen.

Post hæc facto signo Cru-
cis in fronte baptizati, dictis-
que illis verbis : Et hoc signú
† Crucis quod nos fronti eius
damus, tu maledicte diabole
numquam audeas violare. Per
eumdem Christum Dominum
nostrum. ℞. Amen.

Manu super caput eius im-
posita, dicat: Oremus.

Æ Ternam ac iustissimam
pietatem tuam depre-

cor, Domine sacte, Pater om-
nipotes, æterne Deus, auctor
luminis & veritatis, super hunc
(vel hanc) famulum tuum
N. vt digneris eum illumina-
re lumine intelligentiæ tuæ,
munda eum & sanctifica: da ei
scientiam veram, vt dignus sit
frui gratia Baptismi tui, quem
suscepit; teneat firmam spem,
consilium rectum, doctrinam
sanctam, vt aptus sit ad reti-
nendam gratiam Baptismi tui.
Per Christum Dominum. ℞.
Amen.

¶ In Baptismo autem adul-
torum, præter illa quæ suprà
notata sunt, quando supplen-
tur omissa, hæc mutari debet.
Primùm in Exorcismo, **Audi
maledicte Satana**, vbi dicitur
(habitaculu perficiat) dicatur

habitaculum perfecit. Deinde in Exorcismo, Nec te la-
tet, vbi dicitur (vt fiat) dicatur, vt fieret.

ORDO CELEBRAN-
di Sacramentum Ma-
trimonij.

Parochus Matrimonium
celebraturus, publicatio-
ribus factis tribus diebus fe-
stis, si nullum, quod sciat, obstet legitimum impedim.etum
in Ecclesia superpelliceo &
alba stola indutus, adhibito
vno saltem Clerico, superpelliceo pariter induto, qui librū
& vas Aquæ benedictæ cum
aspersorio deferat, coram tribus aut duobus testibus virum

& mulierem, quos parentum
vel propinquorum suorum
præsentia cohonestari decet,
de consensu in matrimonium
interroget vtrumque sigilla-
tim in hunc modum, vulgari
sermone. Ac primò Spōsum.

N. **Vis accipere** N. hîc
præsētem, in tuam legitimam
vxorem iuxta ritum Sanctæ
Matris Ecclesiæ? Respon-
deat Spōsus, **Volo.** Mox Sacerdos Sponsam interroget.
N. **Vis accipere** N. hîc præ-
sentem, in tuum legitimum
maritum, iuxta ritum sanctæ
MatrisEcclesiæ? Respōdeat,
Volo. Nec sufficit consensus
vnius, sed debet esse amborū
& expressus aliquo signo sen-
sibili, siue fiat per se, siue per
Procuratorem.

¶ Deinde detur fœmina à
Patre suo, vel ab aliis amicis
suis. Quod si puella sit, disco-
opertam habeat manum, si vi-
dua tectam. Vir eam recipiat
in Dei fide, & suâ seruandam,
sicut vouit coram Sacerdote:
& teneat eam per manum suâ
dexteram in manu sua dextera
& sic det fidem mulieri per
verba de præsenti, ita dicens,
dicente Sacerdote.

I, N take thee N. to my
Wedded wife, to haue, and to
hold, from this day forward,
for better, for worse, for richer, for poorer, in sicknes
and in health, till death vs depart, if holy Church will it
permit, & thereto I plight
thee my troth.

Manum retrahendo, iterum-

queiungendo, dicat Mulier,
docente Sacerdote.

I, N. take thee N. to my
wedded husband, to haue &
to hold, frō this day forward,
for better, for worſe, for richer, for poorer, in ſicknes
and in health, till death vs depart, if holy Church will it
permit, and therto I plight
thee my troth.

Data ſic vtrimque fide, dicat Sacerdos Ego vos in Matrimonium coniūgo, in nomine † Patris, & † Filij, & Spiritus † ſancti. Amen. Vel a-
liis vtatur verbis iuxta ritum
vniuſcuiuſque Prouinciæ.

¶ Poſtea ponat Sponſus au-
rum, & argentum pro arrha,
& Annulum ſuper librum.
Benedictio annuli.

℣. Adiutorium nostrum in
nomine Domini. ℟. Qui fe-
cit cælum & terram. ℣. Domine exaudi oratione meam.
℟. Et clamor meus ad te veniat. ℣. Dominus vobiscum.
℟. Et cum spiritu tuo.

O remus.

Benedic † Domine An-
nulum hunc, quem nos
in tuo nomine † benedicimus,
vt quæ eum gestauerit, fideli-
tatem integram suo sponso tenens, in pace & voluntate tua
permaneat, atque in mutua
charitate semper viuat. Per
Christum. &c. ℟. Amen.

Deinde Sacerdos aspergat
Annulum aquâ benedicta in
modum Crucis, & Sponsus
acceptum Annulum de manu
Sacerdotis, & manu sua sini-

ſtra tenens dexteram Sponſæ,
docente Sacerdote, dicat:

With this ring I thee wed,
this gold & ſiluer I thee giue,
& with my body I thee wor-
ſhip, & with all my wordly
goods I thee endow.

Tunc inſerat Sponſus An-
nulum pollici Sponſæ, dicens:
In the name of the Father.
Deinde ſecundo digito, dicēs:
& of the Sonne. Deinde tertio digito, dicens: & of the
holy Ghoſt. Deinde quarto
digito, dicens: Amen. Ibíq;
dimittat Annulum.

Mox ſubiungat Sacerdos.
℣. Confirma hoc Deus, quod
operatus es in nobis. ℞. A tē-
plo ſācto tuo, quod eſt in Hie-
ruſalem. Kyrie eleiſon. Chriſte eleiſon. Kyrie eleiſon. P

ter noster, &c. ℣. Et ne nos
indúcas in tèntationem. ℞.
Sed libera nos à malo. ℣. Sal-
uos fac seruos tuos. ℞. Deus
meus sperantes in te. ℣. Mitte
eis Domine auxilium de sancto. ℞. Et de Sion tuere eos.
℣. Esto eis Domine turris fortitudinis. ℞. A facie inimici.
℣. Domine exaudi orationem
meam. ℞. Et clamor meus ad
te veniat. ℣. Dominus vobiscum. ℞. Et cum spiritu tuo.

Oremus.

REspice quæsumus Do-
mine, super hos famulos
tuos, & institutis tuis, quibus
propagationem humani generis ordinasti, benignus assiste,
vt qui te auctore iunguntur,
te auxiliante seruentur. Per
Christum Dominum no-

ſtrum. Amen.

His expletis, ſi benedicendæ
ſint nuptiæ, Parochus Miſſam
pro Sponſo & Sponſa, vt in
Miſſali Romano , celebret
ſeruatis omnibus quæ ibi præ-
ſcribuntur.

DE BENEDICTIONE,
& introductione Mu-
lieris in Eccleſiam
poſt partum.

SI qua puerpera poſt par-
tum, iuxta piam ac lauda-
bilem conſuetudinem ad Ec-
cleſiam venire voluerit , pro
incolumitate ſua Deo gratias
actura, petieritque à Sacerdote benedictionem, ipſe ſuper-
pelliceo & albaStola indutus,

cum ministro aspergillum deferente, ad fores Ecclesiæ accedat, vbi illam genuflecten-
tem, & candelam accensam in
manu tenentem, aqua benedicta aspergat, deinde dicat:

℣. Adiutorium nostrú in nomine Domini. ℟. Qui fe-
cit cælum & terram. Aña.
Hæc accipiet benedictionem.
Psalm.

DOmini est terra, & ple-
nitudo eius orbis terra-
rum & vniuersi qui habitant
in eo.

Quia ipse super maria funda-
uit eum: & super flumina præ-
parauit eum.

Quis ascendet in monté. Domini: aut quis stabit in loco
sancto eius?

Innocens manibus, & mun-

do corde : qui non accepit in
vano animam suam, nec iura-
uit in dolo proximo suo.

H ic accipiet benedictionem
à Domino : & misericordiam
à Deo salutari suo.

H æc est generatio quærentiũ
eum: quærentium faciem Dei
Iacob.

A ttollite portas principes ve-
stras,& eleuamini portę æter-
nales, & introibit Rex gloriæ.

Q uis est iste Rex gloriæ? Dominus fortis & potens, Dominus potens in prælio.

A ttollite portas principes ve-
stras, & eleuamini portæ æ-
ternales: & introibit Rex gloriæ.

Q uis est iste Rex gloriæ? Dominus virtutum ipse est Rex

gloriæ.

G loria Patri &c.

Aña Hæc accipiet benedictionem à Domino, & misericordiam à Deo salutari suo: quia hæc est generatio quærentium Dominum.

Deinde porrigens ad manû mulieris extremam partem stolæ, eam introducit in Ecclesiam dicens: Ingredere in têplum Dei, adora Filium Beatæ Mariæ Virginis, qui tibi fœcunditatem tribuit prolis.

Et ipsa ingressa genuflectit coram Altari, & orat, gratias agens Deo pro beneficijs sibi collatis, & Sacerdos dicit: Kyrie eleison.Christe eleisõ. Kyrie eleison. Pater noster. secretò. ℣. Et ne nos inducas in tentationem. ℞. Sed libera

nos à malo: ℣ Saluam fac ancillam tuã Domine. ℟. Deus
meus speratem in te. ℣. Mitte ei Domine auxilium de sancto. ℟. Et de Sion tuere eam.
℣. Nihil proficiat inimicus in
ea. ℟ Et filius iniquitatis non
apponat nocere ei. ℣. Domine exaudi orationem meam.
℟ Et clamor meus ad te veniat. ℣. Dominus vobiscum.
℟. Et cum spiritu tuo.

O remus.

OMnipotens sempiterne
Deus, qui per beatæ
Mariæ Virginis partum fidelium parientium dolores in
gaudium vertisti: respice propitius super hanc famulã, tuã
ad teplumtuũ pro gratiarum
actione lætam accedentem:
& præsta, vt post hanc vitam,

eiuſdem beatę Mariæ meritis
& interceſſione, ad æternæ
beatitudinis gaudia, cum pro-
le ſua peruenire mereatur.
Per Chriſtum Dominum no-
ſtrum. Amen.

Deinde illam aſpergit iterũ
Aqua benedicta in modum
Crucis, dicens : Pax, & Benedictio Dei omnipotentis , Patris †, & Filij †, & Spiritus
† ſancti, deſcendat ſuper te, &
maneat ſemper. Amen.

BENE-

BENEDICTIO MV-
lieris prægnantis, de
cuius periculo du-
bitatur.

A Diutorium noſtrum in nomine Dñi. ℞. Qui fecit cælum & terram. ℣. Saluam fac ancillam tuam. ℞. Deus meus ſperantē in te. ℣. Eſto illi Domine turris fortitudinis. ℞. A facie inimici. ℣. Nihil proficiat inimicus in ea. ℞. Et filius iniquitatis nō apponat nocere ei. ℣. Mitte ei Domine auxilium de ſancto. ℞. Et de Sion tuere eam. ℣. Domine exaudi orationem meam. ℞. Et clamor meus ad te veniat. ℣. Dominus vobiſ-

D

cum. ℟. Et cum Spiritu tuo.
Oremus.

Omnipotens sempiterne
Deus, qui dedisti famulis tuis in confessione veræ fidei, æternæ Trinitatis gloriã
agnoscere, & in potentia majestatis adorare vnitatẽ; quæsumus, vt eiusdem fidei firmitate, hæc famula tua ab omnibus semper muniatur aduersis. Per Dominum nostrum.
Oremus.

Domine Deus omnium
creator, fortis & terribilis, iustus atque misericors,
qui solus bonus & pius es: qui
de omni malo liberas Israel:
qui fecisti patres electos quoslibet, & sanctificasti eos munere Spiritus tui: qui gloriosæ
Virginis Matris Mariæ cor-

pus & animam, vt dignum filij tui habitaculum effici me-
reretur, Spiritu sancto coope-
rante præparasti : qui Ioannem Baptistam Spiritu sancto
repleri, & in vtero matris
exultare fecisti;accipe sacrifi-
cium cordis contriti, ac feruens desiderium famulæ tuæ
N. humiliter supplicantis,
pro conseruatione prolis de-
bilis, quam ei dedisti cócipe-
re,&custodi pariente tuam,&
defende ab omni dolo,&iniu-
ria diri hostis, vt obstetrican-
te manu misericordiæ tuæ,
fœtus eius, ad hanc lucem veniat incolumis, ac sanctæ re-
generationi seruetur, tibíque
in omnibus iugiter deseruiat,
& vitam consequi mereatur
æternam. Per eundem Do-
        D ij

minum nostrum &c. Amen.

Postea aspergatur aqua benedicta, dicendo Psalm. 66.
Deus misereatur nostri, &c.
℣. Benedicamus Patrem, &
Filium, cum sancto Spiritu.
℞. Laudemus & superexalte-
mus eum in sæcula. ℣. Angelis suis Deus mandet de te. ℞.
Vt custodiant te in omnibus
vijs tuis, ℣. Domine exaudi
orationem meam. ℞. Et clamor meus ad te veniat. ℣.
Dominus vobiscum. ℞. Et
cum spiritu tuo.

Oremus.

Visita quæsumus Domi-
mine cunctam habita-
tionem istam, & omnes insi-
dias inimici ab ea, & à præsenti famula tua longè repelle, & Angeli tui sancti habi-

tent in ea, qui eam & eius prolem in pace cuſtodiant: & benedictio tua ſit ſuper eā ſemper : Salua eos omnipotens
Deus, & lucem eis tuam concede perpetuam. Per Domi-
num noſtrum. ℟. Amen. Be-
nedictio Dei omnipotentis,
Patris †, & Filij †, & Spiritus † ſancti, deſcendat ſuper
te, & ſuper prolem tuam, &
maneat ſemper. ℟. Amen.

RITVS COMMVNI-
candi infirmum.

SAcerdos locum vbi iacet
Infirmus ingrediens cum
SS. Sacramento, dicat: Pax
huic domui. ℟. Et omnibus
habitantibus in ea. Tum de-

positum SS. Sacramentum super mensa, supposito corporali, genuflexus adorat, omnibus in genua procumbentibus, & mox accepta aqua benedicta, aspergit Infirmum, & cubiculum, dicens, Añam:
Asperges me Domine hyssopo, & mundabor: lauabis me, & super niuem dealbabor: & primum versum Psalmi, Miserere mei Deus, cum Gloria Patri. Sicut erat &c. Deinde repetitur, Aña. Asperges me &c. Postea ℣. Adiutorium nostrum in nomine Domini. ℞. Qui fecit cælum & terram. ℣. Domine exaudi orationem meam. ℞. Et clamor meus ad te veniat. ℣. Dominus vobiscum. ℞. Et cum Spiritu tuo.

O remus.

EXaudi nos, Domine san-
cte, Pater Omnipotens,
æterne Deus & mittere digneris sanctum Angelum tuum
de cælis, qui custodiat, foueat, protegat, visitet, atque
defendat omnes habitantes in
hoc habitaculo. Per Christum
Dominum. ℞. Amen.

His dictis accedat ad infirmum, vt cognoscat, num sit
benè dispositus ad suscipien-
dum sacrum Viaticum, &
vtrum velit aliqua peccata
confiteri; & illum audiat, atque absoluat: quamuis priùs
deberet esse ritè confessus, nisi necessitas aliter vrgeat. Postea facta de more Confessione generali, siue ab infirmo,
siue eius nomine à quouis alio

D iiij

Sacerdos dicat : Miſereatur tui &c, Indulgentiam, abſolutionem &c.

Deinde facta genuflectione, accipit Sacramentum de vaſculo, atque illud eleuans oſtendit infirmo, dicens : Ecce **Agnus Dei** , ecce qui tollit peccata mundi : & more ſolito ter dicit : Domine non ſum dignus, vt intres ſub tectum meum; ſed tantùm dic verbo, & ſanabitur anima mea. & Infirmus ſimul cum Sacerdote dicat eadem verba ſi poteſt, ſaltem ſemel, ſubmiſſa voce ; tum Sacerdos dans infirmo Euchariſtiam, dicat : **Accipe frater** (vel ſoror) **Viaticum Corporis Domini noſtri Ieſu Chriſti, qui te cuſtodiat ab hoſte ma-**

ligno, & perducat in vitam
æternam. Amen.

Si vero Communio non da-
tur per modum Viatici, dicat
more ordinario : Corpus Domini noſtri IeſuChriſti cuſtodiat , &c.

¶ Quod ſi mors immineat,
& periculum ſit in mora, tunc
dicto, Miſereatur &c. prædi-
ctis precibus , vel ex parte o-
miſſis, ei ſtatim viaticum præ-
beatur. Poſtea Sacerdos abluat digitos, nihil dicens ; &
infirmo detur ablutio. Deinde dicat : ℣. Dominus vobiſ-
cum. ℟. Et cum ſpiritu tuo.

Oremus.

DOmine ſancte, Pater
omnipotens , æterne
Deus , te fideliter deprecamur, vt accipienti fratri no-

ftro (vel forori noftræ) fa-
cro-fanctum Corpus Domini
noftri Iefu Chrifti filij tui, tam
corpori quàm animæ profit
ad remedium fempiternum :
qui tecum vinit & regnat in
vnitate Spiritus fancti Deus,
per omnia fæcula fæculorum.
℞. Amen.

His expletis, reuertatur Sacerdos ad Ecclefiam, dicendo Pfalmum L audate Domi-
num de cælis, vel alios Pfal-
mos prout tempus feret.

ORDO MINI-
stinstrandi Sacramentum
Extremæ Vnctio-
nis.

CVm peruentum fuerit
ad locum vbi iacet Infir-
mus, Sacerdos cum oleo sacro intrans cubiculum dicit:
Pax huic domui. ℞. Et omnibus habitantibus in ea.

Deinde deposito Oleo su-
per mensam, superpelliceo
stoláque violacea indutus,
ægroto Crucem pie deoscu-
landam porrigit: mox in modum Crucis cum Aqua bene-
dicta, & cubiculum, & cir-
cumstantes aspergit, dicens
Antiphonam, Asperges, &c.

Quod si ægrotus voluerit confiteri, audiat illum, & abfoluat.
Deinde pijs verbis illum con-
foletur, & de huius Sacramen-
ti vi atque efficaciâ, si tempus
ferat, breuiter admoneat, &
quantum opus sit, eius ani-
mum confirmet, & in fpem
erigat vitæ æternæ.

Poftea dicat verficulum.
Adiutorium noftrum in no-
mine Domini. ℟. Qui fecit
cælum & terram. ℣. Domi-
nus vobifcum. ℟. Et cum fpiritu tuo.

O remus.

INtroeat, Domine Iefu
Chrifte, domum hanc fub
noftrę humilitatis ingreffu,
æterna felicitas, diuina prof-
peritas, serena lætitia, charitas
fructuofa, fanitas fempiterna:

effugiat ex hoc loco acceſſus
Dęmonum, adſint Angeli pacis, domúmque hanc deſerat
omnis maligna diſcordia. Magnifica Domine ſuper nos nomen ſanctum tuum, & bene-
dic † noſtræ conuerſationi :
ſanctifica noſtræ humilitatis
ingreſſum, qui ſanctus, & pius
es, & permanes cum Patre &
Spiritu ſancto, in ſæcula ſæculorum. Amen.

O remus ; & deprecemur
Dominum noſtrum Ieſum
Chriſtum , vt benedicendo
benedicat † hoc tabernaculū,
& omnes habitantes in eo, &
det eis Angelum bonum Cu-
ſtodem , & faciat eos ſibi ſeruire, ad conſiderandum mira-
bilia de lege ſua : auertat ab
eis omnes contrarias poteſta-

tes:eripiat eos ab omni formi-
dine, & ab omni perturbatio-
ne, ac fanos in hoc taberna-
culo cuſtodire dignetur. Qui
cum Patre & Spiritu ſancto
viuit & regnat Deus in ſæcula ſæculorum. Amen.

Oremus.

EXaudi nos, Domine ſan-
cte, Pater omnipotens,
æterne Deus, & mittere digneris ſanctum Angelum tuū
de cælis, qui cuſtodiat, foueat,
protegat, viſitet, atque defendat omnes habitantes in hoc
habitaculo. Per Chriſtum
Dominum noſtrum. Amen.

Quæ orationes, ſi tempus
non patiatur, ex parte, vel in
totum poterunt omitti. Tum
de more facta Cōfeſſione generali, Latino, vel vulgari ſer-

mone, Sacerdos dicat: Misereatur tui &c. Indulgen-
tiam &c.

Antequam Parochus inci-
piat vngere infirmum moneat
adstantes, vt pro illo orent, &
vbi commodum fuerit, pro loco & tempore, & adstantium
numero vel qualitate, reci-
tent septem Psalmos Pœni-
tentiales, cum Litaniis, vel a-
lias preces dum ipse Vnctio-
nis Sacramētum administrat.
Mox dicat. In nomine Patris
† & Filij † & Spiritus † sancti extinguatur in te omnis
virtus diaboli per impositio-
nem manuum nostrarum, &
per inuocationem omnium
sanctorum Angelorum, Ar-
chāgelorum, Patriarcharum,
Prophetarum, Apostolorum,

Martyrum, Côfeſſorum, Virginum, atque omnium ſimul Sanctorum. Amen.

Deinde intincto pollice in Oleo ſancto in modum Crucis, vngit infirmum in partibus hîc ſubſcriptis, aptando proprio loco verba formæ in hunc modum. Ad oculos.

PEr iſtam ſanctam Vnctionem † & ſuam pijſſimam miſericordiam, indulgeat tibi Dominus quidquid per viſum deliquiſti. Amen.

Miniſter verò, ſi eſt in ſacris, vel ipſemet Sacerdos, poſt quamlibet vnctionem tergat loca inuncta nouo globulo bombacij, vel rei ſimilis, eáq; in vaſe mundo reponat, & ad Ecclesiam poſtea deferat, côburat, cineréſque proijciat in Sacrarium.

Per istam sanctam Vnctio-
nem, † & suam pijssimam misericordiam , indulgeat tibi
Dominus quidquid per audi-
tum deliquisti. Amen.

Ad Nares.

Per istam sanctam Vnctio-
nem †, & suam pijssimam misericordiam , indulgeat tibi
Dominus quidquid per odo-
ratum deliquisti. Amen.

Ad os, compressis labiis.

Per istam sanctam Vnctio-
nem † , & suam pijssimam
misericordiam, indulgeat tibi Dominus quidquid per gu-
stum & locutionem deliquisti. Amen. Ad manus.

Per istam sanctam Vnctio-
nem †, & suam pijssimam
misericordiam, indulgeat ti-

bi Dominus quidquid per ta-
ctum deliquisti. Amen.

Et aduerte, quòd Sacerdo-
tibus manus non inunguntur
interiùs, sed exteriùs.

Ad Pedes.

Per istam sanctam Vnctione
† , & suā pijssimam misericordiam, indulgeat tibi Dominus quidquid per gressum di-
liquisti. Amen. Ad lumbos,
siue Renes.

Per istam sanctam Vnctio-
nem † , & suam pijssimam
misericordiam, indulgeat tibi
Dominus quidquid per lum-
borum delectationem deli-
quisti. Amen.

¶ Hæc autem vnctio ad lū-
bos, omittitur semper in femi-
nis & etiam in viris, qui ob
infirmitatem vix, aut sine pe-

riculo moueri non poſſunt.

Quibus omnibus peractis,
Sacerdos dicit: Kyrie eleiſo.
Chriſte eleiſo. Kyrie eleiſo.
Pater noſter. ſecreto. ℣. Et
ne nos inducas in tentationē.
℞. Sed libera nos à malo. ℣.
Saluum fac ſeruum tuum. ℞.
Deus meus ſperātem in te. ℣.
Mitte ei Domine auxilium de
ſancto. ℞. Et de Sion tuere
eum. ℣. Eſto ei Domine turris fortitudinis. ℞. A facie inimici. ℣. Nihil proficiat inimi-
micᵒ in eo. ℞. Et filius iniquitatis non apponat nocere ei.
℣. Domine exaudi orationem
meam. ℞. Et clamor meus ad
te veniat. ℣. Dominus vobiſ-
cum. ℞. Et cum ſpiritu tuo.

E ij

Oremus.

DOmine Deus, qui per Apostolum tuum Iacobum locutus es, Infirmatur quis in vobis? Inducat Presbyteros Ecclesiæ, & orent super eum, vngentes eum Oleo in nomine Domini, & oratio fidei saluabit infirmũ, & alleuiabit eum Dominus, & si in peccatis sit remittentur ei: cura quæsumus, Redemptor noster, gratiâ Sancti Spiritus languores istius infirmi, eiusque sana vulnera, & dimitte peccata; atque dolores cunctos mentis & corporis ab eo expelle, plenamque interiùs sanitatem misericorditer redde, vt ope misericordiæ tuæ restitutus, ad pristina reparetur officia. Qui cum

Patre & Spiritu sancto viuis
& regnas in sæcula sæculorum. Amen.

Oremus.

REspice quæsumus Do-
mine, famulum tuum N.
in infirmitate sui corporis fa-
tiscentem, & animam refoue,
quam creasti : vt castigationi-
bus emendatus, se tua sentiat
medicinâ saluatum. Per Christum Dominum nostrum.
Amen.   Oremus.

DOmine sancte, Pater
omnipotens, æterne
Deus, qui benedictionis tuæ
gratiam ægris insundendo
corporibus, facturam tuam
multiplici pietate custodis: ad
inuocationem tui neminis benignus assiste vt famulum tuú
ab ægritudine liberatum, & sa-

E iij

nitate donatum, dextera tua
erigas, virtute confirmes, po-
testate tuearis, atque Ecclesiæ
tuæ sanctæ, cum omni deside-
rata   prosperitate restituas.
Per Dominum nostrum.
Amen.

Ad extremum, pro personę
qualitate salutaria monita
breuiter præbere poterit, quibus Infirmus ad moriendum
in Domino confirmetur, & ad
fugandas Dæmonum tětatio-
nes roboretur.

Denique Aquam benedi-
ctam, & Crucem, nisi aliam
habeat, coram eo relinquat,
vt illam frequenter aspiciat,
& pro sua deuotione oscule-
tur, & amplectatur.

Admoneat etiam domesti-
cos & ministros infirmi, vt si

morbus ingrauescat, vel infirmus incipiat agonizare, statim ipsum Sacerdotem accer-
sant, vt morientem adiuuet,
eiúsque animam Deo com-
mendet : sed si mors immineat, priusquam discedat, Sacerdos animam Deo ritè com-
mendabit.

DE VISITATIONE
& Cura Infirmorum.

SAcerdos intrans in domú
infirmi dicat : Pax huic
domui. ℟. Et omnibus habitantibus in ea. Mox infirmú,
& lectum, & cubiculum af-
pergat aqua benedicta, dicens : Asperges me Domine
&c. Deinde consoletur infir-

E iiij

72 Vifitatio Infirmorum.

mum. Hortetur ad confeffio-
nem, fi vúlt confiteri, illum
audiat & abfoluat. Deinde
dicat: **Chariffime**, Si Dominus vobis præftare dignabitur
fanitatem, nonne proponitis
de cætero pro viribusà peccatis cauere, & eius mandata pro
poffe feruare ? ℞. Propono.
Sacerdos. Adiutorium noſtrú
in nomine Domini. ℞. Qui
fecit cælum & terram. ℣. Dominus vobifcum. Et cum fpiritu tuo. Oremus.

Ntroeat, Domine Iefu
Chrifte, domum hanc fub
noftræ humilitatis ingreffu,
æterna felicitas, diuina prof-
peritas, ferenalætitia, charitas
fruchuofa, fanitas fempiterna:
effugiat ex hoc loco acceffus
Dæmonum; adfint Angeli

pacis, domúmque hanc deferat omnis maligna discordia. Magnifica, Domine, super nos nomen sanctum tuum, & benedic † nostræ conuersationi: sanctifica nostræ humilitatis ingressum, qui sanctus & pius es, & permanes cum Patre & Spiritu sancto, in sæcula sæculorú. Amen. ℣. Dominus vobiscum. ℟. Et cum spiritu tuo.

Sequentia sancti Euangelij secundum Lucam, signat se, & infirmum in fronte, ore, pectore. Si sit femina, se signet, vel alia ipsam.

IN illo tempore : Surgens Iesus de Synagoga, introiuit in domum Simonis. Socrus autem Simonis tenebatur magnis febribus, & rogauerunt

Visitatio Infirmorum
illum pro ea. Et stans super illam, imperauit febri, & dimi-
sit illam : & continuo surgens
ministrabat illis. Cum autem
sol occidisset, omnes qui ha-
bebant infirmos variis languo-
ribus, ducebant illos ad eum.
At ille singulis manus impo-
nēs, curabat eos. ℞. Deo gratias. ℣. Dominus vobiscum.
℞. Et cum spiritu tuo.

Oremus.

REspice Domine famulū
tuum (vel famulam
tuam) in infirmitate corporis
sui laboratam : & animam refoue, quam creasti, vt castiga-
tionibus emendata, continuò
se sentiat tua medicinâ sana-
tum. Per Christum Domínū
nostrum. Amen.

Postea vtramque manum

ponat super caput infirmi, dicens :

SVper ægros manus impo-
nent , & benè habebunt.
Iesus Mariæ filius, mundi sa-
lus & Dominus, meritis & in-
tercessione sanctorum Apostolorum Petri & Pauli, &
omnium sanctorum , sit tibi
clemens & propitius. Amen.
℣. Dominus vobiscum. ℟. Et
cum spiritu tuo.

Oremus.

DOminus Iesus Christus
apud te sit, vt te defen-
dat: intra te sit, vt te cóseruet:
ante te sit, vt te deducat : post
te sit , vt te bene † dicat. Qui
cum Patre & Spiritu sancto
in vnitate perfectâ viuit & regnat in sæcula seculorum.
Amen. Benedictio Dei om-

nipotentis Patris † & Filij &
Spiritus sancti, descendat super te , & maneat semper.
Amen.

MODVS IVVANDI
morientes.

IN grauescente morbo, Sacerdos Infirmum frequentiùs visitabit, & ad salutem diligenter iuuare non desinet: monebitque instante periculo se confestim vocari, vt in tempore præsto sit morienti, sumptoque sanctissimo Viatico, & sacra Vnctione adhibita, si periculum immineat, statim Commendationem animę recitabit.

Hortetur sæpiùs Infirmum,

& excitet, vt dum mente viget, eliciat actus fidei, & charitatis, aliarumque virtutum: Nempe,

Vt firmiter credat omnes articulos Fidei, & quidquid sancta Romana Ecclesia Catholica & Apostolica credit, & docet.

Vt speret Christum Dominum nostrum pro sua immensa clementia sibi fore propitium, & merito eius sanctissimæ Passionis, & per intercessionem beatæ Mariæ, & omnium sanctorum se vitam æternam consecuturum.

Vt toto corde diligat, & maximè diligere cupiat Dominū Deum, ea dilectione qua illum diligunt Beati, Sanctíque omnes.

Vt ob amorem Dei doleat ex corde de omni offensa, qualitercumque contra Dominū Deum, & proximum commiſſa.

Vt ex corde ob amorem Dei parcat omnibus, qui ſibi quoquo modo fuerint moleſti, aut inimici.

Vt ab iis veniam poſtulet, quos aliquando dictis aut factis offendit.

Vt quem patitur dolorem, & morbi moleſtiam, propter Deum in pœnitentiam peccatorum ſuorum patienter toleret.

Vt ſi Dominus ſibi ſalutem corporis præſtare dignabitur, proponat de cætero pro viribus ſuis à peccatis cauere, & eius mandata ſeruare.

Hortetur præterea, vt eo modo quo poteſt, ſaltem ex corde, ita per interualla precetur.

Miſerere mei Deus, ſecundum magnam miſericordiam tuam.

In te Domine ſperaui, non confundar in æternum.

In manus tuas Domine commendo ſpiritum meum: redemiſti me Domine Deus veritatis.

Deus in adiutorium meum intende: Domine ad adiuuandum me feſtina.

Eſto mihi Domine in Deum protectorem.

Deus propitius eſto mihi peccatori.

Dulciſſime Domine Ieſu Chriſte, per virtutem ſanctiſ-

80 Modus inuandi Morietes.
simæ Passionis tuæ recipe me
in numerum electorum tuo-
rum.

Domine Iesu Christe, suscipe
spiritum meum.

Maria mater gratiæ, Mater
misericordiæ, Tu nos ab hoste
protege, & hora mortis suscipe.

Sancte Angele Dei, mihi cu-
stos assiste.

Omnes sancti Angeli, & omnes sancti intercedite pro me,
& mihi succurrite.

Hæc, & his similia poterit
prudens, Sacerdos, vulgari vel
Latino sermone, pro personæ
captu, morienti suggerere.

Ordo commendationis, ani-
mæ, habetur in fine
Breuiarij.

ORDO

ORDO SEPELIENDI
mortuos.

SAcerdos verò antequam
cadauer efferatur, illud af-
pergit Aqua benedicta : mox
dicit Antiphonam, Si iniquitates, & Psalmum , De pro-
fundis clamaui &c. in fine,
Requiem æternam dona ei
Domine, & lux perpetua luceat ei. repetit Antiph. totam.
Si iniquitates &c. Deinde cadauer effertur : Sacerdóíque
de domo procedēs statim gra-
ui voce intonat Antiphonam,
ExultabuntDomino, & Can-
tores inchoāt Psalmum , Mi-
ferere mei Deus fecundum
magnam misericordiam, &c,

F

Clero alternatim prosequen-
te. Ac si lógitudo itineris po-
stulauerit, dicantur alij Psalmi
ex Officio mortuorum : & in
fine cuiusque Psalmi dicitur,
Requiem æternam dona eí
Domine, &c. Qui Psalmi de-
uotè, distinctè, grauíque voce recitari debent vsque ad
Ecclesiam.

Ad ingressum Ecclesiæ repetitur Antiphona :

Domino ossa humiliata. Deinde Ecclesiam ingressi cantant
Resp. Cantore incipiente, &
Clero alternatim respondent-
te, videlicet :

SVbuenite sancti Dei, oc-
currite Angeli Dñi, Sus-
cipientes animam eius, Offerentes eam in conspectu altis-
ssimi, ℣. Suscipiat te Christus

qui vocauit te: & in sinum A-
brahæ Angeli deducant te. Et
repetitur Suscipientes, &c. ℣.
Requiem æternam dona ei
Domine. ℟. Et lux perpetua
luceat ei. Offerentes &c. repetitur.

Deposito feretro in medio
Ecclesiæ, ita vt defuncti pedes, si fuerit laicus, sint versus
altare maius; si verò fuerit Sacerdos, caput sit versus ipsum
Altare, & cereis accensis circa
corpus, statim, nisi quid im-
pediat, dicatur officium mortuorum, cum tribus Nocturnis, & Laudibus, & duo ex
Clero incipiant absolutè In-
uitatoriũ. Regem cui omnia,
viuunt: Venite adoremus, &
repetitur à Clero. Regem, cui
omnia viuunt &c. Psal. V

F iij

nite exultemus, &c. & dupli-
cantur Antiphonæ.

Ad finem Officij post Antiphonam Cantici Benedictus
&c. Ego sum resurrectio, dicitur Pater noster. secreto.
Et ne nos inducas in tentationem. ℞. Sed libera nos à malo. ℣. A porta inferi. ℞. Erue
Domine animam eius. ℣. Requiescat in pace. ℞. Amen.
℣. Domine exaudi orationem
meam. ℞. Et clamor meus ad
te veniat. ℣. Dominus vobiscum. ℞. Et cum spiritu tuo.

O remus.

Absolue quæsumus Do-
mine, animam famuli
tui (vel famulæ tuæ) ab omni vinculo delictorum, vt in
resurrectionis gloria inter
sanctos & electos tuos resus-

citatus (vel refuscitata) refpi-
ret. Per Chriftum Dominum
noftrum. ℞. Amen.

Dum in officio dicuntur
Laudes, Sacerdos cum miniftris parat fe ad celebrandum
Miffam folemnem pro defun-
cto, fi tempus congruens fuerit, vt in die Depofitionis in
Miffali Romano.

Finita Miffa, Sacerdos de-
pofita Cafula, feu Planeta, &
manipulo, accipit Pluuiale
nigri coloris, & Subdiaconus
accipit Crucem, & accedit ad
feretrum, & fe fiftit ad caput
defuncti cum Cruce medius
inter duos Acolythos, feu ce-
roferarios cum candelabris, &
candelis accenfis : & omnes
alij de Clero veniunt ordina-
tim in gradu fuo cum cande-

lis accenfis, & ftãt in circuitu
feretri:tum fequitur Sacerdos
cum Diacono & Affiftente,
aliifque miniftris, & facta rē-
uerentia Altari, fiftit fe contra
Crucem ad pedes defuncti,
retrò aftantibus ei à finiftris
duobus Acolythis, vno cum
thuribulo & nauicula Incenfi,
altero cum vafe Aquæ benedictæ & afperforio, & Acolytho, feu Clerico tenentè librum, abfolutè dicit fequen-
tem Orationem.

NOn intres in iudicium
cum feruo tuo Domine,
quia nullus apud te iuftifica-
bitur homo, nifi per te omniũ
peccatorum ei tribuatur re-
miffio. Non ergo eum quæ-
fumus, tua iudicialis fententia
premat, quem tibi vera fup-

plicatio fidei Christianæ com-
mendat:sed gratia tua illi succ-
curente, mereatur euadere iudicium vltionis, qui dum vi-
ueret, insignitus est signaculo
sanctæ Trinitatis, qui viuis &
regnas in sæcula sæculorum.
℟. Amen.

Deinde Cantore incipiente,
Clerus circumstans cantat se-
quens Responsorium.

Libera me Domine, de
morte æterna; in die illa
tremenda: Quando cæli mo-
uendi sunt & terra : Dum veneris iudicare sæculum per
ignem. ℣. Tremens factus sū
ego, & timeo dum discussio
venerit, atque ventura ira.
Quando cæli mouendi sunt
& terra. ℣. Dies illa, dies iræ,
calamitatis & miseriæ , dies

F iiij

88· Sepultura Mortuorum.
magna & amara valde. **Dum**
veneris. ℣. Requiem eternam
dona ei Domine , & lux perpetua luceat ei. ℣. **Libera me.**
repetitur.

Dum cantatur prædictum
Responsorium , Sacerdos A-
colytho seu Diacono mini-
strante, accipit Incensum de
nauicula, & ponit in thuribulum , & finito Responsorio,
Cantor cum primo Choro dicit , K **yrie eleison.** Et secun-
dus Chorus respondet, **Chri-**
ste eleison. Deinde omnes simul dicunt , K **yrie eleison.**

Mox sacerdos dicat alta
voce: P **ater noster &c.** secretò dicitur ab omnibus : & ipse
interim accipit à Diacono vel
Acolytho aspersorium Aquæ
benedictæ , & facta profundâ

inclinatione Cruci, quæ est
ex aduerso, Diacono seu Ministro genuflectente, & fim-
brias pluuialis subleuante:
Circumiens feretrum (si trã-
sit ante S. Sacramentum genuflectit) aspergit corpus defuncti, deinde reuersus ad locum suum Diacono ministrã-
te, accipit thuribulum & eodem modo circuit feretrum
corpus incensat, vt asperserat:
tum reddito thuribulo ei à
quo acceperat, stans in loco
suo, Acolytho seu alio ministro tenente librum apertum
ante se, dicit: ℣. Et ne nos
inducas in tentationem. ℟.
Sed libera nos à malo ℣. A
porta inferi.℟. Erue Domine animam eius.℣. Requiescat in pace. ℟. Amē ℣. Do

mine exaudi oratióné meam.
℞. Et clamor meus ad té ve-
niat. ℣. Dominus vobiscum.
℞. Et cum spiritu tuo.

Oremus.

DEus cui propriú est mise-
réri semper, & parcere :
te supplices exoramus pro anima famuli tui N· quã hodie
de hoc seculo migrare iussisti:
vt non tradas eam in manus
inimici, neque obliuiscaris in
finem : sed iubeas eam à sanctis Angelis suscipi, & ad pa-
triam Paradisi perduci : vt
quia in te sperauit & credidit,
non pœnas inferni sustineat,
sed gaudia sempiterna possi-
deat. Per Christum Dominú
nostrum. ℞. Amen.

Si defunctus fuerit sacerdos, in Oratione dicatur : pro

anima famuli tui Sacerdotis,
quam hodie,&c.

Finita oratione, Corpus defertur ad sepulchrum, si tunc
deferendum sit, & dum portatur, Clerici cantant

Antiphonam.

IN paradisum deducant te
Angeli : in tuo aduentu
suscipiant te Martyres,
perducant te in ciuitatem
sanctam Hierusalem. Cho-
rus Angelorum te susci-
piat, & cum Lazaro quondam
paupere æternam habeas requiem.

Cum autem peruenerint ad
sepulchrum, si non est benedictum, Sacerdos illud bene-
dicit, dicens hanc orationem.

O remus.

DEus, cuius miferatione
animæ fidelium requief-
cunt, hunc tumulum benedicere † dignare, eíque Angelum tuum fanctum deputa cu-
ftodem, & quorum quarúm-
que corpora hîc fepeliuntur,
animas eorum ab omnibus ab-
folue vinculis delictorum, vt
in te femper cum Sanctis tuis
fine fine lætentur. Per Chriftum Dominum noftrum. ℞.
Amen,

Dicta Oratione, Sacerdos
Aqua benedicta afpergat,
deinde incenfet Corpus defuncti, & tumulum.

Quòd fi corpus tunc ad fe-
pulturam non deferatur, omif-
fo Refponforio In Paradifum
&c, & benedictione fepul-

chri, si iam sit benedictum,
prosequatur Officium vt infra, quod nunquam omittitur,
& intonet Antiphonam. Ego
sum resurrectio. & dicitur
Canticum, Benedictus Dominus Deus Israel, &c. Et repetitur Antipn. Ego sum resurrectio & vita, qui credit in
me, etiamsi mortu⁹ fuerit, viuet, & omnis qui viuit, & credit in me, non morietur in æternum.

Postea Sacerdos dicit: Kyrie eleison. Christe eleison,
Kyrie eleison. Pater noster
&c. interim corpus aspergit.
℣. Et ne nos inducas in tentationem. ℞. Sed libera nos à
malo. ℣. A porta inferi. ℞.
Erue Domine animam eius.
℣. Requiescat in pace. ℞. A-

men. ℣. Domine exaudi orationem meam. ℞. Et clamor
meus ad te veniat. ℣. Dominus vobiscum. Et cum spiritu
tuo.   Oremus.

FAc quæsumus Domi-
ne hanc cum seruo tuo de-
functo (vel famula tua defun-
cta) misericordiam, vt facto-
rum suorum in pœnis non recipiat vicem, qui (vel quæ)
tuam in votis tenuit volunta-
tem, vt sicut hîc eum (vel eã)
vera fides iunxit fidelium tur-
mis, ita illic eum (vel eam)
tua miseratio societ Angelicis
Choris. Per Christum Dominum nostrum. ℞. Amen. ℣.
Requiem æternam dona ei
Domine. ℞. Et lux perpetua
luceat ei. ℣. Requiescat in pace. ℞. Amen. ℣. Anima eius,

& animæ omnium fidelium
defunctorum per misericordiam Dei requiescant in pace.
℞. Amen.

Deinde à sepultura in Ec-
clesiam, vel in Sacristiam re-
uertentes, dicant sine cantu
Antiphonam. Si iniquitates,
cum Psalmo D eprofundis,
Deinde, Requiem æternam
dona eis Domine &c.

Si verò ob rationabilē causam, videlicet ob temporis
angustiam, vel aliorum fune-
rum instantem necessitatem,
prædictum Officium mortuorum cum tribus Nocturnis &
Laudibus dici non potest, deposito in Ecclesia feretro cum
corpore, dicatur saltem primum Nocturnum cum Lau-
dibus, vel etiam sine Laudi-

Sepultura Mortuorum: bus, maximè vbi eiusmodi viget consuetudo, incipiendo ab Inuitatorio, **Regem cui omnia viuũt, Venite &c.** Et postea omnia alia dicantur, quæ supra præscripta sunt dicenda post Officium mortuorum, & Missam.

Quod si etiam ea fuerit temporis angustia, vel alia vrgens necessitas, vt vnum Nocturnum cum Laudibus dici non possit, aliæ prædictę Preces, & suffragia numquam omittantur.

Missa verò, si hora fuerit congruens, ritu pro defunctis, vt in die obitus, præsente corpore non omittatur, nisi obstet magna diei solēnitas, aut aliqua necessitas aliter suadeat & post Missam fiat vt supra.

ORDO

ORDO SEPELIENDI
Paruulos.

CVm igitur infans, vel
puer baptizatus, defun-
ctus fuerit ante vsum ratio-
nis, induitur iuxta ætatem, &
imponitur ei corona de flo-
ribus, seu de herbis aromati-
cis, & odoriferis, in signum
integritatis carnis & virgini-
tatis, & Sacerdos superpelliceo & Stola alba indutus, &
alij de Clero, si adsint, præ-
cedente Cruce, quæ sine ha-
sta defertur, accedunt ad domum defuncti cum Clerico
aspersorium deferente. Sacerdos aspergit corpus, deinde
dicit.

G

Antiph. Sit nomen Domini
benedictum.   Psalm. 112

Laudate pueri Dominum:
laudate nomen Domini.
Sit nomen Domini benedi-
ctum : ex hoc nunc & vsque
in sæculum.

A solis ortu vsq; ad occasum:
laudabile nomen Domini.

Excelsus super omnes gentes
Dominus: & super cælos gloria eius.

Quis sicut Dominus Deus
noster, qui in altis habitat:&
humilia respicit in cęlo & in
terra?

Suscitás à terra inopem:&de
stercore erigens pauperem.

Vt collocet eum cum principibus : cum principibus populi sui.

Gloria Patri & filio &c.

Antiph. Sit nomen Domini benedictum: ex hoc nunc & vsque in sæculum.

Dum portatur ad Ecclesiam dicatur Psalmus Beati immaculati &c. & si tempus superest, dici potest Psalmus, Laudate Dominum de cælis, inferiùs positus , & in fine, Gloria Patri.

Cùm autem peruenerint ad Ecclesiam dicatur Antiph. Hic accipiet. Psal. Domini est terra &c. vt supra in Purificatione mulieris, pag. 44. Antiph. Hic accipiet benedictionem à Domino, & misericordiam à Deo salutari suo : quia hæc est generatio quærentium Dominum.

Postea dicitur, Kyrie eleison , Pater noster. secretò.

G ij

Interim corpus aspergit. ℣.
Et ne nos inducas in tentationem, ℞. Sed libera nos à malo. ℣. Me autem propter in-
nocentiam suscepisti. ℞. Et
confirmasti me in conspectu
tuo in æternum. ℣. Dominus
vobiscum. ℞. Et cum spiritu
tuo.   Oremus.

OMnipotens & mitissi-
me Deus, qui omnibus
paruulis renatis fonte Baptismatis dum migrant à sæculo,
sine vllis eorum meritis vitam
illicò largiris æternam, sicut
animæ huius paruuli hodie
credimus te fecisse : fac nos,
quæsumus Domine, per intercessionem beatæ Mariæ semper Virginis, & omnium Sā-
ctorum tuorum hîc purifica-
tis tibi mentibus famulari, &

in paradiso cum beatis paruu-
lis perenniter sociari. Per
Christum Dominum nostrū.
℟. Amen.

Dum portatur ad tumulum
(& etiamsi non portetur) dicitur Antiph. Iuuenes & virgines.   Psalm. 148.

Laudate Dominum de cę-
lis:laudate eum in excel-
sis.

Laudate eum omnes Angeli
eius : laudate eum omnes virtutes eius.

Laudate eum sol & luna:lau-
date eum omnes stellæ & lu-
men.

Laudate eum cæli cælorum :
& aquæ omnes quæ super cælos sunt laudent nomen Domini.

Quia ipse dixit, & facta sunt:

G iij

ipse mandauit & creata sunt.

Statuit ea in æternum, & in
sæculum sæculi : præceptum
posuit & non præteribit.

Laudate Dominum de terra:
dracones & omnes abyssi.

Ignis, grando, nix glacies, spiritus procellarum: quæ faciut
verbum eius.

Montes, & omnes colles: li-
gna fructifera &omnes cedri.

Bestiæ & vniuersa pecora:
serpentes, & volucres pen-
natæ.

Reges terræ & omnes popu-
li:principes & omnes iudices
terræ.

Iuuenes, & virgines senes cu
iunioribus laudent nomen
Domini : quia exaltatum est
nomen eius solius.

Confessio eius super cælum

& terram : & exaltauit cornu
populi sui.

H ymnus omnibus sanctis ei°
filiis Israel:populo appropin-
quanti sibi.

Et repetitur Antiph. Iuue-
nes, & virgines, Senes cum
Iunioribus laudent nomen
Domini. K yrie eleison.
C hriste eleison. K yrie elei-
son. P ater noster. ℣ Et ne
nos inducas in tentationem.
℟. Sed libera nos à malo.℣.
Sinite paruulos venire ad me.
℟. Talium est enim regnum
cælorum.℣ Dominus vobis-
cum. ℟. Et cum spiritu tuo.
O remus.

O Mnipotens sempiterne
Deus sanctæ puritatis
amator, qui animam huius
paruuli ad cælorum regnum
G iiij

hodie misericorditer vocare
dignatus es ; digneris etiam
Domine ita nobiscum misericorditer agere, vt meritis tuæ
sanctissimæ Passionis, & in-
tercessione beatæ Mariæ semper virginis, & omnium Sanctorum tuorum in eodem re-
gno nos cum omnibus Sanctis
& electis tuis semper facias
congaudere. Qui viuis & regnas, cum Deo Patre in vnitate spiritus sancti Deus, per
omnia sæcula sæculorum. ℞.
Amen.

Deinde Sacerdos corpus &
tumulum aspergat Aqua be-
nedicta, & thurificet simili-
ter: postea sepeliatur.

Cùm autem à sepultura re-
uertuntur in Ecclesiam, dicatur Canticum trium puero-

rum. Dan. 3. Benedicite omnia opera Domini &c. In fine dicitur, Gloria Patri, cum hac Antiph. Benedicite Dominum omnes electi eius, agite dies lætitiæ, & confitemini illi.

Deinde ante altare dicit Sacerdos, Dominus vobiscum. ℟. Et cum spiritu tuo.

O remus.

DEus, qui miro ordine Angelorum ministeria, hominumque dispensas: concede propitius vt à quibus tibi ministrantibus in cælo semper assistitur, ab his in terra vita nostra muniatur. Per Christum Dominum nostrū. ℟. Amen.

DE EXORCIZAN-
dis Obfeſſis, vel etiam Maleficiatis, à Dæ-monio.

Acerdos, ſiue alius Exor-
ciſta ritè confeſſus, aut
ſaltem corde peccata deteſ-
tās, peraĉto, ſi commodè fieri poteſt ſanĉtiſſimo Miſſæ
ſacrificio, diuinóque auxilio
piis precibus implorato, ſu-
perpelliceo & Stola violacea,
cuius extrema pars ad obſeſ-
ſi collum circumponatur, indutus, & coram ſe habens ob-
ſeſſùm ligatum ſi fuerit periculum, eum, ſe, & aſtantes cō-
muniat ſigno Crucis, & aſper-
gat Aqua benedictā, & geni-

bus flexis, alijs respondenti-
bus, dicat Litanias ordinarias,
vsque ad preces exclusiuè. In
fine, Antiph. Ne reminisca-
ris Domine delicta nostra,
vel parentum nostrorum, neque vindictam sumas de peccatis nostris.   Pater noster
&c. ℣. Et ne nos inducas in
tentationem. ℟. Sed libera
nos à malo.

Psalm. 53.

DEus in nomine tuo sal-
uum me fac: & in virtu-
te tua iudica me.

D eus exaudi orationem meã:
auribus percipe verba oris
mei.

Q uoniam alieni insurrexerũt
aduersum me, & fortes quæ-
sierunt animam meam: & non
proposuerunt Deum ante

conſpectum ſuum.

Ecce enim Deus adiuuat me :
& Dominus ſuſceptor eſt animæ meæ.

Auerte mala inimicis meis :
& in veritate tua diſperde
illos.

Voluntariè ſacrificabo tibi :
& confitebor nomini tuo Domine, quoniam bonum eſt.

Quoniam ex omni tribula-
tione eripuiſti me : & ſuper
inimicos meos deſpexit ocu-
lus meus.

Gloria Patri, &c. ℣. Saluum
fac ſeruum tuum (vel ancillam tuam) ℟. Deus meus ſperantē in te. ℣. Eſto ei Domine turris fortitudinis. ℟. A facie inimici. ℣. Nihil proficiat
inimicus in eo (vel ea.) ℟.
Et, filius iniquitatis non ap-

ponat nocere ei. ℣. Mitte ei.
Domine auxilium de sancto.
℟. Et de Sion tuere eũ (vel
eam.) ℣. Domine exaudi orationem meam. ℟. Et clamor
meus ad te veniat. ℣. Dominus vobiscum. ℟. Et cum spiritu tuo.

Oremus.

DEus cui proprium est
miſereri ſemper & par-
cere, ſuſcipe deprecationem
noſtram, vt hunc famulum
tuum (vel famulam tuam)
quem (vel quam) delictorũ
catena conſtringit, miſeratio
tuæ pietatis clementer abſol-
uat.   Oratio.

DOmine ſancte, Pater
omnipotens , æterne
Deus, Pater Domini noſtri
Ieſu Chriſti, qui illum refu-

gam Tyrannū & Apostatam
gehennæ ignibus deputasti;
quique Vnigenitum tuum in
hunc mundum misisti, vt illū
rugientem contereret;veloci-
ter attende, accelera, vt eri-
pias hominem ad imaginem,
& similitudinem tuam crea-
tum,à ruina & Dæmonio me-
ridiano. Da Domine terro-
rem tuum super bestiam, quæ
exterminat vineam tuam. Da
fiduciam seruis tuis contra
nequissimum Draconem pu-
gnare fortissime.,ne contem-
nat sperátes in te, & ne dicat,
sicut in Pharaone, qui iam di-
xit:Deū non noui, nec Israel
dimitto. Vrgeat illum dextera tua potens discedere à famulo tuo N. (vel à famula
tua N.) ne diutius præsumat

captiuum tenere, quem tu ad
imaginem tuam facere dignatus es, & in Filio tuo redemi-
fti : qui tecum viuit & regnat
&c. ℞. Amen.
Deinde præcipiat Dæmoni,
hunc in modum.

PRæcipio tibi, quicumq;
es, fpiritus immunde, &
omnibus focijs tuis, hunc
(vel hanc) Dei famulum ob-
fidentibus, vt per myfteria
Incarnationis, Paffionis, Re-
furrectionis, & Afcenfionis
Domini noftri Iefu Chrifti,
per miffionem Spiritus fancti,
& per aduentum eiufdem Domini noftri ad iudicium, dicas
mihi nomen tuum, diem, &
horam exitus tui, cum aliquo
figno; & vtmihi, Dei miniftro,
licet indigno, prorfus in om--

nibus 'obedias : neque hanc
creaturam Dei, vel circum-
ftantes, aut eorum bona, vl-
lo modo offendas.

Deinde legantur fuper-ob-
feffum hæc Euangelia, vel
vnum, aut plura. Lectio fancti Euangelij, fecundum
Ioannem, Hæc dicens, fignat
fe, & obfeffum in fronte, ore,
& pectore.   Ioan. 1.

IN principio erat Verbum,
& Verbum erat apud Deū,
& Deus erat Verbum. Hoc
erat in principio apud Deum.
Omnia per ipfum facta funt:
& fine ipfo factum eft nihil.
Quod factum eft in ipfo vita
erat : & vita erat lux homi-
num, & lux in tenebris lucet,
& tenebræ eam non compre-
henderunt. Fuit homo mif-
                              fus

à Deo, cui nomen erat Ioannes. Hic venit in teftimoniū,
vt teftimonium perhiberet de
lumine, vt omnes crederent
per illum. Non erat ille lux,
fed vt teftimonium perhiberet de lumine. Erat lux vera,
quæ illuminat omnem homi-
nem venientem in hunc mū-
dum. In mundo erat,& mun-
dus per ipfum factus eft : &
mundus eum non cognouit.
In propria venit , & fui eum
non receperunt. Quotquot
autem receperunt eum, dedit
eis poteftatem filios Dei fieri:
hus , qui credunt in nomine
eius. Qui non ex fanguinibus,
neque ex voluntate carnis,ne-
que ex voluntate viri : fed ex
Deo nati funt. Et Verbum caro factum eft : & habitauit in

H

nobis (& vidimus gloriam
eius, gloriam quasi vnigeniti
à Patre) plenum gratiæ &
veritatis. ℞. Deo gratias.

L ectio sancti Euangelij secundum Marcum. Marc. 16.

IN illo tempore dixit Iesus
discipulis suis: Euntes in
mundum vniuersum, prædi-
cate Euangelium omni creaturæ. Qui crediderit & baptizatus fuerit, saluus erit: qui
verò non crediderit condem-
nabitur. Signa autem eos, qui
crediderint, hæc sequentur.
In nomine meo dæmonia
eijcient: linguis loquentur
nouis: serpentes tollent: & si
mortiferum quid biberint, nō
eis nocebit: super ægros manus imponent, & bene habe-
bút. ℞. Deo gratias.

Lectio sancti Euangelij secundum Lucam. Luc. 10.

IN illo tempore: Reuersi
sunt septuaginta duo cum
gaudio dicentes ad Iesum:
Domine , etiam dæmonia
subijciuntur nobis in nomine
tuo: Et ait illis: Videbam Sa-
tanam sicut fulgur de cęlo ca-
dentem. Ecce dedi vobis potestatem calcandi supra serpentes , & scorpiones , & super omnem virtutem inimici,
& nihil vobis nocebit: verũ-
runtamen in hoc nolite gau-
dere , quia spiritus vobis subijciuntur : gaudete , autem ,
quod nomina vestra scripta
sunt in cælis. ℟. Deo gratias.
℣. Domine exaudi oratione͂
meam, ℟. Et clamor meus ad
te veniat, ℣. Dominus vobis-
H ij

cum. ℞. Et cum fpiritu tuo.
    O remus.

OMnipotens Domine,
    verbum Dei Patris,
Chrifte Iefu, Deus & Dominus vniuerfæ creaturæ, qui
fanctis Apoftolis tuis dedifti
poteftatem calcādi fuper fer-
pentes & fcorpiones, qui inter cætera mirabilium tuorū
præcepta, dignatus es dicere,
Dæmones effugate : cuius
virtute motus tanquam fulgur de cælo Satanas cecidit:
tuum fanctum nomen cum
timore & tremore fupplici-
ter deprecor, vt indigniffimo
mihi feruo tuo, data venia
omnium delictorum meorū,
conftantem fidem & poteftatem donare digneris: vt hunc
crudelem dæmonem, brachij

tui sancti munitus potentiâ
fidenter,& securus aggrediar,
per te Iesu Christe Domine
Deus noster, qui venturus es
iudicare viuos & mortuos, &
sæculum per ignem. ℞.
Amen.

Deinde muniens Obsessum
signo Crucis, circumposita
parte Stolæ ad collum eius,&
dexterâ manu sua capiti eius
impositâ,constanter&magna
cum fide , dicat ea quæ se-
quuntur. ℣. Ecce † Crucem
Domini fugite partes aduer-
sæ. ℞.Vicit leo de tribu Iuda
radix Dauid. ℣. Domine
exaudi orationem meam. ℞.
Et clamor meus ad te veniat.
Dominus vobiscum. ℞. Et
cum spiritu tuo.

O remus.

DEus, & Pater Dñi nostri
Iesu Christi , inuoco
nomen sanctum tuum, & Cle-
mentiã tuam supplex exposco
vt aduersus hunc, & omnem
immundum spiritum , qui ve-
xat hoc plasma tuum , mihi
auxilium præstare digneris.
Per eumdem Dominum no-
strum Iesum Christum Filium
tuum , qui tecum viuit & regnat in vnitate Spiritus sancti
Deus, per omnia sæcula sæculorum. ℞. Amen.

¶ Exorcismus.

EXorcizo te immundissi-
me spiritus, omnis incur-
sio aduersarij, omne phantasma , omnis legio, in nomine
Domini nostri Iesu Christi †
eradicare, & effugare † ab hoc

plafmate Dei. Ipfe tibi imperat, qui te de fupernis cælorum in inferiora terræ demer-
gi præcepit. Ipfe tibi imperat,
qui mari, ventis, & tempefta-
tibus imperauit. Audi ergo, &
time Satana, inimice fidei,
hoftis generis humani, mortis
adductor, vitæ raptor, iuftitiæ
declinator, malorum radix,
fomes vitiorum, feductor ho-
minum, proditor gentium, in-
citator inuidiæ, origo auari-
æ, caufa difcordiæ, excita-
tor dolorum : quid ftas, & re-
fiftis, cum fcias Chriftu Dominum vires tuas perdere? Illum metue, qui in Ifaac im-
molatus eft, in Iofeph venum-
datus, in agno occifus, in homine crucifixus, deinde inferni triumphator fuit.

H iiij

Tum sequentes Cruces faciat in fronte obsessi.

Recede ergo in nomine Patris †, & Filij †, & Spiritus † sancti : da locum Spiritui sancto, per hoc signum † Crucis Iesu Christi Domini nostri. Qui cum Patre & eodem Spiritu sancto, viuit & regnat Deus, per omnia sæcula sæculorum. ℟. Amen. ℣. Domine exaudi orationem meam. ℟. Et clamor meus ad te veniat. ℣. Dominus vobiscum. ℟. Et cum spiritu tuo.

Oremus.

DEus conditor & defensor generis humani, qui hominem ad imaginem tuam formasti : respice super hunc famulum tuum N. (vel hanc famulam tuam N.) qui (vel

quæ) dolis immundi fpiritus
appetitur, quem ventus ad-
uerſarius, antiquus hoſtis terræ formidinis horrore circū-
uolat, & ſenſum mentis hu-
manæ ſtupore defigit, terrore
conturbat,& metu trepidi ti-
moris exagitat. Repelle Domine virtutem diaboli, falla-
céſque eius inſidias amoue ;
procul impius tentator aufugiat ; ſit Nominis tui † ſigno
(ſignat in fronte) famulus
tuus (vel famula tua) munitus, & in anima tutus & corpore.

Tum tres Cruces ſequentes
faciat in pectore dæmoniaci.

Tu pectoris † huius inter-
na euſtodias. Tu viſcera † re-
gas. Tu † cor confirmes. In
anima aduerſatricis poteſtatis

tentamenta euanescant. Da
Domine ad hanc inuocatio-
nem sanctissimi nominis tui
gratiam, vt qui hucusque ter-
rebat, territus aufugiat, & vi-
ctus abscedat, tibique possit
hic famulus tuus (vel famula
tua) & corde firmatus, &
mente sincerus debitum præbere famulatum. Per Domi-
num nostrum Iesum Christũ
filium tuum, qui tecum viuit
&c. ℞. Amen.

¶ Alius Exorcismus.

ADiuro te Serpens anti-
que, per Iudicem viuo-
rum & mortuorum, per facto-
rem mundi, per eum qui habet potestatem mittendi te in
gehennam, vt ab hoc famulo
Dei N. qui ad Ecclesiæ sinũ
recurrit, cum metu & exerci-

tu furoris tui feftinus difcedas. Adiuro te iterum (fignat
in fronte †) non mea infirmitate, fed virtute Spiritus fancti, vt exeas ab hoc famulo
Dei N. quem omnipotens
Deus ad imaginem fuam fe-
cit. Cede igitur, cede, non
mihi, fed miniftro Chrifti.
Illius enim te vrget poteftas,
qui te Cruci fuæ fubiugauit.
Illius brachium contremifce,
qui deuictis gemitibus inferni
animas ad lucem perduxit. Sit
tibi terror corpus hominis †
(in pectore) fit tibi formido
imago Dei (in fronte.) Non
refiftas, nec moreris difcede-
re ab homine ifto, quoniam
complacuit Chrifto in homine habitare. Et ne contemnē-
dum putes, dum me peccato-

rem nimis esse cognoscis: imperat tibi Deus †. Imperat tibi maiestas Christi.†. Imperat tibi Deus Pater †. Imperat tibi Deus Spiritus †san-
ctus. Imperat tibi Sacramentum † Crucis. Imperat tibi
fides sanctorum Apostolorum
Petri †& Pauli, & cæterorū
Sanctorum. Imperat tibi martyrum †sanguis. Imperat tibi cōtinentia †Confessorum.
Imperat tibi Christianæ fidei
mysteriorum † virtus. Exi
ergo transgressor. Exi sedu-
ctor, plene omni dolo & falla-
cia, virtutis inimice, innocen-
tium persecutor. Da locū di-
rissime, da locum impijssi-
me, da locum Christo, in
quo nihil inuenisti de ope-
ribus tuis, qui te spoliauit, qui

regnum tuum deſtruxit, qui te
victum ligauit, & vaſa tua di-
ripuit, qui te proiecit in tene-
bras exteriores, vbi cũ mini-
ſtris tuis erit præparatus inte-
ritus. Sed quid truculente re-
niteris? quid temerarie de-
trectas? Reus es omnipotenti
Deo, cuius ſtatuta trangreſ-
ſus es. Reus es Filio eius IESV
Chriſto Domino noſtro, quẽ
tentare auſus es, & crucifige-
re præſumpſiſti. Reus es hu-
mano generi, cui tuis perſua-
ſionibus mortis venenum
propinaſti.

Adiuro ergo te, Draco ne-
quiſſime, in nomine Agni †
immaculati, qui ambulauit
ſuper aſpidem & baſiliſcum,
qui conculcauit leonem &
draconem, vt diſcedas ab hoc

homine, (fiat in fronte †)
difcedas ab Ecclefia Dei,
(fiat fignum Crucis fuper cir-
cunftantes †) contremifce,
& effuge, inuocato nomine
Domini illius, quem Inferi
tremunt, cui Virtutes cælo-
rú, & Potestates & Domina-
tiones fubiectæ funt, quem
Cherubim & Seraphim inde-
feffis vocibus laudant, dicentes, Sanctus, Sanctus, Sanctus, Dominus Deus Sa-
baoth. Imperat tibi Verbum
† caro factum. Imperat tibi
natus † ex Virgine. Imperat
tibi Iefus † Nazarenus, qui
te, cùm difcipulos eius con-
temneres, elifum atque pro-
ftratum exire præcepit ab homine; quo præfente, cum te
ab homine feparaffet, nec

porcorum gregem ingredi
prȩfumebas. Recede er-
go nunc adiuratus in no-
mine † eius, ab homi-
ne quem ipfe plafmauit.
Durum eft tibi † velle refi-
ftere. Durum eft tibi † contra
ftimulum calcitrare. Quia
quanto tardius exis, táto magis tibi fupplicium crefcit
quia non homines contem-
nis, fed illum qui dominatur
viuorum & mortuorum, qui
venturus eft iudicare viuos &
mortuos, & fæculum per
ignem. ℞. Amen. ℣. Domi-
ne exaudi orationem meam.
℞. Et clamor meus ad te veniat. ℣. Dominus vobifcum.
℞. Et cum fpiritu tuo.

Oremus.

DEus cæli , Deus terræ,
Deus Angeloru̅, Deus
Archangelorum , Deus Pro-
phetarum, Deus Apostoloru̅,
Deus Martyrum , Deus Vir-
ginum, Deus qui potestatem
habes donare vita̅ post mortem , requiem post laborem,
quia non est alius Deus præter te, nec esse poterit verus,
nisi tu creator cæli & terræ,
qui verus Rex es , & cuius
Regni non erit finis ; humiliter maiestati gloriæ tuæ sup-
plico , vt hunc famulum tuu̅
de immundis spiritibus libe-
rare digneris. Per Christum
Dominum nostrum. ℞.
Amen.

Prædicta omnia quatenus
opus fuerit repeti possunt, donec

nec Obsessus sit omnino libe-
ratus. Iuuabit præterea pluri-
mum super Obsessum deuo-
tè sæpéq; repetere Pater noster, &c. Aue Maria, &c.
Magnificat &c. Symbolum
item Sancti Athanasij Quicumque vult, &c. Item septem Psalmos pœnitentiales,
aliásque pias preces & Orationes, pro deuotione Sacerdotis exorcizantis, & populi
circunstantis.

Oratio post liberationem.

ORamus te Deus omni-
potens, vt spiritus ini-
quitatis amplius non habeat
potestatem in hoc famulo
N. (vel famula tua N) sed
vt fugiat, & non reuertatur.
Ingrediatur in eum (vel in
eam) Domine, te iubente,

I

bonitas, & pax Domini nostri
Iesu Christi , per quem re-
dempti sumus , & ab omni
malo non timemus, quia Dominus nobiscum est. Qui viuit & regnat , cum Deo Patre in vnitate Spiritus sancti
Deus, per omnia sæcula sæculorum. Amen.

BENEDICTIONES

variæ.

¶ Benedictio Loci , seu
Domus.

Adiutorium nostrum in no-
mine Domini. ℟. Qui fecit
cælum & terram, ℣. Domi-
nus vobiscum. ℟. Et cum
spiritu tuo.

O remus.

Benedic † Domine Deus omnipotens locum istú (vel domum istam) vt sint in eo (vel in ea) sanitas, castitas, victoria, virtus, humilitas, & mansuetudo, plenitudo legis, & gratiarum actio Deo Patri & Filio, & Spiritui sancto: & hæc benedictio maneat super hunc locum, & super habitantes in eo, nunc & semper. ℟. Amen. Et aspergat aqua benedicta.

¶ Benedictio Thalami. Adiutorium nostrum in nomine Domini. ℟. Qui fecit cælum & terram. ℣. Dominus vobiscum. ℟. Et cum spiritu tuo. O remus.

Benedic † Domine thalamum hunc, v t omnes ha-

I ij

bitantesin eo in tua pace cõsi-
stant, & in tua voluntate per-
maneant, & senescãt, & mul-
tiplicentur in longitudine
dierum, & ad regna cælorum
perueniant. Per Christum
Dominum nostrũ. ℞. Amen.
Deinde aspergatur aqua benedicta.

℥ Benedictio carnium in
Paschate.

Adiutorium nostrum in no-
mine Domini. ℞. Qui fecit
cælum & terram. ℣. Domi-
nus vobiscum. ℞. Et cum spiritu tuo.

Oremus.

DEus, qui per famulum
tuum Moysen, in libe-
ratione populi tui de Ægy-
pto, Agnum occidi iussisti, in
similitudinem Domini nostri

Iefu Chrifti & vtrofque po-
ftes Domorum de fanguine
eiufdem agni perungi præce-
pifti: tu benedicere † & fan-
ctificare digneris hanc creaturam carnis, quam nos famuli tui ad laudem tuam fumere
defideramus, per refurrectionem eiufdem Domini noftri
Iefu Chrifti. Qui tecum viuit & regnat in fæcula fæculorum. ℞. Amen. Et afperga-
tur aqua benedicta.

¶ Benedictio Ouorum.
℣. Adiutorium noftrum in
nomine Domini. ℞. Qui fe-
cit cælum & terram. ℣. Dominus vobifcum. ℞. Et cum
fpiritu tuo.   Oremus.
SVbueniat quæfumus Do-
mine tuæ benedictionis†
gratia huic Ouorum creatu-

ræ, vt cibus falubris fiat fidelibus tuis, in tuarum gratiarum actione fumentibus, ob refurrectionem Domini noftri Iefu Chrifti, qui tecum viuit & regnat, in fæcula fæculorum. ℞. Amen. Afpergat aqua benedicta.

¶ Benedictio Panis.

℣. Adiutorium noftrum in nomine Domini. ℞. Qui fecit cælum & terram. ℣. Dominus vobifcum. ℞. Et cum fpiritu tuo.   Oremus.

Domine Iefu Chrifte, panis Angelorum, panis viuus æternæ vitæ, benedicere † dignare Panem iftū, ficut benedixifti quinque panes in deferto; vt omnes ex eo guftantes, inde corporis & animæ percipiant fanitatem.

Qui viuis & regnas in sæcula
sæculorum. ℞. Amen. Et aspergat aqua benedicta.

¶ Benedictio ad quodcum-
que comestibile.

℣. Adiutorium nostrum in
nomine Domini. ℞. Qui fecit
cælum & terram. ℣. Domi-
nus vobiscum. ℞. Et cum spiritu tuo.   Oremus.

BEnedic † Domine crea-
turam istam N. vt sit re-
medium salutare generi hu-
mano: & præsta per inuocationem sancti nominis tui, vt
quicumque ex ea sumpserint,
corporis sanitatem, & animæ
tutelam percipiant. Per Christum Dominum nostrum.

FINIS.